Exploding Myths
That Jews Believe

Exploding Myths That Jews Believe

Jeremy Rosen

JASON ARONSON INC.
Northvale, New Jersey
Jerusalem

This book was set in 11 pt. New Century Schoolbook by Pageworks of Old Saybrook, CT, and printed and bound by Book-Mart Press, Inc. of North Bergen, NJ.

Library of Congress Cataloging-in-Publication Data

Rosen, Jeremy.
    Exploding myths that Jews believe / Jeremy Rosen.
        p.   cm.
    Includes bibliographical references and index.
    ISBN 0–7657–6135–1
    1. Judaism—Doctrines. I. Title.

  BM601.R55   2000
  296.3—dc21

                                        99–057348

Printed in the United States of America on acid-free paper. For information and catalog, write to Jason Aronson Inc., 230 Livingston Street, Northvale, NJ 07647–1726, or visit our website: www.aronson.com

Contents

Preface

As a teenager I was sent to study at a yeshiva in Israel that had been set up by former colleagues of my father from Mir Yeshiva in Lithuania. The Rosh Yeshiva of Be'er Yaacov, Rabbi Moshe Shapiro, was a jovial, brilliant man whose learning was well beyond my level of comprehension at the time, yet he could make a *sugya* sound simple and exciting to a young mind. His delight in life and love for learning were infectious. A different influence on the yeshiva was that exerted by the Mashgiach, the more somber and serious Rabbi Shlomo Volbe. He was rumored (as if to cover up a scandal) to have studied philosophy in Berlin before coming to Mir. I remember once having the gall to ask him what I should do if I had difficulty proving that God existed. "Don't worry," he told me, "It may take time, a lot of time. Meanwhile learn Torah and do good deeds."

Eight years later I arrived at Mir Yeshiva in Jerusalem after having studied philosophy at Cambridge. I still could not prove God's existence, but by then it did not matter because I had learned that "proof" was a rather weak and ineffectual device in matters of spirit and metaphysics. Still, I was fascinated by linguistic analysis and very much influenced by the giant shadow that Wittgenstein cast over Cambridge philosophy.

I had a letter on me from Reb Laizer Yehuda Finkel, *z'l*, (who had been my father's, *z'l*, Rosh Yeshiva when Mir was in Eastern Europe before the Second World War), allowing me to come and learn (it was his policy to accept any son of a former Mirrer man). Sadly, he had died by the time of my arrival in 1965 and when I turned up I was shown into the apartment of Reb Nochum Trokker, *z'l*, the son-in-law of Reb Chaim Shmulevitz, *z'l*. He asked me where I had been learning and I said that I had just come from university. He said that the yeshiva was full, but I persevered and told him that I had been at Be'er Yaacov for several years beforehand and he relented temporarily. "What did you study in university?" he asked. "Philosophy," I replied. "Oh," he said, "You really ought to go to Merkaz HaRav Kook." I showed him the letter I had from Reb Laizer Yehuda. "All right," he said, "But I warn you: I do not want any philosophy in Mir."

I obeyed his order because I had come to Mir to learn, not to philosophize, but his fear of philosophy was based on a position that probably goes back to Spinoza—if not to the Greeks. It is that philosophy in some way is inimical to Torah, that philosophy is a sort of atheism. No doubt there were and are plenty of philosophers who were and are atheists. No doubt the association of philosophy with Mendlessohn and the challenge of "Haskala" (Enlightenment; the eighteenth-century secular movement of Russian origin) gave it a bad name in certain circles. At Cambridge, philosophy was the means of analyzing thoughts and ideas, and, of course, language. It was and is a fantastic tool to aid clear thinking. Much as I enjoyed philosophy, it was a welcome return to studying Torah, to something more related to the act of living and real moral problems rather than abstract ones.

During my time at Mir I heard many wonderful *shiurim* from Reb Chaim, Reb Nochum, and others. It was the spiritual and intellectual highlight of my student years. But there was never any question of an open, questioning debate on theological issues. I knew I could ask anything in learning but nothing in philosophy. Unquestioning acquiescence was assumed, total obedience without question. Incredible brilliance was mustered to challenge every letter of the Gemara and its armor bearers but no such inquiry was expected or encouraged on matters of belief. It struck me as strange that no one seemed at all bothered, but I focused on what I perceived was the priority, Torah, and suppressed any tendency to philosophize.

When I came to get my *Semicha* (rabbinic ordination) years later, after studying very hard and avoiding controversy, Reb Nochum gave me a little lecture. He told me to be very careful how I spoke and how I phrased my words of wisdom in the alien environment of a Diaspora Jewish community of *Balei Batim*. He thanked me for suspending my philosophy and told me that now, perhaps, would be the time to return to it and apply it for the sake of Torah. He was a remarkable man.

Throughout my teaching career in school and the rabbinate I have sought to stimulate minds, to challenge and to provoke, to encourage people to think for themselves rather than to provide answers. No one answer satisfies every mind. No one generation's philosophy suits every other generation. Thinking, like fashion or even like science, has its trends and movements and changes. People have to find their own ways to deal with issues and a good teacher helps by showing ways, teaching methodology. Nowadays many have no interest in philosophy or in abstractions—and I am not going to argue with them. Not everyone is suited to a life of questioning even if Saadya Gaon thinks it desirable and Maimonides thinks it the only way to understand and know God. But there are inquiring minds who feel dissatisfied with the conventional responses. I hope this book will do no more than open some minds to different ways of looking at old problems. In the end, to use a simile, loving is more important than knowing how to love. For me, Jewish religious experience lies at the center of my spiritual world. Philosophy is its assistant.

I have chosen to go back to biblical and talmudic sources primarily because they are the purest expression of Jewish thinking. I strongly believe that much of Jewish thought and practice in the years of the Diaspora were influenced directly by external conditions or were reactions to pressure imposed upon Jewish life. I believe that the current lack of interest in theological thinking and in philosophical method is very much a reaction against what were in practice as well as in theory, for a very long time, alien and antagonistic cultures. It is impossible for our Jewish psyche not to be affected by what two thousand years of subjugation achieved, culminating in the atrocities that European culture spawned this century. Yet just as we have responded by intensifying Torah and rebuilding Jewish life as the strongest, most effective reply to our enemies, so too I believe we need to renew our theological dynamism as a response to assimilation.

I often hear people complain about religious authority. I wonder how much of this is a front. I am an individual and I love individuality, and individualism requires of people that they create their own religious life. No excuses. In the final analysis this is the overriding issue. But at the same time, as Jews we are part of a community and required to contribute. There is a great deal that is unsatisfactory about all religious structures, bureaucracies, and authorities. They tend, inevitably, to be concerned with preserving authority and power. They tend to overlook individual sensitivities in pursuit of a wider picture. I believe that spirituality is about the importance of every human being as a "child of God," but the only way of dealing with problems is by engagement—not by the opposition of a full-frontal attack, because whatever the reservations about authority may be, any body of thought and law requires a controlling element. But if this control cannot be ameliorated or influenced by engagement, then, as Hillel the Elder said, "When everyone is gathering in then you can spread out, but when everyone else spreads out, then you should gather in," which is a prelude to Bar Kappara saying, "What is the essential quotation that encapsulates the principles of the Torah? 'Know Him in everything you do and He will help you walk the straight path.'"[1] This was my late father's, *z'l,* motto and the one he gave to the school he founded.

I owe everything I am as a Jew for the better to my father Kopul Rosen, *z'l* (who died at the age of 49 when I was just 18). He was a giant among men, both in size and charisma and I have not seen his like. And to my wise and gracious mother Bayla Brana, *a'h.* For my failings I accept responsibility.

My deepest gratitude for great love and encouragement goes to my wife, Suzanne, and to my children, Anushka, Jacky, Natalia, and Avichai. They are the joy of my life.

Finally, I am honored to be part of a family dedicated to Jewish life: my brothers, Rabbi Dr. Michael Rosen and Rabbi David Rosen and my sister, Ayellet Rosen Gillis. We have been touched by the magic of our parents.

New York

Notes

1. Talmud Bavli *Brachot* 63a.

Chapter 1

Myth:
Good Jews Have
to Believe in God

1

Jewish life is pervaded by assumptions. There are assumptions about who a good Jew is and what a good Jew is. There are assumptions about who believes what. One group of Jews makes assumptions about other groups of Jews, religiously, politically, and socially. And every other non-Jewish group makes assumptions about Jews.

We know that there are many different opinions and ideologies within the "broad church" of the Jewish people, but Jewish Law, Halacha, does act as a sort of constitution that describes the development of the behavioral tradition, certainly for two millennia and probably for three. However, the same clear structure does not apply to theological issues. Since medieval times there have been various lists of beliefs to which Jews must adhere. The most famous is Maimonides'[1] Thirteen Principles of Faith. This has become so universally accepted that it finds expression in most prayer books both by itself and in the lyrical poem *Yigdal*.

In fact these lists of creeds were direct responses to Christian and Islamic attacks on Judaism. It was felt necessary at times to counter the charges that Judaism was not a "proper" religion. Although in the Talmud there are examples of "required belief" there is no actual list of defining beliefs, and it was not until the end of the first millennium that these Jewish creeds began to emerge. The trouble is that Maimonides wrote and thought within a Greek philosophical framework. He regarded himself as a follower of the Aristotelian school. Many elements of the philosophy that Maimonides took for granted no longer help many of us in our philosophical thinking, yet his list of what Jews are expected to believe is taken for granted and rarely examined.

These chapters are written to look at many of these and other theological assumptions to see what it really is that we are expected to believe and exactly how we can reconcile traditional beliefs with critical thinking in the scientific and rational world in which we live on the one hand and the exciting freedom of mysticism on the other.

2

The formative years of the Bible occurred long before Greek philosophy made its appearance. If the golden age of Socrates is approximately two and a half thousand years ago, King David predates it by about five hundred years—and many of the biblical texts are even earlier than that by several hundred years at least.

The Bible does not speak in rational, scientific terms. Its language is predominantly what we would call poetic. This should not be confused with meaning something fanciful, imaginative, and therefore not based in reality, but means rather that the style of writing has to be understood on more than the surface value. There is a music to the language that conveys as much as the actual words, but one has to be able to listen to and understand the music. A scientific experiment uses language in a very different way. It is strictly descriptive and is terse and precise; the language is the servant of the experiment. Poetry uses language much more creatively, both to describe something and also to create a mood, an impression. In both the words are symbols, but they have different functions.

The language of the Bible is very different from everyday language the way we or indeed the way Greek philosophers used it. It is designed to bring a spiritual dimension of existence into everyday life so that there is an immediate connection between human life and (let us call it) Divine life. This connection is prescribed through narrative, through instruction, and through song. The language of the Bible has a strong group dynamic designed to reinforce the identity of a small group of believers in an alien world. Its agenda is clearly a spiritual one. It is pre-rational. It is not rational. This does not mean that it is illogical, just that its parameters are different parameters than the ones to which we in the West have been conditioned for so long. So for the first thousand years of Jewish existence, the relationship with God was not conducted on a philosophical basis. The language used to describe God and human beings communicating was not a language of scientific accuracy, of philosophical logic, but rather of poetry. The Jews of that period were not called upon to bring philosophical proofs of their beliefs nor were they expected to submit their feelings to rational analysis. Does this mean that they were not "good" Jews? I think not!

For the next phase of Jewish history, the Second Temple and the talmudic period, Jews lived under different and alien cultural influences. The language and ideograms of their discourse were heavily influenced by a way of thinking that was Greek, Roman, or Christian. The rabbis strongly objected not just to the cultural baggage of Greece but also to the very rational, almost exclusively rational, approach of its great philosophers. They objected because they felt that logic was an incomplete way of looking at the world—as did the Greeks themselves in a way, though their antidote was a strange collection of gods cavorting with humans and fighting amongst themselves. The monotheism of Judaism found this offensive and ridiculous. This is one of the reasons that the rabbis encouraged the mystical tradition and why it developed so strongly as a counterbalance to the rational.

The clearest example of this conflict between the logical and the mystical is the episode that Talmud records concerning Elisha Ben Abuya who became an apostate and was henceforth called Acher, Someone Else, The Unmentionable.[2] Four major second-century rabbinic leaders are described as entering the orchard. The orchard, *Pardess*, in this context, is a code word for the mystical experience of God. "Four entered into the orchard: they were Ben Azai, Ben Zoma, Acher, and Rabbi Akiva. Rabbi Akiva said to them 'When you reach the stones of pure marble do not say, "Water, water" because it says (Psalms 101): "Whoever speaks lies cannot survive in My Presence."'"

Ben Azai dies, Ben Zoma goes mad, Acher "cuts away at the roots"—that is to say, cannot accept the traditional structure—and only Rabbi Akiva comes out "in peace." There are, of course, different ways of understanding this incident. The context is the chapter in the Mishna that starts by limiting general inquiry into *Maaseh Bereshit*, how the world was created, and *Maaseh Mercava*, a code for what we call mysticism, a connection with God that transcends normal physical limitations in the way that the prophet Elijah was taken up to God in a chariot of fire. The Mishna suggests that very few people are equipped for these lines of investigation and that they require learning, experience, and a good guide.

According to the Mishna, these esoteric subjects should be studied only with expert teachers and only after one has acquired a solid basis in "revealed" Torah before turning to the "hidden" Torah. In the course of the discussion in the Gemara, this episode is recounted. Rabbi Akiva warned his friends not to take their experiences at face value. Just because something looks like water does not necessarily mean that it is water. He was arguing against a rational, material way of observation in the context of spiritual experience. For whatever reasons, the first two had such a profound experience that it changed them in a destructive way and Acher simply had no patience for or interest in the mystical experience and abandoned Rabbi Akiva's religion for Greek Philosophy, for pure reason.

Later in the same chapter the Gemara records an exchange in which Elisha Ben Abuya is quoted as wondering whether there are two Divine forces at work in this world. This is pure Greek: Plato in his Republic suggests that because God is good, He cannot be the source of evil; evil must come from another power. The link between Acher and Greek thought is clear. This is the same Acher who disputes the rabbinical concept of the afterlife as the place where humans are rewarded or punished for their behavior.

Rabbi Yaakov[3] describes a situation in which a father sends his son up a tower to chase away a mother bird before taking her fledglings. These are two actions that the Bible says will bring long life (Exodus 20:12 and Deuteronomy 22:6). Nevertheless the child falls and dies. In response to the question of where the long life is, the rabbis reply that the actual long life is the eternal life after death. According to tradition (and the Maharsha, commenting on the incident) it was this incident that led to Elisha Ben Abuya's apostasy.

Elisha stands for the rational school and Rabbi Akiva stands for the mystical school. Rabbi Akiva is known to us as the supporter of Bar Cochba's nationalist rebellion against Rome. Indeed, for a while Rabbi Akiva thought that Bar Cochba was the Messiah[4] and there are in various collections today coins that Bar Cochba minted describing him-

self as the Messiah. Extreme nationalism is often associated with a metaphysical attachment to land and abstractions of nationhood. Thus Rabbi Akiva's association with Bar
Cochba says something about Rabbi Akiva's political ideology.

But Rabbi Akiva also asserted that The Song of Songs
was the holiest book of the Bible.[5] The Song of Songs is a
beautiful flow of passionate poetry, its holiness deriving from
the understanding that the real "lovers" are God and Israel.
The metaphor is that passion rather than intellect is the
way to experience God, so that when Rabbi Akiva says that
The Song of Songs is fundamental to Jewish life he is asserting the primacy of emotion and poetry as the way of really
drawing closer to God, following an established theme that
runs through the prophetic tradition of the Bible.

Isaiah describes the relationship between Israel and God
as one of husband and wife[6] and goes on to describe the
pleasure of the relationship in marital terms.[7] The prophet
Hosea makes the analogy of Israel as a faithless wife the
central theme of his message[8] and sees the reconciliation as
one in which the relationship is not one of domination but
"pleasurable coexistence." The pre-Greek Jewish way of
expressing closeness to God is the very antithesis of a philosophical approach.

3

Opposition to Greek language and wisdom[9] recurs in the Talmud. This opposition came not just from rabbis who disapproved of pagan manifestations of Greek culture such as
theaters and circuses for their emphasis on the physical but
because of the political hegemony that the successors of
Alexander imposed on the Jews. Just as important, the
rabbis opposed the strictly rational intellectual approach to
life. Many of the debates between rabbis and one Roman

general or emperor or another recorded in the Talmud are indeed paradigms of the rational/nonrational divide. Issues such as resurrection in the last chapter of Talmud *Bavli Sanhedrin* are challenged by non-Jews on a rational basis and defended by the rabbis nonrationally. Rabbinic approval of high ranking families teaching their children Greek was excused as being necessary for affairs of state, but certainly the emotional antagonism was profound even if economic necessity required some interaction—as indeed is the case today.

Just as the Stoic and the Epicurean approaches to life find resonance in Jewish thought, so too do rationalism and mysticism. Both coexisted in Judaism, but two thousand years of living under alien theological systems resulted in two things: Those Jews who explored their religious thinking in a systematic way inevitably used rational, philosophical systems and tools. The tools they used were those of the philosophical world, the non-Jewish and Greek philosophical tradition that both the early Church Fathers and the Arabic *Mutakallimun* theologians used. These imposed an artificial restriction on mental processes. They led, for example, to the assumption that one needed proofs of the existence of God in the same way that one would seek proofs of mathematical formulae. But proofs are very limited things. Descartes, the great French philosopher, realized that it was all but impossible to prove one's existence and his solution— *Cogito Ergo Sum*, I Think Therefore I Am—is no proof of anything other than, perhaps, that there is a thought. Thus when philosophical proofs came to be challenged, the bottom fell out of their justifications.

The mystics, on the other hand, went to the other extreme and spoke in exciting symbols and metaphors that— precisely because they rejected any kind of rational scrutiny—opened the way for lesser minds to introduce magic, hocus-pocus, and trivialization. Even attempts to bring some logic into Chassidism avoided the rational issues because of the fundamentalist atmosphere in which the attempt was born.

We should not be caught up in only one or the other of these two great traditions. We should be able to draw on both the logical and the mystical in our modern attempt to understand the complete person. We should be able to draw on a whole range of mental tools and experiences in order to get as complete a picture of our world and its many levels of being and experience as possible. I want to try and span the two conflicting ways of thinking, the logical and the mystical. We currently live in a society that increasingly seeks to meld the rational and the mystical, in thought, spirit, and medicine. This combination seems to me to be the most appropriate way to lay bare the essentials of Jewish belief.

For the most creative period of postbiblical Jewish thought, the Midrash rather than theology was the vehicle for expression. The midrashic approach of the rabbis is indeed not a philosophic one. It is syncretic rather than systematic. It brings lots of different ways of thinking, imagining, and talking together. It is certainly prephilosophical and was more the precursor of a mystical approach to God than a rational one. One can understand rabbinic thought only through this earlier framework. Midrash is usually a way of using a biblical verse to convey, directly or indirectly, a religious idea. More often than not this was done orally, in private study or in a public sermon. Many of the ideas were hyperbolic and in some cases manifestly contrary to the accepted Halacha. Often *midrashim* are introduced with the statement "He saw that his audience was dozing and so he said," clearly something that would wake them up for its controversy. A typical example is the statement that it is better to put out a human light than to put out a soul on *Shabbat*.[10] Such a system, allowing for flexibility, is a wonderful way of seeing the range of rabbinic ideas. This is why there is no attempt to come to conclusions or to decide on a single accepted position in midrashic thought. And this is why to understand the essence of Jewish theology one must turn not to philosophy but to Midrash.

4

The idea, or the experience, of God is the fundamental principle on which the life of Judaism is based. The Torah talks about loving God and knowing God but nowhere talks about proving the existence of God. While behavioral commands are phrased as "Say to the Children of Israel that they must (or should)," no such phraseology is used with regard to the abstract aspects of the Torah. There is no statement like "Speak to the Children of Israel and say to them, 'This is what you must believe.'" The Torah contains no actual command to believe that is phrased as a command, as opposed to actions that are commanded. The first of the Ten Commandments, which is usually taken to refer to a belief in God, does not say "You must believe that there is God," and there is nowhere else in the Torah a formulation that we would recognize as a categorical, theological imperative. This is not to say that ideas play no part or indeed that the theological importance of God can be underestimated but rather it is to emphasize that whereas the Torah specifically commands actions and actions are the criteria for testing Jewish eligibility both civilly and religiously, there is no detailed description of what a person is expected to believe. Even the last chapter of the talmudic folio of *Sanhedrin* that talks about who has no part in the world to come[11] does not deprive a Jew of his or her identity for a theological incapacity. All we are told is *Mida Keneged Mida*, you are paid back "measure for measure." If you do not believe in an afterlife, you do not get one! This similarly applies to the other issues mentioned there.

Whereas halachically there is an elaborate structure of authority, a clear demarcation of hierarchy, a clear statement of what constitutes rebellion against authority, no such defined position exists on what we might call theological issues. Whereas Maimonides in the eleventh century is accepted as an absolutely crucial voice, a *Rishon* (a major "first wave" posttalmudic authority), in the halachic process and any disagreement falls within defined parameters, no such respect is accorded to his Aristotelian philosophic system. If his Thirteen Principles have come now to be accepted as a handy guide or menu of Jewish Thinking (despite the theoretical opposition of giants like Crescas and Albo), there is no obligation to accept an Aristotelian description of what constitutes a Perfect Unity as opposed to a Platonic or indeed (anachronistically) a Wittgenstinian one. Maimonides thought of perfect unities the way a Greek did. If I use the phrase "God is a perfect unity," it does not mean anything to me at all. I understand that there is only one God, but I do not understand what a perfect unity is. I think I know what Aristotle or Maimonides meant, but I cannot be sure.

If God is the paramount feature of a religious life, then in what way does the Torah seek to convey His importance? Not, as others do, by insisting on a statement of belief. This does not mean that God is any less essential or fundamental, just that there are different ways of relating.

5

The whole of the Torah is an encounter with God. From Adam and Eve through Cain and Abel and on to Enosh, Enoch, and Noah, the search for the appropriate relationship underlies the narrative. Adam and Eve have no relationship with God. They are given instructions and punished for their disobedience. Cain is the first to try to relate in an act of devotion by bringing the first sacrifice.[12] Perhaps his method was inadequate. Abel"s offering was accepted. Enosh calls on God,[13] perhaps an attempt at verbal contact rather than sacrificial. Enoch walks with God and is taken away.[14] There is clearly something wrong with his relationship; otherwise he might have been chosen before Noah. It is not before Avram that we see the example of the correct relationship between God and man. Avraham, Yitschak, and Yaakov are all shown engaged in different ways with God and humans, but they are all manifestly preoccupied with and dominated by their relationship with God.

From Moses onward this relationship is bifurcated into a personal and a national experience. The nation is made up of different people on different levels. Debate and uncertainty enter the situation. The existence of God is not challenged; what is asked for is a description, a name, or reassurance, as after the golden calf episode. One might even say that the Torah **is** God, so dominant is His presence. We look back and seeing it through modern eyes can only wonder that a people which had experienced Divine intervention at first hand could nevertheless on occasion rebel or act as though it had not had much effect. But the Torah talks about the people's experiences, not its state of mind except immediately after crossing the Red Sea when it says that "They believed in God and in Moses His servant."[15] Of course this puts belief in God on the same footing as belief in Moses. Clearly the word "belief" functions very differently in the biblical mind from the way we, in a post-Christian world, regard it.

6

The Hebrew word *EMuNa*, normally translated "belief," a way of thinking about the absolute, means something very different in the Torah. There it means "to be convinced of something." It is the same distinction we make in English between "I believe in God" and "I believe in you." To "believe that" something is the case and to "believe in" something or a person are two different sorts of statements. To "believe that" is usually a statement about material facts, scientific or even ethical, and it usually requires some evidence to support it. If I believe it will rain tomorrow, or that base metal can be turned into gold, or that good people are rewarded for their deeds, then I need some sort of factual information to support these beliefs. On the other hand if I believe in you, I am saying that I have come to be convinced of your friendship or reliability. I base this as much on feeling as I do on evidence. Of course many people remain convinced that someone loves them long after the evidence shows that he or she does not, but "belief in" is far more a matter of feeling than "belief that." "I believe that you are my father" is likely to be said only if someone has challenged the paternity in the first place and there is some doubt. Otherwise a person simply says "I am your father," which is precisely how God addresses us in the opening verse of the Ten Commandments. Look at the way the word "believe" is used in the Torah.

What are the other uses of "belief," *emunah*? Sarah asks, "Is it really the case (*UMNam*) that I will give birth?"[16] Joseph threatens his brothers, "We will see if what you say can be verified (*VaYeaMNu divreichem*)."[17] Jacob does not believe (*HeEMiN*) his sons when they tell him that Joseph is alive.[18] We can see that we are talking about conviction, certainty, trust. When Moses has to keep his arms high while Joshua fights Amalek, he needs Aharon and Chur to hold his hands up. With their support, the hands of Moses remain up until sunset. His hands were *EMuNa*, firm.[19] When a woman suspected of adultery appears before the priest he makes a declaration to which she has to assent. Her agreement is described as her affirming, "*AMeN, AMeN*."[20] Thus we have a word that connotes firmness, agreement. It is not a word that connotes theological or philosophical proof. A fascinating use of the root of the word for belief is the word for a nurse. God will care for Israel as a "nurse cares (*OMeN*) for a child."[21] At the end of Deuteronomy[22] Moses describes the Jewish people as backsliding and a "people with no credibility, trust," children with no *EMuN*.

Of course there are plenty of quotes that emphasize the faith or lack of faith that the people had in God and in Moses, but the meaning of this faith is not an abstract or intellectual affirmation. Rather it is a statement of trust, conviction. God is described as being *NeEMaN*,[23] reliable, in just the same way as Moses is described as *NeEMaN*. This is important because conviction and certainty, certainly with regard to people, often comes about as a result of intangible or emotional responses. It is feeling that decides certainty just as much if not more than theory.

We can apply a similar analysis to the word for truth. In our culture truth is usually an absolute. There can only be "The truth, the whole truth, and nothing but the truth." Hence the association of the word "truth" with God and the implication that was such a vital tool of Christian missionaries that there could only be one true religion. However, if you look at the word *EMeT*, truth, in the Torah, a different kind of usage emerges, one that is more empirical and less absolute.

Eliezer, the servant of Abraham, uses the word *emet* in thanking God for having directed him to Rebecca and either bestowing *emet* or leading him down the correct path toward his goal.[24] When the patriarchs ask for a favor they ask both their children and God to deal with them in a way that is *emet*, correct, appropriate. In this Genesis context, *emet* implies actions or support that are correct, beneficial, and trustworthy. This continues into the Book of Judges where, in Chapter 9, the word *emet* it is used several times to mean "to do the right thing."

In Exodus[25] when Jethro advises Moses to look for a team of men to assist, he is told to look for "men of truth who hate corruption." The book of Deuteronomy[26] uses the word empirically—"Is it true that this event actually happened?"—so that when we examine the nature of the word and apply it to God, it is clear that we are talking about experiencing behavior in man and God that is dependable and honest. It is a quality of God that reinforces our love for Him and our commitment to Him. In man, similarly, it is reassuring and a matter of confidence-building. It tells us something about the nature of God and about the nature of man without implying absolutes or a monochromatic concept that excludes other possibilities. So it was in classical Judaism that there was room to accept and even appreciate other religions that were monotheistic and to allow for "the pious of the nations of the world," who would achieve spiritual greatness and the World to Come. More important is the fact that if "truth" is empirical, then it allows for intellectual uncertainty and experiment. This is the very opposite of the fundamentalist position, which implies a stasis—that the idea is fixed, defined, and impervious to modification.

7

The Torah is primarily concerned with behavior; it is the action that defines, not the thought. Thus in rabbinic Judaism it is the act of breaking Jewish law in public that results in a person being barred from giving testimony in a court of Law.[27] It is the commitment to Law that defines membership in the group, once one's genealogy or conversion has gained one initial acceptance. After all, this is the only way a person's affiliation can be reliably tested. Anyone can say whatever he or she wants. I can say I believe in men from Mars. I guess I would be prepared to say that I believe in lots of strange things if I thought my life was in danger. Perhaps once, people were frightened to take the Lord's Name in vain. But even then, the Torah knew full well that a Credo was no basis for reliable verification. This is why there is no such statement in the Torah as "Speak to the Children of Israel and tell them they must believe." This is a meaningless statement. God is to be experienced and one must attempt to understand.

The Torah talks about "knowing" God in the way that a

man "knows" his wife, and about loving God in the way lovers
know each other. These terms are not necessarily intellectual terms. One brings a lot of sensual and emotional experiences and sensitivities to play in the act of knowing and
loving another human being, which does indeed involve the
mind and the thought process—but not exclusively. The
Greek way, and hence Maimonides' way, to God is through
pure intellect, the intellect in contradistinction to matter.
The two eternal substances that in Greek thought are caught
in a primordial battle are intertwined and indivisible in
biblical Judaism, but I am arguing that it is through a
mystical rather than a rationalist position that one can understand God in the Jewish experience.

The need to prove the existence of God is redundant and
irrelevant in Judaism, whereas the need to experience is essential. "Taste it and see," says the psalmist. Yet there is no
single way, no single formula that is "the correct one" to come
to God. There may be revealed ways to behave but there are
not prescribed ways to think.

This is not to say that the world of ideas is irrelevant in
Judaism. There are indeed ideas that play an important part
in our religious tradition, but they play this part in a very
different way and in a far less precise manner than they do
in other Western religious traditions. Theology is the science of the Christian religious world; it is incidental to the
Jewish. Just as Maimonides says that one can only say what
God is not—one cannot describe the indescribable—so too,
Judaism is essentially concerned with avoiding negative
ideology. Its approach is not to reject even if one is uncertain about what to accept.

If one looks at the talmudic statements of a theological
nature, the argument is against the ideological heretic. The
Talmud recounts, at the end of *Sanhedrin*, those who have
no portion of the World to Come. They are the deniers; those
who say there is no life beyond the grave; those who know
precisely that the Torah is not the word of God. It is the

atheist rather than the agnostic, the denier rather than the doubter, who creates the problem for traditional Judaism. It is the person who eats forbidden food as an act of ideological defiance who is rejected rather than the one who gives in to weakness and eats out of self-indulgent appetite.[28] We are all in the second category to some extent or another. This is the biblical understanding of the inclination of man: There is a constant struggle. Biblical Judaism sees every person, including King David, as caught in this behavioral battle. The way to survive is by accepting the presence and the influence of the Divine, but this is something to be experienced and lived with. It is not a door one goes through. It is not a state one enters to be saved. Rather it is a constant engagement with a constant stream of experiences that reinforce the commitment to the way of living that reinforces the experience of and the commitment to the Divine. It is not a formula. It is not a Credo. It is an act of devotion and love.

This is why it is myth to say that one must believe. A myth is a misleading story, a fictional narrative. It may deal with important issues, but it deals with them in a misleading way. God is essential to Jewish spiritual experience, it is simply not the case that there is a required formulation of exactly what one has to believe to pass the test of Jewish identity.

Notes

1. Rabbi Moses Ben Maimon, born in Cordova, 1135, and died in Egypt, 1204, was one of the greatest authorities on Jewish Law and a world renowned philosopher.
2. Talmud Bavli *Chagigah* 14b.
3. Talmud Bavli *Kiddushin* 39a, *Chullin* 142a.
4. Talmud Yerushalmi *Taanit* 4:5.
5. Mishna *Yadaim* 3.

6. Isaiah 54:4–7.
7. Isaiah 62:4–5.
8. Hosea 2.
9. Talmud Bavli *Bava Kama* 82b and 83a.
10. Talmud Bavli *Shabbat* 30b.
11.Talmud Bavli *Sanhedrin* 90a and b.
12. Genesis 4:3.
13. Genesis 4:26.
14. Genesis 5:24.
15. Exodus 14:31.
16. Genesis 18:13.
17. Genesis 42:20.
18. Genesis 45:26.
19. Exodus 17:12.
20. Numbers 5:22.
21. Numbers 11:12.
22. Deuteronomy 32:20.
23. Deuteronomy 7:9.
24. Genesis 24.
25. Exodus 18:21.
26. Deuteronomy 13:17 and 22.
27. Talmud Bavli *Eruvin* 69b.
28. Talmud Bavli *Sanhedrin* 27a.

Chapter 2

Myth:
We Can Know
What God Is

1

One of the major problems most thinking people have with the idea of God is the way God is portrayed. He is a big Daddy in the sky, sitting on a golden throne among thick clouds surrounded by white gowned angels with oversized bird's wings. Once a year He takes out a huge tome and with a quill starts writing the names of the people He determines are going to have a good year. What do we really have to think about God?

The Bible could well be described as a book that is "God intoxicated," but there is hardly any actual description of God. God is the hero, the beginning and the end. God is engaged with and argues with human beings. He (gender is unimportant; it is a convention and no more) is exalted and accepted. To us moderns it seems strange that nowhere does the Bible call upon us in specific words to believe or indeed tell us exactly what God is. Yet there is a very definite assumption that without God there would be nothing. God himself, or itself, uses different words to describe Himself and uses riddles in Self Description. What can we distill from the Torah?

"In the beginning God created the heavens and the earth."[1] The word used for God there is *Elohim*, a word that is elsewhere used to describe human judges as well as other gods in the idolatrous world. Other words used to describe God are *Adonai* (my Master); *El* (the God above); *El Elyon* (The God above all others); *El Shaddai* (God of the spirits); *Yah* or the full *YHVH*, sometimes erroneously transliterated as Yahweh.

Various attempts have been made to systematize and explain the different usages. Wellhausen, the founder of so called "Higher Biblical Criticism" and the JEPD scheme of describing different editors of different parts of the Torah, thought that the different authors of the texts used different names for God and that this could identify them. But since different names often occur in the same sentence this does not work unless you set about a wholesale re-editing of the text, which itself would be like cutting off the legs of a human being so that the body could fit onto the bed.

Umberto Cassutto is excellent in demolishing Wellhausen but not quite so good in answering the questions that remain. He suggests that *YHVH* is used specifically in spiritual terms where a special engaged relationship between man and God is being described. Thus in the first chapter of creation when God is focused on the material ingredients of creation the word *Elohim* is used, but as soon as there is interaction with mankind the phrase *YHVH Elohim* is used.

Many other theories are offered, including a popular one that *Adonai* or *YHVH* is used specifically in relation to Israel, the Jewish People, whereas the word *Elohim* and its associate words are used to describe the more universal relationship of God to the world in general. This is a beautiful idea but it does not work in every case. No theory really satisfies. We are left with the conclusion that God has many names, many facets, and that a person sees God according to his or her own level of experience and intellect.

If we use the Torah as the basis for trying to understand what God is, we find two types of statements. Some statements describing God are really descriptions of His "qualities" as manifested to humans. So Moses' thirteen attributes of God,[2] thirteen qualities to which he appeals in asking God to forgive the Children of Israel for the golden calf, cannot be taken as either Self Description or a formula for describing God objectively, otherwise God would have used them Himself when Moses asked for a description at the burning bush.

Similarly the famous *Shema Yisrael*, "Hear Israel, *YHVH* is our God, YHVH is One,"[3] is Moses instructing the nation and providing it with an encapsulating formula, a sort of slogan. To say that God is "one" can mean that there is not more than one, or, as the philosophers would have it, that "God is perfect unity." Yet Maimonides, for example, asserts that one cannot give a positive description of God.[4] As God says to Moses, "No man can see Me and live,"[5] and so we have to try to create a picture in our minds that will help us to understand what we are talking about when we use the word "God." The primary source, of course, is the Torah itself.

2

God tells us about His actions. We see Him creating and instructing mankind and then, in a way, standing back and watching him destroy himself. The Torah shows us a process of spiritual evolution that reaches to Abraham, the founding father of the tradition. We see how from the start mankind tried to find different ways of relating to God and God to mankind: Adam receives instructions. He disobeys. He is questioned by God and is simply punished. There is

no dialogue. Cain tries to reach God through sacrifice. He
fails, yet here at least God engages him and gives him words
of support and encouragement. Abel's sacrifice is accepted
but there is no communication.[6] Various characters progress
or regress through the early chapters of Genesis. Enosh calls
in the name of God.[7] Enoch walks with God and disappears.[8]
Humanity acts corruptly and God decides to destroy it. Noah
and his family are saved, and yet there is nothing written
about the nature of his relationship with God other than
that he was a good man in his generation and he walked
with God.[9] Before the flood God speaks to Noah, but only to
instruct him. During the flood there is no dialogue at all,
and after the flood God speaks to Himself (to His heart)
rather than discuss anything with Noah. Noah, like Adam,
is given instructions. He is a tool. It is not until Abraham
that we find engagement with God.

Abraham's relationship is the example we are asked to
idealize. Closeness to God influences and improves his closeness to mankind. He is able to argue a case, as with the
destruction of Sodom, yet he is unwilling to challenge God
over the near sacrifice of his son. God introduces Himself to
him, saying that He is the God Who has taken him out of Ur
of the Chaldees.[10] Is this the first contact Abram has with
God, or is it simply the first statement of commitment? The
Midrash contains a tradition that Abram recognized God as
a child and destroyed his father's idols, but there is nothing
of this said in the Torah. All we have is God appearing to
Abram and making certain promises and predictions. There
is no self-description or command to believe, yet there is a
phrase that is usually translated to the effect that "Abraham
believed in God[11] and it was (He thought or considered it to
be) a 'good thing.'" In fact, looking carefully at the context,
it really should be translated "And Abraham accepted what
God had just told him and God was satisfied with him."
Either way, there is no description of God.

It is not until Moses, at the burning bush, asks God to

describe Himself, to help persuade the Hebrew slaves that salvation is at hand, that God obliges with a definition: "And God said to Moses, 'I will Be What I Am,' and He said, 'Speak to the Children of Israel and tell them, '"I Will Be' has sent me to you.""[12]

On first reading this sounds like a riddle, almost as though Moses is being palmed off with no answer—a sort of "mind your own business." But the Hebrew gives a clue. The Hebrew is *EHYEH ASHER EHYEH*, which literally means "I will be what I will be," except that the future and the past are interchangeable and "I will be" could equally be "I was." In other words, God is unlike anything material, which is subject to change. A nonphysical force can make guarantees of continuity that a physical power cannot. The Hebrew letters *YHVH* are the same letters that are used in the Hebrew words for past, present, and future.

Given the times, this seems a brilliantly simple way of God describing Himself in a nonphysical way. But this first description is in response to a doubt; it is a reaction. Ideally one would not need to ask God for a description. God gives one only in response to Moses, who has to go face the Children of Israel and needs something to say that will persuade them. Of course, how this description of God is received by the slaves is a different issue, and we can see that despite Moses' assurances and God's miracles, there was plenty of room left for large numbers to question the nature of both Moses and God.

Is this why God also presented Moses with a range of wonders—the burning bush, the staff that became a snake, the hand that became leprous and was cured—some of which the Egyptian magicians were able replicate? God is indeed a wonder beyond the capacity of many to grasp. This is why we are sometimes presented with hints and images that on the one hand obscure reality and give excuses for doubt. On the other hand, only via these "miracles" can some people be brought closer to an understanding of the infinite power that is God. Something above and beyond humans needs either to be shrunk for them to comprehend or to be presented through its impact rather than its reality.

It is in response to one of these periods of national doubt that God admits that "(When) I appeared to Abraham, Isaac, and Jacob it was as *El Shaddai* and I did not make known to them My Name *YHVH*."[13] Does this mean that Abraham's conception of God was inadequate? We should deduce from this, rather, that understanding God on one level is not enough. God manifests Himself on different levels to different people and one needs lots of names and lots of definitions to come close to understanding the wondrous complexity of *YHVH*. This is one of the reasons that Maimonides in his Guide to the Perplexed emphasizes that one cannot say what God is, only what He is not.

This is why in my discussions about God I normally prefer to use the word *Makom*, a rabbinic usage, for God, because it avoids both the history of the misuse of God's Name and the cultural particularism of a male overlord. *Makom* is used in the Mishna primarily in the context of God's relationship and interaction with people. The Mishna describes God, in the context of protectively passing over the homes of the Children of Israel, as *Makom*.[14] Choni HaMeagel, the miraculous rainmaker who stood in his circle and would not move until rain came down, treated God as a friend, much to the disgust of Shimon Ben Shetach, and there the Mishna also speaks of God as *Makom*.[15] Job is described as a fearer (respecter) of *Makom*[16] and the use of *Makom* in *Pirkei Avot* is primarily in the context of the link between those whom God loves and those who establish good relations with other humans.[17]

The explanation for calling God *Makom* is in the Midrash:[18] "The Holy Blessed One is the dwelling place of the world but the world is not the dwelling place of *Makom*," and in the *Pesikta Rabtai*:[19] "God is the *Makom* (place) of the world but the world is not the *Makom* (place) of God."

The clear implication is that God transcends the material world. Unlike the pantheist who says that God is the world and no more, this stresses that God is the world but also much more. Unlike the deist who says that God is beyond but not here, *Makom* asserts the presence of God here. This very down-to-earth word *Makom*, "place," suggests a certain immediacy and intimacy. This is why we comfort mourners with the phrase "May *HaMakom* comfort you." It is why *Makom* recurs so much in the Pesach Haggada. How one intellectualizes this notion is very subjective, and precisely because it is so complex, the Torah nowhere commands us to believe, to accept a specific formula that defines God and requires our acceptance.

This is behind the beautiful explanation of why the *Amidah* prayer, the central piece of traditional prayer, said at least three times daily, starts off "The God of Abraham, the God of Isaac, and the God of Jacob." The phrase is unnecessarily repetitive and could simply be said "The God of Abraham, Isaac, and Jacob." It is also strange that the word for God is *Elohei* which literally means "the Gods of." Leaving aside the poetic rhythm of the beat of the repetition, there is a message here. The Midrash describes each one of the fathers as having a different character and being defined by a different adjective. Each one saw God through his own experience and character and so each one had a subjective, perhaps different concept or understanding of God. By thinking of this at the start of prayer, we are invited to discover our own routes to God.

3

The first of the Ten Commandments says, "I Am the Lord your God Who took you out of the Land of Egypt."[20] It is a statement—not a command. It is the primary statement and foundation of Torah, but it is not phrased as though it were a theological statement. It is as much a requirement to feel and to experience God as it is a theological definition. It is true that the Torah commands us to love and to respect God, but love and respect can be achieved through experience and feeling and not necessarily by abstract thought. On the contrary, as Chassidism loudly proclaimed, it is feeling that can find the way directly to God rather than abstruse reasoning. Similarly, when the Torah says that we should "Know the Lord your God,"[21] it continues, "and you will bring to your heart (the realization) that *YHVH* is God." "Bringing to one's heart" is a metaphor for feeling rather than thinking, which is usually associated with the brain. This emphasizes the emotional. Knowledge need not be intellectual. After all, if Adam "knew" his wife and she conceived, we do not assume that this was an intellectual process.

The Torah, therefore, in my view, intentionally takes God out of abstraction and puts Him firmly in the realm of experience. But then what are we to make of the incident after the golden calf in which God says to Moses, "No person can see me and live,"[22] and then places him in a crack in a rock and passes by so that he can see the back, or afterimage, of God? The message seems to me to be clear: Communication between God and man is possible through various means and channels. It is true that the level of specific revelation that Moses attained was the highest achieved in the Bible. As God told Miriam and Aharon, Moses was unlike any other person with whom God communicated: "Mouth to mouth I spoke with him."[23] Nevertheless this does not mean that the totality of God was circumscribed in these encounters or that Moses was able to fully comprehend beyond the limits of human understanding. Thus Moses was put in the cleft in the rock, and God covered his face as He passed by and let him see His afterimage. The implication of this, though, is that when God was talking "mouth to mouth" to Moses, on Mount Sinai, Moses was not experiencing even an afterimage. He was receiving a message, a whole series of laws and ideas, from God, but through channels that had no recognizable physical shape or representation. The experience Moses had of God's afterimage happened only once. This illustrates the limits of human understanding, however great the human or close the relationship with God. It also raises one of the issues that makes the nature of Divine communication so complex. To adapt the well-known aphorism: "The God that is small enough for my mind is not big enough for me." We, as humans, can therefore only imagine and use only human, material terms to describe what we experience.

At the time God received Moses on Sinai, some of the high ranking Israelites "saw the God of Israel (and It was) like sapphire stone and as pure as the sky."[24] Did they really see God? How could that be if Moses, for all his closeness to God, could not? Or did they experience some sort of blinding flash, some sort of awareness that God was beyond anything earthly and therefore only symbolically describable in earthly terms? Consider our concept of "perfection." Can we really imagine absolute perfection? Or can we just think of something better, faster, or more beautiful than anything we have come across so far? It is not possible, despite the assertions of the Greek-influenced theologians, to have a positive concept of perfection. I would argue that it is not possible to have a positive concept of unity. The idea of a "perfect unity" can only mean not more than one. The limits of human understanding are best illustrated in the mystical tradition.

We mentioned in the previous chapter the episode of the four who entered the orchard:[25] Ben Azai, Ben Zoma, Acher, and Rabbi Akiva. Rabbi Akiva said to them, "When you reach the pure marble stones do not say, 'Water, Water,' because "No one who speaks falsehood can abide in My presence." (Psalms 101) The narrative uses the word "orchard" as a synonym for the mystical experience of God, or sometimes for the afterlife, an existence beyond this world entering into the closest possible proximity to the palace of the Divine ("This world is like an orchard before the palace.")

But this experience, because it is a mystical one, cannot really be understood on a rational level. The similarity to the experience of the elders with the sapphire stones in Exodus 24 is remarkable and certainly not coincidental. What Rabbi Akiva is saying is that one must not judge by appearances. If one sees stones that look like water one must be careful not to give expression to the thought because of the human capacity for delusion or miscomprehension, in which case one would be excluding from one's mind the possibility of a totally different kind of experience. The elders who believed they saw the "feet of God" and thought it was like pure sapphire stones might have made the mistake that Rabbi Akiva was warning about 1,500 years later. Those earlier seekers were able to translate their experience into their own physical realm and that is why the Torah says that they responded or celebrated by eating and drinking, the archetypal way of linking spiritual and physical pleasure as reflected in the way our tradition celebrates festive occasions. For some, however, a profound mystical experience is too much to handle, as illustrated by Ben Azai and Ben Zoma in their different ways. For others, it is offensive to rational preconceptions. Elisha Ben Abuya, the great rabbi, became Acher, Someone Else, when he abandoned Judaism for Greek philosophy. Only Rabbi Akiva's balanced and considered view allowed him to go through the experience and come out unharmed—precisely because he was open to the mystical, as illustrated by his claim in the Mishna *Yadaim* that the Song Of Songs is the holiest book of the Bible because it is an analogy for the experience of God.

4

The Talmud consistently presents God in quasi-human ways. The aim is to intensify the immanence of God and His presence, close to and involved in His people and in humanity. The Talmud depicts God praying,[26] mirroring the way humans pray. As we pray to God, so He prays to Himself that His qualities of mercy should override His anger at human frailty and that He should judge us leniently. A little earlier[27] God is said to wear tefillin. As our tefillin celebrate our commitment to God in the choice of Torah excerpts included in the four compartments on the head and rolled into one on the arm, so God's tefillin celebrate His commitment to us by including the quotation "Who is like you Israel, a unique nation on earth."[28] The idea of mutual engagement, of a relationship, is the crucial issue here. This relationship can only be on a mystical level.

Similarly, the idea that God appears to humans in different ways at different times can be understood only in human, mystical terminology; it makes no sense rationally. "God appeared at the Red Sea as a Fighting Warrior but on Sinai as a Merciful Elder."[29] Nor can we understand other than metaphorically the idea that God suffers because of our failures. This is a recurring theme, beautifully illustrated in the story of Elijah encountering Rabbi Yossi turning into a ruin to pray and asking him what he heard. "I said that I heard a voice moaning like a dove and saying, 'Woe to My children, because of whom I destroyed My house and burnt My halls and exiled them amongst the nations.' He [Elijah] said to me 'As you live, not only once but three times a day the voice says this. Yet, whenever the Jewish People come into the synagogues and study houses and say, 'May His great name be blessed.' The Holy One Blessed Be He nods His head and says, 'Happy is the king who is praised in His own home. But how sad it is for a father who has to exile his children. And it is even worse for children to be exiled from their father's table.'"[30]

This state of alienation yet closeness is affirmed in the Midrash, and this is how the rabbis characterize the relationship with God. It is certainly not a philosophical approach. This is the meaning of an often-used phrase taken from Ezekiel's vision of God: In the vision, God is described as "hovering toward," wanting to come close yet at the same time "drawing away."[31] This has been taken to mean that God is trying to come closer to us but as He approaches us He withdraws—or, as the mystics suggest, we withdraw. This withdrawal is either because of our imperfections, which 'drive God away,' or it is in the nature of the difference between the Divine and the human: There is an inherent attraction and yet an inevitable distance.

The yearning to get closer to God is a recurrent feature of the mystical tradition, beautifully illustrated by the phrase in the haunting poem by the sixteenth-century mystic Eliezer Azikri that some congregations sing on *Shabbat*, *Yedid Nefesh*: "My soul is sick of love for You," or, as another poet says: "My soul thirsts for my eternal, living God." Yet there is an inevitability of distance simply because of the different natures and realities of humanity and God. The rabbis portray God almost equally desperately wanting humans to come closer in order to consummate the union of the spiritual and the material.

This is hardly rational, but it is the way language is used to draw us nearer to a real understanding of what God is. Talking about it is inadequate, like trying to describe butter to someone who cannot taste it. Trying to describe an experience does not work; one can only encourage others to try for themselves and then the talk can be based on common ground.

All the other names that are used to call or describe God in the Torah are similarly approximations that make sense to humans in their cultural contexts. They are meant neither to be taken literally nor to be definitions; rather they are pointers, hints at something greater. A God that is like a superman, capable of doing wonderful things whenever and wherever a priest requires it, makes sense in a context of idol worshippers. A God of spirits makes sense in a world of spirit worshippers.

This is why the very word "God," in English, is so disturbing. Its context is one of two thousand years of people using this word to mean different aspects of a supposedly monotheistic concept that has been divided and trinitized and used as an excuse for political oppression, torture, domination, and hypocrisy. Only if we break from using this word can we free ourselves from cultural imperialism and try to rediscover the specifically Jewish idea of *Makom.*

Like any experience, there is always some doubt and uncertainty. There will always be moments when we are less convinced or more convinced. The experience of God is an encounter that involves us in constantly trying to get closer and to understand. It is not a matter of affirming or discovering a formula and then entering a new state of certainty. This is why the Torah shows a constant struggle in the minds of its greatest personalities, from Abraham's uncertainty as to what God wanted when he went up the mountain to sacrifice his son to Moses's struggle with God and need for reassurance after the golden calf episode. It is this struggle that is the paradigm for us to follow, not the medieval philosophers formulae of certainty as though God were a mathematical proposition like a Euclidian proof.

It is for this reason that "proof" of the existence of God is irrelevant and unnecessary. Proofs are to show others. Proofs are the medieval tools of theologians. They are the abstractions that obscure the emptiness, the vacuum that an absence of experience creates. Judaism calls on us to feel and to experience God rather than to play fanciful intellectual games with Him. The myth here is the impression that one has to have a very precise notion or concept of what God is. To be obliged to relate to something and come to terms with an experience is not the same as saying "This is what it is that you must believe."

Notes

1. Genesis 1:1.
2. Exodus 34:6.
3. Deuteronomy 6:4.
4. Maimonides' Guide to the Perplexed, 1.LII (Friedlander).
5. Exodus 33:20.
6. Genesis 4.
7. Genesis 4:26.
8. Genesis 5:22.
9. Genesis 6.
10. Genesis 14:7.
11. Genesis 15:6.
12. Exodus 3:14.
13. Exodus 6:3.
14. Mishna *Pesachim* 10:5.
15. Mishna *Taanit* 3:2.
16. Mishna *Sotah* 5:5.
17. Mishna *Avot* 2:9, 3:10 et passim.
18. Midrash Rabba *Bereshit* 68:10.
19. *Pesikta Rabtai* 21:10.
20. Exodus 20:2.
21. Deuteronomy 4.
22. Exodus 33:20.
23. Numbers 12:8.
24. Exodus 24:10.
25. Talmud Bavli *Chagigah* 14b.
26. Talmud Bavli *Brachot* 7a.
27. Talmud Bavli *Brachot* 6a.
28. 1 Chronicles 17.
29. *Pesikta Rabtai* Exodus 14.
30. Talmud Bavli *Brachot* 3a.
31. Ezekiel 1:14.

Chapter 3

Myth: Judaism Defines the "Soul"

"They called the soul by five names. *Nefesh, Ruach, Neshama, Yechida, Chaya. Nefesh* is blood . . . *Ruach* is the spirit that rises and descends . . . *Neshama* is the personality of a person . . . *Chaya*, even if all the limbs are dead, it still survives in the body . . . *Yechida*, all limbs are in pairs but this one it remains unique."[1]

What is a soul? Do we all have one? What happens to it when we die? These are questions we ask as children but are rarely answered and so we push them to the recesses of our minds and carry on with the business of living. We replace the uncertainty with a cliché and stock responses, using the word "soul" pretty casually in day-to-day conversation without really examining what we think or believe.

There is no specified command in Jewish texts to believe in the existence of a soul and yet it is taken as axiomatic that we have one—indeed it seems to be so obvious that it does not even need to be posited. Ideally, of course, this is as it should be. Spiritual phenomena should be so immediate and obvious to us that we should not need to prove anything. If a parent meets a child after a long absence, one does not expect the parent to say, as they run to embrace, "You have got to believe it is me!" (unless of course someone has called into question the issue of paternity). Nevertheless, in talking about the soul we do have a problem both in defining it and in the relationship it has to God and as the element of a human that is supposed to survive after death. All talk about afterlife and resurrection implies a function for the soul, whatever it might be.

If we accept convention, "soul" is something Divine in humans that has an existence of its own and survives and is unaffected by physical change. It is the link between humans and God, usually a result of something placed by God within humans as an afterthought or addition following the completion of the physical body. There is an old English expression, a euphemism for dying: "to give up the ghost." "The Ghost" is a Christian term for "The Holy Spirit," one of the elements of the Trinity. It has some similarity to the word *Shechina* or to the idea of "The Spirit Of God." "To give up the ghost" suggests that God gives a part of Himself to humans and when humans die they "give up" that "ghost" for its return to God. Is this what we mean when we talk about the soul?

In the Torah we see several different words used to describe "soul" or "spirit." The rabbis added even more words, yet the assumptions that have been handed down can be and in practice are challenged and varied throughout both the Bible and the Talmud.

There are three main words used in the Torah for what we call "soul." The first is *ruach*, "spirit," which appears initially as a word to describe the presence of God: "And the spirit of *YHVH* was hovering over the deep."[2] Some commentators suggest that God caused a wind to blow, like the one that divided the Red Sea for the Israelites, but most take this to mean the *Shechina*, the presence of God. Since God cannot be confined to any one place or said to be in any one place, the rabbis devised a way of talking about the presence of God without implying the totality of His Being. This is the *Shechina*, the presence; literally it means "The Dwelling" or "Where She is," the place where God has chosen to have an impact. It does not have an independent reality or function in the way that "The Holy Spirit" is often understood. Later on, when talking about the flood, the Torah says that God will destroy "All flesh that has the spirit of life," using the same word, *ruach*.[3] Thus the word *ruach* is applied both to God and to all living creatures as though it is a common link.

There is an altogether different use of *ruach* to describe a human passion. When Jacob hears that his son Joseph is alive, the Torah says that "His heart missed a beat (fainted) because he did not believe them,"[4] but then when he is reassured "his soul (*ruach*) comes alive again." There *ruach* means his spirit as an aspect of his personality or state of mind. When describing the jealous husband who suspects his wife of infidelity the Torah says that a "spirit of jealousy overcomes him," and the term used for this feeling is *ruach*.[5] This only underlines the ambiguity of the word.

The second word for "soul" is *nefesh*, as in: "And *YHVH* said, 'Let the earth produce all kinds of living souls, animals, reptiles, and beasts,' and it was so."[6] When forbidding the Israelites to drink blood, the Torah says, "For the life of a person (*nefesh*) is in the blood."[7] *Nefesh*[8] is used almost interchangeably with *adam*,[9] "person," to describe a human who brings a sacrifice, in the book of Leviticus. Significantly, when the Torah institutes the law of fasting on Yom Kippur, the term it uses is "Afflicting your souls," using the word *nefesh*.[10] Though the affliction referred to could simply be fasting, a physical act, in this context it is clearly meant to have penitentiary and therefore spiritual connotations as well. This is a clear indication of the dual role of *nefesh*. Throughout the Torah, the words *nefesh* and *ruach* seem to be used in similar situations having a heavily spiritual content; nevertheless both are applied to "All living beings," animal as well as human.

The third word for "soul," one that in the Torah (but not in rabbinic literature) is only used of humans, is the word *neshama*: "And *YHVH Elohim* formed man from the dust of the ground and He breathed into his nostrils the breath (soul) of life."[11] This "breath of life" does not necessarily refer to a spiritual endowment from God. Later on in the Torah, when talking about Cannanite tribes that have to be destroyed because of their corruption and the threat they present to the newcomers, the word *neshama* is used simply to mean all living humans: "Do not let any breathing being (*neshama*) live."[12]

The Torah also uses the words *neshama* and *ruach* together describing the destruction of life by the flood: "Everything that had the breath of the spirit of life (*nishmat ruach*) in its nostrils, that was on dry land, died."[13] Thus the distinction between the ways the two words are used is blurred and it is ambiguous as to whether it applies to all life or only human life.

If we rely only on the Torah we are left with a confusing picture. The words that we suppose to connote a special relationship between humans and God are used for animals as well, and the one word that might indicate a special spiritual relationship with God applies to all humans, including idol worshippers.

Turning to the later books of the Bible the picture is even more confusing. *Ruach* and *nefesh* are the words that the psalmist uses most often to describe what we would call "soul" and yet the clearest quote that we could select to indicate the link between soul and God is in Proverbs: "For the light of God is the soul (*neshama*)."[14] The most challenging quotation comes from Ecclesiastes, attributed to King Solomon: "For what happens to humans and what happens to animals, is the same thing: As this one dies so does the other and there is one spirit for all and there is no way in which man is better than animals. Everything is meaningless. Everything goes to the same place; everything came from dust and returns to dust. And who knows if the spirit of man rises upwards and the spirit of the animal goes down into the dust?"[15]

2

The use of these "soul" words in the Talmud is just as ambiguous. The word *nefesh* is used to describe a normal human being: "Whoever keeps alive (or destroys) a person (*nefesh*) it is as though he has saved (or destroyed) the whole world."[16] "Saving a life (soul, *nefesh*) overrides the laws of *Shabbat*."[17] Human food is described as *ochel nefesh* in talking about preparing food for *Shabbat*.[18] *Nefesh* is also used to describe a human characteristic, such as "a bitter spirit"[19] or a spirit of self-denial[20] (and, of course, echoing the terminology of the Torah, it is used in the context of Yom Kippur as it is with regard to the jealous husband). The word is used for a "tough character," a "modest character," and a "reliable character."[21] A similar analysis of the way the word *ruach* is used seems to indicate a more specifically human element, but not necessarily a spiritual one: "Rabbi Levitas of Yavneh said 'Be of very low spirit (humble) because the end of man is worms.'"[22] Yet at the same time the Talmud also uses the word in relation to animals: "The righteous understand the souls (*nefesh*) of their animals."[23] It is also used to describe any living being.[24]

It is the word *neshama* that in the Talmud seems to be the one that corresponds most to our attempts to identify the "soul" of theology. "The sound of the soul as it leaves the body"[25] is a clear indication that the soul is an essential condition of life. Consider, however, Antoninus's question, which really sounds as though it comes from a Christian theologi-

cal stance: "Antoninus asked Rebbi, 'When is the soul placed
in the body, at conception or at birth?' He (Rebbi) said, 'At
birth.' He (Antoninus) said, 'From conception,' and he pro-
duced a quotation from the Book of Job to support his position."[26] In light of the very different attitudes in Judaism
and Christianity toward the fetus and abortion, this is a fascinating historical quote, but either way it reiterates the idea
that human life requires the soul for survival.

A more mystical approach, still using the same word,
neshama, concerns the extra spiritual dimension a person
has that is particularly heightened on days of religious significance in the calendar: "On Erev *Shabbat* God gives man
an extra soul and when *Shabbat* ends He takes it away."[27]
One might have thought that the soul is an independent
entity regardless of the circumstances but it seems from this
that a soul can be stimulated by special occasions. And if
the soul is part of a person's created makeup it should have
come with the creation of man in the first place, yet there
is disagreement on this as well. "God breathed the soul into
man on Friday,"[28] is one opinion; a contradictory one is that
"God breathed the soul into man on *Shabbat*."[29] All three of
these quotes, regardless of the variations, reinforce the notion
that "soul" is the spiritual dimension of human beings. This
is reiterated in the much later use of *neshama* in the traditional prayer book. All variations of liturgy still commonly
include these two prayers: On waking every day we echo
Abaye's prayer, "I give thanks to You, living and eternal King,
for returning my soul (*neshama*) to me," and on *Shabbat*
morning we recite the *Nishmat* prayer, "The soul of every
living being will praise your name *YHVH* our God."

With these different words, names, and uses, and with
the differences of opinion, the question still remains: "What
exactly did the rabbis understand the soul to be? Is it a part
of God in man? Is it a sense? Can it be changed or even
obliterated? How are we to understand it?

3

"When he (Abaye) awoke he would say, 'My God the soul (*neshama*) that You have given me is pure. You have breathed it into me and You maintain it within me and You will take it away from me one day and return it to me in the Future to Come. For as long as the soul is within me I thank You *YHVH* my God and God of my fathers, Master of the Universe, Lord of all souls. I bless you *YHVH* Who returns souls to dead bodies.'"[30] From this we could deduce that the soul is to be identified with consciousness. After all, if it is returned when one wakes, the clear implication is that it was removed when the body sleeps. One of the explanations given for the ritual obligation of washing one's hands when waking from sleep is that on waking one returns to a state of sanctity after sleeping, when one is in a less sanctified level of existence. Just as ritual requires washing before eating, immersion of vessels in water before being dedicated to laws of *Kashrut*, immersion of a convert in preparation for a new life, or a woman's immersion to record the transition into a new phase, so the body needs sanctification when it receives the soul again. The body without the soul is in a state of incompleteness, even inferiority. Of course, this is very Greek. The idea that the body, as matter, is inferior to mind, as spirit, is the cornerstone of both the Platonic and Aristotelian ways of looking at the world.

There is a famous parable of Rabbi Yishmael that while treating soul and body as two different forces does not attribute superiority or inferiority to either one. Rabbi Yishmael taught, "It (the question of responsibility for human actions) can be compared to a king who had an orchard containing choice, ripe fruits. The king appointed as guardians a lame person and a blind person and said to them, 'Take care of my choice fruits.' After a few days the lame one said to the blind one, 'I can see choice fruits in the orchard.'

The blind one said, 'Let us eat them.' The lame one said, 'How can I get there?' The blind one said, 'And I cannot see.' So the lame one rode on the blind one and they ate the fruits. After a few days the king came into his orchard and said, "Where are my choice fruits?' The blind man said, 'My master the king, can I see?' The lame man said, "My master the king, can I walk?' The king was wise. He made the lame man ride on the blind man and as they started walking he said, 'This is what you did and you ate my choice fruits.' So in the Future to Come, the Holy One Blessed Be He says to the soul, 'Why did you sin against Me?' She will say, 'Master of the Universe, I did not sin against You. The body sinned. From the moment that I came out of the body I have been like a pure bird hovering in the air. How could I have sinned against You?' He says to the body, 'Why did you sin against Me?' He will say, 'Master of the Universe, I did not sin against You. The soul sinned. From the moment that she has left me I am like a stone cast down on the ground. How could I have sinned against You?' What will God do to them? He will throw the soul into the body and judge them both."[31]

Rabbi Yishmael's narrative, although not suggesting that one is any better or worse than the other, would indicate that the soul is rather like the *yetser hatov,* the "good incli-nation "that contrasts with the "bad inclination." Both forces battle for control of the human being. It is an important distinction between rabbinic interpretation and Christian thought that the rabbis did not totally accept the notion of a "good" mind or soul locked in an evil body. Indeed, they have difficulty with the notion of Good and Evil in general because everything is perceived as coming from one Divine source: "We bless God for the bad in the same way that we bless Him for the good."[32] In the Gnostic tradition, evil is accorded independent power; it is represented as the force of darkness, the Satan. Greek philosophy could not accept— at least, Plato's narrator in the Republic could not accept— the idea of a totally good God being responsible for evil. Thus the rabbinic tradition allowed for the neutrality of the body and different influences within man battling for supremacy. It was not a battle of "states," the state of sin versus the state of grace; it was a battle of wills affecting specific actions. Indeed, there could be occasions when the "bad inclination" could really be good; otherwise no one would get married, build a house, or plant a vineyard.[33] Yet this inclination does not appear to be inborn. It is something that arrives in youth: "There is an inclination in the heart of man that is bad from youth."[34] From this one might deduce that the neutral human is subject to different influences that develop early in life, which is almost Freudian. However there is still no clear concept of what it is that influences man to battle this negative inclination. The Greeks and their heirs thought it was the mind, but this creates as many philosophical problems as it answers. Dualism leads to the idea of "the ghost in the machine," the good mind controlling the bad body. There is no resonance for this in biblical literature or in most of rabbinic thinking.

Nevertheless, it is clear that the soul was indeed perceived as a sort of piece of God. "Just as God sees but is not seen, so the soul sees and is not seen. Just as God fills the world, so the soul fills the body. Just as God nourishes the world, so the soul nourishes the body. Just as God is pure, so the soul is pure. Just as God dwells in the inner chambers, so the soul dwells in the inner chambers."[35]

Once again we have entered the metaphysical; indeed this seems to be just as important a way of looking at the soul as the rational. "The son of David will not come until all the souls in the bodies have been used up."[36] This implies a solid state of soul energy whose function it is to direct humanity in a Godly way. There is a hint here at the idea that there is a sort of stock of souls that God has created, and they are "sent down" to guide human beings. They have a mission to complete; if they fail, they must continue returning to bodies after death until they have succeeded in doing what they were designed for. This is similar to the idea of the personal guardian angel or *mazal* whose task it is to protect its charge. Only when the human race has used up its souls to improve its state and no longer needs their input can we reach the neo-heavenly state of messianic days on earth. Yet for all this we are no nearer understanding what the words really signify and if they have any relevance for us.

4

One way of reconciling the various words used for "soul" is to talk about their each having different functions. By medieval times it was common to speak about an animal soul and a divine soul. This would explain the Torah's implication that animals have souls while drawing a distinction that elevates humanity above the animal. This was taken further by the mystics to indicate that even among humans some had the divine soul and others did not. There is even a view that only Jews have this divine soul and this explains the special relationship between God and Israel. This is a clear example of how religious absolutism can justify inhuman behavior to humans. If one believes that a human who does not share your spiritual belief is relegated to the level of an animal, it is easier to treat them inhumanely. Nevertheless, the different words used to describe soul could indeed be referring to different elements within the human being similar to the way that the different words used to describe God were understood by the rabbis to indicate different "qualities" or manifestations.

It is an artificiality of our scientific world to attempt to create rigid categories and scientific formulae. It has its usefulness in certain areas, but not in every area. The human is, as we well know, a complex organism. There are many different functions and dimensions that can be recognized even if they cannot be accurately defined or scientifically analyzed. "Personality," "Consciousness," and "Conscience" are concepts that are still difficult to define. "Spirituality" is another classic example.

Thus we talk about mind, human consciousness, conscience, and sensitivity without clearly knowing what we are talking about. It is the same with aesthetics. We know that people appreciate art, without being absolutely certain what the nature of the attraction is. Is it shape or color or proportion? Is it something triggered by visual laws or by intellectual laws? Does it depend on the eye or brain, and what part of the brain? All we can do is to try to log as many different elements as we can while encouraging everyone to experience as much as possible while trying to make sense of what it is that they see.

The different words do indeed indicate elements that we are pretty certain mean different things to us, and they are all vital for human existence and experience on differing levels. Just as medicine is now prepared to incorporate other types of healing without denying its rational, experimental foundations, so too talk about "soul" must incorporate the metaphysical as well. Consciousness, awareness of the difference between actions and how they affect others as well as ourselves, sensitivity to other creatures, and awareness of the Divine all combine to create a person who we will describe as having a large soul. Some of these elements can be isolated, and humans can function on different levels—on primitive as well as elevated planes. The more elements one employs the fuller one is using one's capacities as a human to fulfill one's potential and justify one's creation. So the different words that are used are needed to describe different aspects of what "soul" is.

Similarly we speak of "mind" as a general word to describe a very wide range of different functions. We use the "mind" to calculate, to communicate, and to appreciate the arts. The word "spirit" is also used in various ways. The

French use the word devoid of any religious connotation to describe the creative aspect of the human mind. In French a person described as *spirituel* may be an atheist. In English "spirit" is also used to describe the dynamism of a person, but "spiritual" has only transcendental connotations. The words for "soul" in Hebrew include both of these areas.

5

The animal soul, the human soul, and the divine soul are all aspects of human life that go toward creating what we call "personality." This is why consciousness, the awareness of ourselves and our actions, is needed to see the fully aware person in action. This overall application of "soul" clearly is rooted in the physical world and has no relevance once the body has died and decomposed, but there is a spiritual soul that connects us with God, a transistor for picking up Divine wave bands. It is a capacity that can be enlarged, enhanced, or destroyed. Maimonides believed in two types of soul; there is "the soul that is part of the body and the soul that has no part of the body, called 'mind.'"[37] "The reward of the righteous is the next world, which is a life without death and a good that contains no bad. . . . They will benefit from this delight and be included in this good. The punishment for the wicked is that they will not get this life and they will be cut off and die. Anyone who does not achieve this life dies with no eternal life and is cut off for his wickedness and dies like an animal." But it is only the soul that has no relationship to the physical that continues into the world beyond the grave.

Maimonides thought that this soul is the eternal mind. The kabbalists called it "The part of God from above" that is given to us to use, to develop or to squash. Whether this is figurative or literal, it is a challenge to us to increase the spirituality within our lives and within our personalities.

The more we are simply material, the more of us there is that disappears with our deaths. The more we appreciate, value, and contribute to the Divine, the more there is to continue in spirit and as part of God. If the metaphorical bubble of spirit is trapped within our bodies, when it is released at death it must return to its source. If our souls are Divine they must return to the Divine. In death we return our souls to God.

The concept of "soul" calls us to rise to our greatest height, to use our potential and to reach beyond our limitations to God. The soul is part of our makeup. It is the in-built equivalent of spiritual instinct that gives us an extra dimension to use for our own benefit and improvement. A great deal may depend on whether we choose, or sometimes whether we are trained, to take advantage of it. It is the challenge of a spiritual life.

"When *adam* was created he was from one end of the earth to the other; because he did wrong, God placed His hand on him and shrank him."[38] It is the soul that enables us to restore our greatness, yet here too there is no command, "You shall believe that there is a soul." Soul talk runs through midrashic literature but nowhere can it be said to be defined in a rigorous way. It is an idea that hovers rather than a formula that is tied to specific words. The myth is that we know about "soul" in the same specific way that we know what the heart or the brain is and how they work.

Notes

1. Midrash Rabba *Bereshit* 14:9.
2. Genesis 1:2.
3. Genesis 6:17.
4. Genesis 45:26.
5. Numbers 5:14.
6. Numbers 1:24.

7. Deuteronomy 12:23.

8. Leviticus 4:2.

9. Leviticus 1:2.

10. Leviticus 16:29.

11. Leviticus 2:7

12. Deuteronomy 20:16.

13. Genesis 7:22.

14. Proverbs 20:27.

15. Ecclesiastes 3:19–21

16. Talmud Bavli *Sanhedrin* 37a.

17. Talmud Bavli *Shabbat* 132a.

18. Talmud Bavli *Shabbat* 60b.

19. Talmud Bavli *Moed Katan* 14b.

20. Talmud Bavli *Nedarim* 81a.

21. *Masechet Kalla Rabtai* 3:9.

22. Mishna *Avot* 4:4.

23. Mishna *Avot* 50a.

24. Talmud Bavli *Eiruvin* 15a.

25. Talmud Bavli *Yoma* 20b.

26. Talmud Bavli *Sanhedrin* 91b.

27. Talmud Bavli *Beitza* 16a.

28. Midrash Ruth Rabba 7.

29. Pesikta deRav Cahana 23.

30. Talmud Bavli *Brachot* 60b.

31. Talmud Bavli *Sanhedrin* 91a, *Vayikra Rabba* 4:5.

32. Talmud Bavli *Brachot* 48b.

33. Midrash Rabba 9:9.

34. Genesis 8:21.

35. Talmud Bavli *Brachot* 10a.

36. Talmud Bavli *Yevamot* 63b.

37. Maimonides *Yad HaChazaka Hilchot Teshuva* 8:1 and 8:3.

38. Talmud Bavli *Chagigah* 12a.

Chapter 4

Myth: We Know What Was Given to Moses on Sinai

1

The Torah is the word of God, we are told. How do we know this? Is the Torah we have today the same Torah that Moses received three and a half thousand years ago from God on Sinai? Wasn't the language different then? Didn't they write differently then? How do we explain the variations and discrepancies in the text? Do we really have to take this tradition literally?

When the Torah is lifted up in synagogues it is customary to say, "And this is the Torah that Moses placed before the Children of Israel, by the word of God through the hand of Moses." The Mishna asserts, "Moses received the Torah from Sinai."[1] This is an indication of the "pedigree" of the Torah and its fundamental importance as the constitution that is the very basis of Jewish history and tradition, but this statement is no more than a very general assertion. The

Mishna goes further, dogmatically, in stipulating the importance of the issue as a criterion for identification with Jewish spiritual continuity: "Someone who says that the Torah does not come from Heaven has no part of the World to Come."[2] Incidentally, it is worth noting that text does not suggest that this disqualifies one from being a Jew. Nevertheless, it is such a vital principle that according to the rabbis it is one of the defining points for acceptance as a committed member of the community. It is not just accepting Torah as the Jewish constitution that is required; according to this formulation one is required to accept that it came directly from God.

When it says that Moses received the Torah from Sinai, "Sinai" is more than an experience on a mountain. "Sinai" is another way of saying "from God on Sinai." Torah comes from God. The wording of this Mishna about accepting Torah from God is strange because it is negative rather than positive. That is, we are not commanded to assert that it does come from God; rather we are told that we must not deny it. This distinction actually does make sense. To be sure of something is very difficult. One must lay oneself open to a range of ideas and experiences and cannot be sure when certainty may be reached. To deny involves an act of faith far more certain and arrogant than to accept the *possibility* of something. Denial does not allow for doubt; one is saying absolutely that one knows for certain that something is not the case. It is this arrogance that the rabbis were keen to exclude, rather than the honest doubter.

We are bound to wonder what actually happened so long ago. How did God transmit? How did God "talk?" Was Moses a passive receptacle or did Moses himself play a part in the process of revelation? Was he conscious or not? What did he see or feel while he was receiving? Was it entirely or partially Divine? The Talmud is very definite in saying that "Even if he says that the Torah comes from Heaven apart from one sentence that God did not say but Moses said on his own (initiative), this is as though he has 'Scorned the word of God' (Numbers 15). Even if he said that all the Torah comes from Heaven except for one detail, one logical deduction, one comparison of texts, then it is as though he has 'Scorned the word of God.'"[3] This goes well beyond saying that the Torah was given on Sinai. It says that even deductions, innovations in Jewish law that may be made later, were given on Sinai as well. This surely sounds like hyperbole.

It sounds as though the rabbis are trying very hard to establish the authority of Torah and are making assertions for popular consumption. Could this be true? Yet Maimonides with all his philosophical training makes this statement one of his Thirteen Principles: "I believe with complete conviction that all the Torah that we now have in our hands is the one given to Moses." What did he mean when he said "Torah?" Sometimes "Torah" is used to describe the Five Books of Moses and sometimes it is used to describe the whole corpus of Jewish law. Is Maimonides agreeing with the Midrash that uses "Torah" to mean everything beyond the text of the Torah or not? The fundamental importance of accepting Torah as the will of God is essential, he says, but he does not suggest—either here, in his introduction to his *Sefer HaMitzvot* or the Mishna, or in his "Eight Chapters" that discuss the tradition and its transmission—that anything developed subsequently has the same authority as the original text of the Torah.

These statements tell us a great deal about the agenda of the rabbis. We know that they had to battle very hard for their understanding of what the Torah was. Their first struggles were against the Sadducees, the priestly party that resisted rabbinic interpretation, internally, and the Samaritans, the neo-Jews who rejected a great deal of the established Jewish canon, externally. Then they had to deal with the Christians, who rejected the validity of the laws of the Torah altogether because a New Testament had been given,

and the Kaarites, who were heirs to the Sadducees in rejecting the Oral Law. It is hardly surprising therefore that they
fought to maintain both the sanctity and the integrity of the
Torah tradition. However, in their polemic some of them
made categorical statements that are difficult to understand,
and some of these statements have entered Jewish thinking
as necessary dogma.

2

What actually happened on Sinai? On the face of it Moses
received the Ten Statements, usually but inaccurately called
the Ten Commandments (they are called *Asseret HaDibrot*
not *Asseret HaMitzvot*, "Ten Statements or Principles" not
"Ten Commands"). After all, the two tablets of stone with
these ten statements were all that Moses brought and then
smashed when he saw the golden calf. Then, after sorting
out the mess, he went back up Sinai to receive a second
version. It is the Ten Statements that are described as being written by the finger of God, engraved on and through
stone on both sides, that are most obviously referred to in
talk about a work of Divine uniqueness.[4]

But the text of the Torah seems to suggest that in addition to the tablets of stone there was also a Book of the
Covenant, which one might reasonably expect to refer to the
whole of the Torah: "And he took the Book of the Covenant
and he read it to the people and they said, "Whatever God
tells us we will do and understand."[5] Rashi[6] in his commentary on this verse says that the Book of the Covenant is the
Torah from *Bereshit* to when the Torah was given—but if
this is so then there was a text in existence before the Sinai
revelation because this reading took place beforehand. There
were other contemporaneous texts that we have lost, such
as the Book of the Wars of God.[7] What was this? Was it Divine
too? One could argue that on Sinai God excluded some and

validated other earlier texts, and this would solve a lot of problems raised by obscure references in Genesis that seem to refer to lost traditions such as the Nephillim,[8] the Sons of the Judges,[9] and the Great Sea Serpents.[10] However, the word "Torah" itself is mentioned as being given to Moses on Sinai in the verse "And God said to Moses, 'Come up the mountain to Me and I will give you the tablets of stone and the Torah and the commandments, which I have written down to teach them.'"[11] Here is a clear textual basis for the idea that Moses received much more on Sinai than just the tablets, although not necessarily in written form.

The question, however, remains: Exactly what Moses did receive? "Why is the law of *shmitta* (the seventh-year release of land, slaves, and commerce) connected to Sinai? Were not all the commandments given on Sinai? It is to teach that just as with *shmitta* all the principles as well as the details were given on Sinai, so every single commandment was given, principles and details, on Sinai."[12] And further, "Even that which an old student finally teaches in front of his master has already been said to Moses on Sinai,"[13] The Gemara itself realizes that this creates a practical problem: "Could Moses have learned all the Torah in forty days? But God taught him the general principles only."[14] Such a position also offers a solution to the problem of Moses not knowing how to deal with the cases of the son of an Egyptian father who cursed using God's name[15] and the gatherer of wood on *Shabbat*.[16] Moses, when faced with a crisis, had to detain the principal while he clarified exactly what God wanted. There were specific details that Moses was uncertain about. It is inevitable that human fallibility will in the course of time lead to error or ambiguity. How often do we forget what we have been told? The problem was not just one of principle but also of practicality.

The rabbis are further divided as to how Moses wrote down the Torah: "Rabbi Yochanan said in the name of Rabbi Beena, 'The Torah was given in scrolls because it says

(Psalms 40): "Because I said that I have come (revealed Myself) through the book of scrolls that I have written.'" Rabbi Shimon Ben Lakish said, 'The Torah was given complete (sealed) because it says (Deuteronomy 31): "This book of the Torah has been presented.""[17] Given the assumption now accepted as the norm in conventional minds, that the Torah was written down at one moment immediately after revelation, this divergence of opinion is significant even within a fundamentalist context. Rashi takes the surface meaning even further to suggest that final compilation took place very late indeed in the biblical narrative. Rabbi Beena's position means "As each part was taught to Moses he wrote it down. At the end of forty years when all the parts were complete, he joined them and sewed them with sinews." Rabbi Shimon ben Lakish's position is that "Nothing was written until the end of forty years when all the sections had been taught. What had been taught to Moses during the first and second years was kept orally until they came to be written down."

Of course this is not very interesting to those who attribute the Torah to a much later editor. For them none of this is a problem. The narrative is not to be taken literally. It also ignores the problem of script because the script we have nowadays was initiated by Ezra almost a thousand years after Sinai.[18] Was the script used at Sinai the one archaeologists believe was in use at that time, the early Hebrew script, the one Moses wrote in? Surely not the one that Ezra brought back from Babylon? Yet the Talmud talks about the tradition that the tablets of stone were carved through both sides. How then did the middle of the letters *mem* and *samech*, which are totally surrounded by the outlines of the letters, stand up suspended and not fall out?[19] The answer the Talmud gives is that it was a miracle. In fact if the commandments were written in an earlier script then other letters, like the *ayin*, would have been problematic, not these two. Within the traditional world, these issues were not even considered, yet what we can see is that the differing views of the rabbis speak of greater variety and ambivalence than is normally allowed. The traditional point of view accepts unreservedly the Divine influence and authorship without even attempting to understand the means and the mechanisms. These remain obscure. We know nothing of how anything was actually transmitted. Apart from the tablets we know only by midrashic deduction that Moses descended and started teaching first Aharon, then the priests, and then the elders. The Talmud gives a very moving expansion of this as Aharon moves aside and listens to Moses repeating the Torah to his sons, and then they move aside as the elders come in. It is a lesson in the methodology of oral transmission[20]—but it was oral; there is no hint of a text available to them at that stage.

3

The law that Moses received was not the end of the matter. It must have included within it the means of further deduction and evolution. There is the role of the priest and the judge and the framework of consultation and majority opinion, all incorporated in the Torah itself. The rabbis accepted the reality that once the original revelation had been given, it was up to man to take it further.

The classic narrative is that of the debate over Achinai's oven, a seemingly incidental issue of ritual purity affecting an oven that could be taken apart and reassembled, thus changing its status. "The rabbis declared it impure (contrary to Rabbi Eliezer's view). On that day Rabbi Eliezer replied (to the rabbis) with all the arguments in the world but they still did not accept him (his point of view). He said, 'If the law is like my (position) let this carob tree be uprooted a hundred *amot* from its place as proof (some say four hundred).' They said, 'We do not accept proof from a carob tree.'

He said, 'If the law is like my (position) let the spring of water prove it.' The waters started flowing in the opposite direction. They said, 'We do not accept proof from a spring.' He said, 'If the law is like my position let the walls of the study hall prove it.' The walls started to lean over to fall. Rabbi Yehoshua rebuked them and said 'Why are you intervening in a dispute between wise men?' The walls did not fall out of respect for Rabbi Yehoshua but did not return to the upright position out of respect for Rabbi Eliezer, and they stayed leaning. Rabbi Eliezer said, 'If the law is like my position let the Heavens prove it.' A voice came down and said, 'Why are you arguing with Rabbi Eliezer? The law always goes according to him.' Rabbi Yehoshua stood up and said, 'It is not in heaven.' (Deuteronomy 30) What did he mean, 'It is not in heaven?' Rabbi Yirmiya said that the Torah has already been given from Sinai and we do not pay attention to a Heavenly voice because the Torah has already said, 'You incline your decision toward the majority' (Exodus 23) Rabbi Natan met Elijah and said to him, 'What did God do at that moment?' He said, 'God smiled and said "My children have defeated me."'"[21]

The rabbis showed their right to decide law on the basis of a majority decision, which in a sense, Almighty God is not allowed to intervene. What could be a clearer statement of the fact that after the initial revelation it is the oral tradition, invested in human beings, that carries the power to decide? Sinai allows the tradition to evolve.

This need not affect the integrity of the original revelation. It simply indicates how that revelation was taken further. There is another narrative that appears to challenge the idea that everything was given in predigested form at one moment. It concerns Moses being shown around Heaven and wondering why God is busy putting little crowns on the letters of the Torah (itself showing the evolution of the script).

God tells him it is because one day Rabbi Akiva will deduce whole piles of laws from the nuances of the script. He wonders why he rather than Rabbi Akiva was chosen to be the medium of Divine revelation. "Rav said that when Moses went up on high he found God tying crowns to the letters (of the Torah). He said, 'Why are You doing this?' He said, 'In the future, after several generations, there will be a man called Akiva Ben Yosef who will deduce piles of laws from every little spike on every letter.' He said, 'Show him to me.' He said, 'Go to the back.' He went and sat eight rows back and did not understand what they were saying. He felt weak. Then one of the pupils asked where a law came from and (Rabbi Akiva) replied that this was a Law (Tradition) from Moses on Sinai and he (Moses) felt better."[22] Rashi clarifies, saying that "He felt better . . . because he had been quoted even though he had not received (that particular law)." Thus a tradition attributed to Moses might well be something that Moses knew nothing about. Rashi felt no compunction in contradicting the midrashic tradition that everything was given, even future laws. The issue is more of promoting reverence for the tradition than deducing its exact chronological provenance.

Not only were the rabbis aware of some of the problems with the original process, but they also accepted that many traditions may have been lost over the years. This is how the Talmud[23] and Maimonides indeed, explain the various conflicts over major legal issues, including biblical ones and the often contentious debates between the schools of thought of *Beit* Hillel and *Beit* Shammai. But they also projected this process of uncertainty further back, right to the moment of Moses's death. "It was taught that one thousand seven hundred deductions, comparisons of texts, and points of the scribes were forgotten while they were mourning for Moses. Rabbi Abahu said that they were all reinstated through the logical deductions of Othniel Ben Kenaz."[24]

4

The question is whether this is a zero-sum issue. Do you have a choice simply between believing or denying? The skeptics will point to the discovery of a book of law at the time of Josiah to support the contention that the law evolved and that what came to be accepted as the text of the Torah emerged over time. King Josiah led a revival of religious life and repaired the Temple, which had fallen into disrepair. In the course of the work a book was discovered, a *Sefer Torah*.[25] The king read the book and tore his clothes in despair when he realized how far the people had strayed. He gathered everyone together and read what is called *Sefer HaBrit*, the Book of the Covenant, which is similar to the terminology used in Exodus to describe the book that Moses read before going up to Sinai. It is a symbolic renewal of the Sinai covenant (or as some might argue, the initiation of it). The king commanded the nation to celebrate Passover together "as written in the Book of the Covenant."[26] The Book of Kings goes on to say that "No Pesach had been celebrated like this since the time of the Judges who judged Israel and all the days of the Kings of Israel and Judea."

This echoes the language of the Book of Joshua regarding the circumcision ceremony after the crossing of the River Jordan and the initial conquest.[27] Here there is a statement that no one had been circumcised during the forty years in the wilderness. This seems surprising given Moses' own experience when he did not circumcise his children.[28]

One can take these statements at face value but one can also understand them to be making a polemical point. Josiah may have discovered a new book altogether. One possibility is that it was the Book of Deuteronomy because the Passover in Exodus seems to have applied only to the freed slaves, whereas in Deuteronomy it is clearly for future generations. Another possibility is that the Torah had been preserved by a few elite "sons of the prophets" and was an esoteric text rather than a public one. Another possibility is simply that there had been a long period of backsliding and idolatry, something the text seems to bear out. Which of the options one is likely to choose depends on one's preconceived position.

Some respond to this by saying that it does not matter how the Torah came about. What matters is that the Torah is the basis of Jewish religious life today. If one wants to experience Jewish religious traditions and feel the integrity of at least a two and a half thousand years of tradition then one has to participate in a religious tradition that takes the Torah as its core. It matters not, according to this position, whether it is a matter of spiritual men trying to discover what God wants or God telling men how to transmit what He wants. Even if the tradition is man-made it still has a constitution and even if one challenges the constitution and tries to change it one still has to support and propagate the tradition as the particularly Jewish contribution to society.

The traditionalists want to preserve the Divinity of the Torah. Among them are those who love to use computer codes that are said to confirm the perfectly integral authorship of the Torah. Sadly (or not), Christians and Muslims can do exactly the same with their texts too. But being committed to the Divinity of the Torah can also be based on the experience of reading the Torah itself. There is a very special poetry and feel to the text that strikes some people as very special. Its law and its language is so remarkable, so unlike any contemporary or near-contemporary alternative text, that it must be exceptional. The resilience of its principles and the fact that its moral message has not been bettered nor an alternative to the Ten Commandments been found also point to its supernatural origin. Then there is the experience of a life lived according to Torah and the way it creates an atmosphere and a framework for spirituality (when followed in depth and not superficially). These all combine to provide an experience of Torah that suggests its

Divine origin, as opposed to a literary or historical analysis that seeks to dissect it and suggest that its primitive origins contrast with a supposedly more progressive scientific culture that holds different criteria for excellence, consistency, structure, and simplicity. A spiritual or mystical outlook is concerned more with intensity and experiential criteria and will indeed depend on what one is looking for. To quote the English historian J. Collingwood, "There is no such thing as History, only Historians."

5

The fact is that the rabbis disagree both as to the actual nature of what happened on Sinai and to the content of the revelation. Therefore one is bound to ask how they could insist on people being asked to assent to something so imprecise. When one is asked to assert something, one needs to know clearly what it is he or she is being asked to assert. Whether intentionally or not, the rabbis left these details vague. Even if one agrees that every jot and tittle was given, the questions remain: In what form? and In how much detail? This is why, it seems to me, the rabbis were much more definite about denying the possibility of revelation. Denial requires, intellectually, a great deal more certainty or arrogance. It is possible that the very vagueness of the terms "Torah from Heaven" and "Torah from Sinai" and the fact that they are interchangeable, is a further indication of the importance of the general principle rather than the precise details.

This is not to suggest that there was no revelation or that the importance of the Torah as the lodestone of the tradition is any less. My purpose is simply to point out that insisting on acceptance of Divine revelation was more a matter of accepting the authority of the tradition than it was an actual statement about the historical event of revelation.

About this we cannot speak. We were at the bottom of the mountain, not up on top to witness the actual transmission. Once again, the rabbis show philosophical genius in not expecting a theological formulation. They are concerned with the practical commitment to a way of life and a particular way of understanding and interpreting Torah. The issue is not what happened so much as what is and how authority is perceived and protected. The authority that God adds works both to emphasize the mystery, sanctity, and the greatness of Torah and indeed to protect it from manipulation and transience. Obedience and commitment do not necessarily require blind acceptance but they do require an agreement to engage with Torah and to try to feel the presence of God in it. The principle is that at a moment in history a people was granted a revelation and the result of this is its religious constitution. The myth is the assumption that we know exactly what happened. We know the results, but cannot know what actually went on up there in the smoke and the clouds.

Notes

1. Mishna *Avot* 1:1.
2. Mishna *Sanhedrin* 11:1.
3. Talmud Bavli *Sanhedrin* 99a.
4. Exodus 32:15 and 16.
5. Exodus 24:7
6. Rabbi Yitzchaki, born in Troyes, France, 1040, and died 1105, was the greatest commentator on the Bible and the Talmud.
7. Numbers 21:14.
8. Genesis 6:4
9. Genesis 6:2.
10. Genesis 1:21.
11. Exodus 24:12.

12. *Torat Cohanim Emor*.
13. Talmud Yerushalmi *Peah* 13:1.
14. Midrash Rabba *Shemot* 41:6.
15. Leviticus 24:3.
16. Numbers 15:32.
17. Talmud Bavli *Gittin* 60a.
18. Talmud Bavli *Sanhedrin* 21a.
19. Talmud Bavli *Megillah* 2b.
20. Talmud Bavli *Eiruvin* 54b.
21. Talmud Bavli *Bava Metzia* 59b.
22. Talmud Bavli *Menachot* 29a.
23. Talmud Yerushalmi *Sanhedrin* 1:4.
24. Talmud Bavli *Temura* 17a.
25. 2 Kings 22:8.
26. 2 Kings 23:21.
27. Joshua 5.
28. Exodus 4:24.

Chapter 5

Myth: We Know What Happens after We Die

1

Most religious people assume that there is more to life than this world and that there is some form of existence beyond. Where does this idea come from? Maimonides in his Thirteen Principles does not specifically mention "life after death" but he does talk about "resurrection." Is "resurrection" a synonym for "afterlife" or are they two very different ideas?

Death itself is a fascinating and sometimes frightening issue, but the Torah treats it in a very relaxed way as though there is nothing remarkable in a natural process. The Torah implies that Adam and Eve were originally created to live for ever and it was only by making the mistake of disobeying God that they were "sentenced" to die: "On the day you eat from the tree, you will die."[1] Of course, this is ambiguous. First, what is the difference between the tree of knowledge and the tree of life? But even without this issue there are two possible meanings for this statement. It could mean that Adam and Eve would die specifically as a punishment for disobeying God, as would later humans who transgressed specific moral instructions (like Cain) or biblical laws. It could also mean that as a punishment for the first primeval disobedience, all of humanity would suffer death just as women would suffer the pains of childbirth. Either way the fate of mankind is expressed: "You are dust and you will return to the dust."[2] It sounds very final.

"And Chanoch (Enoch) walked with God, and he was not because God took him."[3] This too is ambiguous. What is the difference between dying and being taken away by God? Could it be that when God takes someone he or she goes to another world whereas someone dying simply "gives up the ghost" and decomposes? The Midrash Rabba explains that Enoch was indeed a good man but that he was taken away before he could do wrong. This implies that his good behavior was in some way unstable or only skin-deep. There is a tradition that Enoch thought that a monastic expression of faith was the ideal and he withdrew to a hermit's life away from humanity. God removed him, supposedly, to teach us the lesson that one must integrate into the society of other human beings and try to influence them. His fate could simply have been death, but the text allows for the possibility that God took Enoch to Him, that he was elevated to a higher realm. If this is the case then here we have the first hint at something beyond the grave.

The word for grave is either *kever* or *sheol*. These are the words most frequently used in the Torah for what happens to the body. *Sheol* in particular has Canaanite connotations of a frightening underworld where King Mot (*mavet*, "death") rules and cannibalizes the bodies that are sent down to him. It is possible that "to bury" as in *kever*, is simply to put in the ground; whereas *sheol* implies an underworld from which it is possible to emerge, as the Graeco-Roman myths of Orpheus, Eurydice, and Persephone recount. This would be supported by the phrase "God takes down to the grave (*sheol*) and brings up."[4] None of this emerges necessarily from the way the words are used in the Torah; we are simply theorizing.

Another biblical word, used in Psalms is *dumah*, "silence,"[5] a very final end that fits in well with David's views that only the living can praise God. But this too tells us nothing about anything beyond the grave.

Abraham's death is described this way: "And Abraham (expired, became body) and died in good old age and he was gathered to his people."[6] Similarly, "Isaac (expired, became body) and he was gathered to his people in good old age."[7] And finally, "Jacob (expired, became body) and he was gathered to his people."[8] This same expression, used exclusively of the patriarchs (plus Yishmael), might signify something beyond the grave. The idea seems to be that one expires first, perhaps losing consciousness or ceasing to breathe. Then in the second stage, one becomes simply a physical carcass. After these two phases the dead person goes on to the final state of death, which might allude to the escape of the soul and its return to God. Again, this is not necessarily implicit in the text.

But what of the idea of "joining one's people?" This could simply mean that one goes where all of one's ancestors have gone: into the earth. Of course, the Egyptians and other contemporaneous civilizations believed in life after death and prepared their elite for the future. In a way it would have been strange had the Children of Israel not shared some of these ideas. Nevertheless we are in the realm of speculation for there is no explicit statement.

Apart from the reference in Samuel, the first explicit statement that shows that the concept of afterlife is a well-known idea appears in Ecclesiastes: "For what happens to humans and what happens to animals is the same thing: As this one dies so does the other and there is one spirit for all and there is no way in which man is better than animals. Everything is meaningless. Everything goes to the same place; everything came from dust and returns to dust. And who knows if the spirit of man rises upwards and the spirit of the animal goes down into the dust?"[9] From this it is clear that the subject was one of debate at the time, and indeed from the fact that the author challenges it we can deduce that it was the common assumption. Of course there are different opinions as to exactly when "that time" was and who wrote the book itself. There is a clear division between the traditionalists and the academics.

The clearest statement in the Bible that a person continues in some form or another after death comes from Daniel: "And you will go to your end, and rise again to meet your destiny in the end of days."[10] Despite the obscurity of its meaning, it is an unambiguous statement that death is not the end of the story.

Daniel's talk about dying and then rising indicates, as does that of Ecclesiastes, that there was a well-accepted idea that his audience would have instantly recognized about living on or surviving after death. But what exactly was this concept? Egypt, of course, had a very sophisticated idea of what happens after death, even though this afterlife was reserved for a select few. Jewish ideology, however, appears to have intentionally distanced itself from Egyptian thought in its early years. The early books of the Bible were written against a background of reaction against Egypt and so it is likely that we must look to Babylonian culture, which gave much more expression to eschatological ideas than did the early biblical culture. Just as Babylon introduced the synagogue to Jewish life, so it seems that ideas of what heaven was like, such as what functions angels and other spirits had, was considered much more in Babylon and this inevitably influenced rabbinic thinking. What emerged was a complicated mélange of different concepts that were molded to fit the rabbinic agenda without there being a rigid philosophical system. As the rabbis say in the context of messianism, "Rabbi Chiyya the son of Abba said in the name of Rabbi

Yochanan, 'Whatever all the prophets prophesied concerned the days of the Messiah but as far the World to Come is concerned, "No eye has seen it God, apart from You Who have made it for those who wait."'"[11] The crucial issue for them was that "there is more to life" than that which we see and experience now.

2

What does the Talmud tell us about this next phase? The most common term used to describe it is *Olam HaBaah*, "the World to Come." The earliest reference in rabbinic literature comes in *Avot*: "Rabbi Yaacov said, 'This world is like a corridor; prepare yourself in the corridor so that you can enter the palace.'"[12] This clearly posits two states of existence. It also indicates that this world must be seen positively, not as a "Vale of Tears" to be suffered but as a testing ground to be used correctly and merit a next stage. However, there is no attempt to explain what the "Palace" is.

Rabbi Yaacov goes on to say, "One hour of good deeds and repentance in this world is better than all the World to Come, and one hour of peace of mind in the next world is better than all this world." The use of paradox is a common rabbinic tool. It seems as though Rabbi Yaacov is saying that this world is better than the next, but actually he is suggesting that it will take an act of repentance in this world to merit the next and that therefore in pure value terms, the act that earns eternal bliss must be considered of greater objective value. On the other hand when it comes to evaluating the actual pleasure, Rabbi Yaacov suggests that whatever degree of pleasure we have in this material world is exceeded by far in a nonmaterial world.

This is not just a restatement of the Greek assertion of the superiority of spirit over matter. Neither is it a simple comment on physical pleasure that is often satisfied and that however overpowering the desire for which may be at one moment can pass completely in another. It is a statement of priorities. The rabbis certainly regarded moral values and the pursuit of study and prayer as superior goals to physical pleasure and yet they regarded physical pleasure both as a handmaiden of the abstract and as a legitimate way of worshipping God and celebrating His creation.

This is already rooted in biblical attitudes. The emphasis on sacrifice as a means of celebration involves eating and "rejoicing in all the good that God has given." Most of the sacrifices commanded or offered were in practice sacrifices in which the donor participated and after giving dues to the Temple and the priests, ate himself. The repeated emphasis in the biblical text on rejoicing on festivals was linked to eating and drinking. There is a remarkable incident in which some of the important Children of Israel, at Sinai, "saw" God. Immediately they responded with a very physical celebration: "And they saw God and they ate and they drank."[13]

Yet this same incident is used by the rabbis to show that true proximity to God is beyond this world: "The World to Come is not like this world. In the next world there is no eating, no drinking, no reproduction, no business, no envy, no hatred, and no competition; just the righteous sitting with crowns on their heads, enjoying the brightness of the Presence (of God). As it says, 'And they saw God and they ate and they drank (Exod. 24).'"[14]

This emphasizes also the rabbinic reluctance to go into too much detail. "Yosef the son of Rabbi Yehoshua became ill and he passed out (died and returned to life). His father asked him, "What did you see there? He said, 'A world that was upside down. Those on high (here) were low there and those low (here) were high there (Rashi says that this refers only to material wealth, whereas Rabbeyna Channanel in the *Tosafot* suggests it has more to do with authority).' He replied, 'You saw a very clear (true) world. But how are we perceived there?' He replied, 'As we are here.'"[15] There is no physical description of "the palace," just of the standards of judgment being different from most of those applied by humans on earth.

Most people who have an interest in other religions will be familiar with the fact that in Islam, the Next World is indeed described in very physical terms as a wonderful garden, a place of water and maidens and music. But the analytical Muslim theologian will argue nevertheless that such expressions should be understood as analogies, given that material beings cannot really grasp the reality of something nonmaterial. In effect, apart from talking about the pleasure of the proximity to God, the rabbis avoid going into any detail. They do not like to make too many analogies. The Garden Of Eden is one and "the palace" is another, but without specifying details this is as far as they go. The rabbis are eager to assert the promise of something better but feel no obligation to specify what it is like. "These are the things for which a person eats the fruit (interest) in this world while the capital remains for the World to Come: honoring one's father and mother, being kind (to others), bringing (making) peace between a person and his friend, and studying Torah more than all the others."[16] That is, among the duties and pleasures, Torah is the greatest and the reward in the Next World is greater than in this—but again, this is an assertion rather than a clarification.

3

There is, of course, a very close connection between the notion of another world and the issue of whether humans are rewarded and punished for their actions. Since there does not appear to be a clear and direct connection on earth between being good and being rewarded, the rabbis looked for some explanation or some other criterion for what reward might be. The prevailing view is that "The reward for the righteous is in the future to come,"[17] and furthermore that "There is no reward altogether for (performing) *mitzvoth* in this world."[18] Nevertheless the majority opinion as reflected in the text of the prayer book seems to be that we do have some reward in this world, though of course the far greater payback will come later. Based on the statement quoted above from the Mishna, the morning service contains this extract: "These are the things for which a person eats the fruit (interest) in this world while the capital remains for the World to Come: honoring one's father and mother, being kind (to others), bringing (making) peace between a person and his friend, and studying Torah more than all the others." The following talmudic extract is added: "These are the things that a person enjoys the fruits of in this world and the principle remains for the World to Come (this is based on commercial terminology; the usufruct is the benefit one derives from property while the property rights themselves may well belong elsewhere). These are honoring parents, acts of kindness, getting early to the house of study (morning and evening), hospitality, visiting sick, helping brides get married, escorting the dead, concentrating on prayer, bringing peace between a man and his wife, and the study of Torah is worth them all."[19]

Another way of trying to explain another world without going into physical details is to make comparisons with spiritual experiences in the present. Thus the assertion that "This world is like the eve of *Shabbat* and the next world is like *Shabbat*,"[20] is an attempt to describe the difference by referring to the spiritual pleasure of *Shabbat*. Experiencing the anticipation is pleasurable, but not as good as *Shabbat* itself. By breaking away from a purely physical yardstick, the rabbis are trying to make analogies that are immediate and recognizable.

Once again the rabbis are eager to emphasize that this world also has its values and pleasures. The pursuit of these is an obligation and a preparation. Still, the reality is that the rabbis are promising something that has no real meaning other than as an abstract promise. It is an assertion of hope rather than of actuality, yet it is also predicated on the belief in a spiritual content to humanity that would not necessarily disappear with physical death. Within the context of rabbinic understanding both of God and of soul, there is a consistency and a logic in their position despite the difficulty in articulating anything substantial. In effect, human existence, as opposed to animal existence, is dependent on the spiritual dimension and the extent to which it is allowed to play a part in a person's life.

What I find particularly noteworthy is the idea that the "World to Come" has both national and universal references. On the one hand the rabbis emphasize that every Jew has a place in the World to Come: "All Israel has a place in the World to Come,"[21] which seems to be saying that arrival in the next world is almost automatic. On the other hand, the rabbis add on many extra promises to the effect that if one does this or does not do that, then he or she is guaranteed a place in the next world. A typical example is "Whoever responds, 'Amen, let His great Name be blessed,' is guaranteed to be a son of the World to Come."[22] This may be a relatively minor issue but there are dozens of similar assertions applicable to a range of major ethical and ritual deeds. Thus the rabbis are reinforcing the idea that it is a person's behavior that is crucial. Being Jewish provides a framework and a pattern of living that, if followed, is likely to enhance the spiritual life of a person and thus offer entry to a higher level of spiritual existence.

Yet this promise is not restricted to Jews alone: "Even a Canaanite servant who lives in Israel is guaranteed to be a daughter of the World to Come."[23] This is indeed in the context of asserting the importance of the Land of Israel, but it is symptomatic of an attitude of universalism that found its most notable expression in the assertion that "The pious of the nations of the world have a place in the World to Come,"[24] which Maimonides quotes as an important principle.[25]

4

This debate about who has or has not a part in the World to Come highlights an interesting anomaly. The rabbis seem to use the ideas of "the World to Come" and "Resurrection" interchangeably. Do they think that they are one and the same? The Mishna says, "All Israel has a place in the World to Come . . . and these do not, the person who says that resurrection is not from the Torah."[26] Then the Gemara goes on to ask "Why so much (such an extreme punishment)? It is taught that since he rejects resurrection therefore he has no part in resurrection because God always deals measure for measure."[27] But the Mishna was not talking about resurrection; the Mishna was talking about the World to Come! Which one do they mean, or are they synonymous? Of course one could argue that one cannot merit resurrection unless one's soul continues to the next world and survives death. Yet the ambiguity is intriguing. One is also bound to ask why Maimonides does not include in his Thirteen Principles "I believe in the World to Come" but does include as essential a belief in resurrection.

The possibility that these two terms are interchangeable is very important for creative thinking. It means that neither should be taken at simple face value but need to be understood on an altogether more esoteric level. It means, in effect, that if one wants to remain committed to a traditional position and at the same time be intellectually open, these ideas must be dealt with on a mystical rather than a rational level.

Another issue that is relevant is exactly what the rabbis meant by *Gan Eden* and *Gey Hinnom*, the Garden of Eden and the Valley of Hinnom—or as we would say in a Christian world, Heaven and Hell. Both terms are used eleven times (perhaps coincidentally) in both the Babylonian and the Palestinian Talmud (and eighty-two times in the Midrash Rabba and commonly throughout the allied texts) to indicate a state of heavenly bliss for the righteous and a state of heavenly punishment for the wicked. In origin the Garden of Eden, as the place in which God put His new human creatures, was an earthly place of bliss, and one supposes, the paradigm for a trouble-free existence. It was chosen as a symbolic and evocative name, holding out the promise for the future in terms that would make sense or at least create a mental picture of relevance to the average Jew. The term "Valley of Hinnom" similarly has biblical origins, first mentioned in the Book of Joshua as a place where children were passed through fire to the idol Moloch. In conjuring up an awful fate that would befall the sinner, this was an equally evocative word picture. Unlike other traditions, however, the Talmud did not go into great detail to describe either one.

Not only that, but Maimonides in his *Hilchot Teshuva*, describing the next world, does not use either of these expressions at all. Once, in *Hilchot Yesodei HaTorah*, he describes the idol worshippers as descending to the "Lowest level of Geyhinom," but does not use the expression "Gan Eden" at all (and it almost goes without saying that neither expression is found in his "Guide"). This underlines their relative unimportance other than as figurative symbols. In describing what happens to the good and the wicked, however, he is quite explicit: "The good that is kept for the righteous is the life of the World to Come, which is a life without death and good without bad. . . . the reward of the righteous is that they will benefit from this delight and be in this good and the punishment for the wicked is that they will not get this life and they will be cut off and die. Anyone who ever does not achieve this life dies with no eternal life and is cut off for his wickedness and dies like an animal."[28]

5

There is another term, much used by the rabbis, that is similar but to exactly equivalent to "the World to Come" and this is the expression "the Future to Come." Some of the ways in which "the Future to Come" is used seem to be referring to a radically different physical world in which the world order changes and is very different from the present: "In the Future to Come produce will grow every month and fruit every two months,"[29] or "In the Future to Come there will be no death."[30] Other ways refer to the messianic era. For example: "In the Future to Come all idol worshippers will bring gifts to King Messiah."[31] Others imply that "the Future" will be after a general resurrection has already taken place: "In the Future to Come Abraham our father will sit at the entrance to Gey Hinnom and he will not let anyone who is circumcised go down,"[32] or "In the Future to Come the son of David will be in the middle; Adam, Seth, and Methuselah on his right hand; and Abraham, Moses, and Jacob on his left."[33]

Still others imply a certain evolution in the human condition that will modify the sort of requirements that the Torah makes on people. "In the Future to Come God will permit everything He has forbidden."[34] "In the future the books of prophets and writings will be canceled but the five books of the Torah will not be canceled."[35]

It seems that the rabbis looked to the future in many different ways. Both in the way they saw this world and in the way they looked forward to another, they were animated by several ideas. First, they believed in a God Who had control over the universe and that this God approved of certain behavior and disapproved of others. Given this, they recognized that this world was a strange place in which, on the surface, God's justice did not seem to make sense. The only way they could reconcile this was by suggesting that true reward and punishment came at a later stage, either when this world changes or in another one altogether. This important assertion was for them more a matter of asserting their faith in Divine Justice and Providence than in a particular process or circumstance. This is why they were so adamantly opposed to those who absolutely denied the possibility of Divine Intervention or the limitless capacity of the Divine. This why their statements were directed toward those who denied rather than toward insisting on what exactly should be believed. This gives us a great deal of freedom to formulate our own concepts of exactly what a life after death is like and what our own attitudes to death should be.

It is not directly relevant here but worth mentioning that in general the attitude to death as found in the Bible was not one of dread and fear. If anything, rabbinic opinion tended to see death as a natural process to be welcomed: "And God saw everything that He had made and behold it was very good (Genesis 1:31) 'very good' is death."[36] If we believe that death leads to a world in which there is no pain or suffering then logically it must be a preferable existence, particularly if old age brings debility and loneliness. The Jewish version of Rip Van Winkle, Choni the Circle maker, slept for seventy years. When he returned he found no one who recognized him and he requested permission to die,[37] so long life is not always a blessing. King David adds the remarkable phrase "The dead cannot praise God; neither those who go down to silence. But we will praise God from now and for ever, Halleluyah."[38] It seems that King David thought that this world was the one worth emphasizing.

So we talk blithely about the Next World. The myth is that we know what it is, but to quote the prophet, "No one has seen it; only You, God."

Notes

1. Genesis 2:17.
2. Genesis 3:19.
3. Genesis 5:24.
4. 1 Samuel 2:6.
5. Psalms 115:17.
6. Genesis 25:8.
7. Genesis 35:29.
8. Genesis 49:33.
9. Ecclesiastes 3:19–21.
10. Daniel 13:14.
11. Talmud Bavli *Sanhedrin* 99a.
12. Mishna *Avot* 4:21.
13. Exodus 24.
14. Talmud Bavli *Brachot* 17a.
15. Talmud Bavli *Bava Batra* 10b.
16. Mishna *Peah* 1:1.
17. Mishna *Avot* 2:16.
18. Talmud Bavli *Kiddushin* 39a.
19. Talmud Bavli *Shabbat* 127a.
20. Talmud Bavli *Avoda Zara* 50a.
21. Mishna *Sanhedrin* 10:1.
22. Talmud Bavli *Brachot* 57a.
23. Talmud Bavli *Ketubot* 111a.
24. *Tosefta Sanhedrin* 13.
25. Maimonides' *Yad HaChazaka Hilchot Teshuva* 3:5.
26. Mishna *Sanhedrin Chelek* 1 and 2.
27. Talmud Bavli *Sanhedrin* 99a.
28. Maimonides' *Yad HaChazaka Hilchot Teshuva* 8:1.
29. Talmud Yerushalmi *Shekalim* 10:2.
30. Ecclesiastes Rabba 1:7.
31. *Shemot* Rabba 35:5.
32. *Bereshit* Rabba 48:7.
33. *Massechet Kalla* 87a.
34. Midrash *Tehillim* 146:4.

33. Talmud Yerushalmi *Megillah* 1:7.
36. Midrash Rabba *Bereshit* 9:5.
37. Talmud Bavli *Taanit* 23a.
38. Psalms 115.

Chapter 6

Myth: Our Present Bodies Will Be Brought Back to Life on Earth

1

The concept of resurrection is a very difficult one to come to terms with. If it means that after death our bodies may be returned to life in a recognizable form, our rational minds are bound to raise a long list of very practical problems. What about overpopulation? Will everyone be resurrected or only a very limited number of good people? At what stage in a person's life and in what form will bodies come back? Will they come back with false teeth and limbs or without? Will they have gray hair or dark? What about the martyrs who were burned to death? No, I am not being facetious since Cleopatra raises precisely this sort of very practical problem in the Talmud: "Queen Cleopatra asked Rabbi Meir, 'I can understand that dead come alive as it is written "And they will grow out of the city like grass grows out of the earth," but when they get up, will they get up naked or with their clothes on?' He said, 'We can learn from wheat, if wheat is buried naked but rises in several clothes so the dead who are buried in garments, how much more so?'"[1] Amusingly, we can see that fashion was then as now, the preoccupation of the wealthy and the powerful.

Before we take up these issues, let us examine the history of the concept. Although the rabbis suggested that resurrection is mentioned in the Torah, the examples they give are far from obvious. Rabbi Meir said, "Where do we have (a basis for) resurrection in the Torah? Because it says, 'Then Moses and the children of Israel will sing this song.' It does not say 'sang' but "they will sing.' From here (we have evidence of) resurrection in the Torah."[2] Of course the word *yashir*, "he will sing," can be used identically in the past and the future tenses. It is one of the features of Hebrew grammar that certain tenses can be used both ways and that a *vav* in front of a future verb turns it into the past tense. No one has ever suggested that in the original text in Exodus it does not mean that Moses sang, in the past tense, on being delivered from the Egyptians. So obviously this is not the literal textual meaning but rather a device to back up a rabbinic position as being sanctioned by tradition.

There is no explicit, unambiguous, or direct reference in the Torah to resurrection. This does not mean that it could not have been implicit. The phrase the rabbis use, *min haTorah*, "from the Torah," does not mean necessarily "written in the Torah." It could mean that the idea derives its authority from the Torah. There are lots of things we can assume from the Torah without their being explicitly stated. It does not actually say, for example, that God has no body, though most (but by no means every)[3] great rabbis have taken this for granted. So it is possible that there are hints or implications in the Torah.

The nearest we get to a suggestion of an existence beyond the grave is the deduction that might be made from the phrase used of Abraham, Isaac, Yishmael, and Jacob that when they died they were "gathered to their people."[4] This is interesting because this phrase is only used of these important men and no one else. Were they unique in the way they died? Or is this a reference to their seminal position as the founders of the monotheistic tradition?

It is not until Samuel that we get an explicit statement that "God puts to death and brings to life, brings down to the grave and takes up,"[5] but this does not necessarily imply resurrection. It says, in its poetic context, that God is capable of bringing the dead back to life in the way that some of the biblical prophets could bring dead children back from the grave. In talking about "soul" we quoted the lines from Ecclesiastes, "For what happens to humans and what happens to animals is the same thing: As this one dies so does the other and there is one spirit for all and there is no way in which man is better than animals. Everything is meaningless. Everything goes to the same place; everything came from dust and returns to dust. And who knows if the spirit of man rises upwards and the spirit of the animal goes down into the dust."[6] Can this be taken to imply resurrection? Certainly talk about souls rising suggests that there is an afterlife, but this may mean no more than that they return to their source, not that they are reconstituted or subsequently returned to a reconstituted body. In neither of these cases do we have any clear and unequivocal statement about a general resurrection of dead bodies.

2

The first clear statement, it might appear, about actual resurrection comes from the vision of Ezekiel, in exile in Babylon, seeking to comfort the Jewish people in their despair at having lost their land and autonomy:

And the hand of God was on me and the spirit of God took me out and placed me in a valley and the valley was full of bones. And He moved me about the bones, around and around and there were many over the surface of the valley and they were very dry. And He said to me, "Son of man, can these bones live?" And I said, "My God Elohim, You know." And He said, "Prophesy over these bones and say to them 'Dry bones, listen to the word of God. Thus says God, Elohim, to these bones, I am going to bring spirit into you and you will live. And I will give you sinews and make flesh come and enclose you in skin and I will put spirit in you and you will live.'" And I prophesied as I had been commanded and as I was prophesying I heard a sound and then a whirlwind and the bones drew closer to each other. And I saw that there were sinews and flesh coming and skin on top but there was no spirit. And God said to me, "Prophesy to the (wind) spirit, prophesy son of man and say to the wind (spirit), 'Thus says my God Elohim, from the four winds, come spirit and breathe into these corpses and they will live.'" And I prophesied as He commanded me and the spirit came and they stood on their feet a huge and very large army. And He said to me, "Son of man, these bones are <u>all</u> (my emphasis) of the house of Israel. They say, 'Our bones are dried, we have lost hope, it has been decreed against us.' Therefore prophesy and say to them, 'Thus says God Elohim, I am going to open up your graves and I am going to take you out of your graves and I will bring you, my people, to the land of Israel. And you will know that I am YHVH when I open your graves and when I take you up, my people, from your graves. I will put my spirit into you and you will live and I will lead you to your land and you will know that I am YHVH, I have spoken and I will do, says YHVH.'"[7]

I underlined the word "all" because at the time not all of the house of Israel was dead. The Judeans were very much alive in Babylon even though they might have been depressed in exile and even though they might have doubted they would ever see a reborn Jewish state in Israel. Even if "the House of Israel" referred to the Northern Kingdom of Israel, there too the so-called Ten Lost Tribes were not completely lost.

I have emphasized the word "all" in the phrase "these bones are all of the house of Israel" because I think this unambiguously indicates that Ezekiel is talking about the "dead" morale of the Jewish people in general, and the burden of his message is that however bad things appear God will revive the fortunes of the people and give them back their land and state. It is an immediate message of hope that was in fact accomplished in the return to Zion that Cyrus permitted. Still, it is hardly evident that this is a commitment to a select group to be resurrected at some future date.

Nevertheless, some of the rabbis of the Talmud were inclined to think that there was something unique about this specific message and saw it as an actual event rather than as a parable. "Rabbi Eliezer said, 'The dead whom Ezekiel brought back to life stood on their feet and sang a song and then died. What song did they sing? God puts to death with justice and revives with mercy.' Rabbi Yehoshua said, 'God puts to death and revives, takes down to the grave and takes up.' Rabbi Yehuda said, 'In truth it was a parable.' Rabbi Nechemia said to him, 'If it was true why call it a parable and if it was a parable why call it truth?' Rabbi Eliezer the son of Rabbi Yossi HaGlili said, 'The dead whom Ezekiel revived went up to the land of Israel and married women and gave birth to sons and daughters.' Rabbi Yehuda Ben Bateira got up and said, 'I am one of their grandchildren and these are their tefillin that my grandfather left me. Who were the dead that Ezekiel revived?' Rav said, 'They are the sons of Ephraim (the ten northern, lost, tribes).'"[8]

Rabbi Eliezer takes the view that what Ezekiel prophesied actually happened but that it was a single remarkable event that showed the capacity of God to achieve the miraculous. Hence their song, which was reminiscent of the song sang by the Israelites to celebrate their miracle of surviving the crossing of the Red Sea. Rabbi Yehuda understands that the narrative was a parable. Rabbi Nechemia, in analyzing Rabbi Yehuda's comment, recognizes that Rabbi Yehuda may be saying that it is a parable but has difficulty understanding the way Rabbi Yehuda is expressing himself. It is almost as though his ambiguity is intended to keep his options open. What Yehuda Ben Bateira is saying could also be understood two ways: He could be saying that the story is a parable referring to the revival of the Jewish people, from whom he is descended, and his tefillin were those worn by the returnees who rebuilt the Temple and reestablished the Jewish presence in Israel. He could, on the other hand, be taken at face value. Either way, it is hard to see any clear, unambiguous principle emerging from Ezekiel's vision.

Perhaps Daniel offers a clearer position: "Many of those who sleep in the earth will awake to eternal life and others to shame and everlasting disintegration."[9] This seems to be a much clearer statement of the expectation that after death the good will awake and return to some sort of life but the bad will not. The book ends with a promise that "Happy is he who waits and arrives at the one thousand, three hundred and thirty-fifth day. And you, go to the end, and you will rest and then get up (to face) your fate at the end of days."[10]

Nevertheless, the phrase *ketz yamim*, usually translated "the end of days" with its eschatological connotations, is misleading. It need not mean some distant day way into the future. For example, the phrase is used in the Cain and Abel narrative: *MiKetz Yamim*, meaning "after a few days had passed."[11] The basis for considering this as the foundation of the concept of revelation is also insubstantial and at best a matter of tradition rather than textual authority.

3

By the time of the Mishna, the belief in resurrection had become formalized: "All Israel has a place in the World to Come. . . . These do not, the person who says that resurrection is not from the Torah."[12] Of course, the very phrase "All Israel has" is a polemical statement that asserts the importance of an idea. Just as the rabbis say that "All Israel is responsible, one for the other,"[13] what they are expressing is a wish rather than a reality. Furthermore, this statement about "All Israel" is not phrased in a way that we normally associate with legal exhortations. The terminology of legal, halachic statements in the Mishna and the Talmud is far stricter and precise. "A person has an obligation to" or "It is forbidden to" are the common forms of statements of what is or is not to be done. You would think that a similar phrase would be appropriate here too, such as, "It is an obligation on every Jew to believe that." It seems that the formulation of this Mishna is directed toward those who reject a position rather than toward exhorting people to believe. Given the battles that the rabbis had with internal schisms, the Sadducees, the followers of Boetus, the Sectarians, the Samaritans, the Christians, and the Greeks and Romans, it is hardly surprising that they were eager to reinforce their position. We have seen how they did this when we looked at their defense of revelation. However, this does not disguise or repudiate the fact that the rabbis did not formulate ideological issues in the same way they did legal ones. Not only that, but there is some ambiguity as to exactly what they meant.

4

The Mishna talks about resurrection and its source in the Torah. However, the Gemara goes on to question this generalization: "Why so much (such a harsh penalty as being deprived of a place in the World to Come)? The Tana taught: He rejected resurrection, therefore he has no part of it because God always deals measure for measure."[14] In effect the person who rejects the idea of resurrection as being referred to in the Torah, not of resurrection itself, is nevertheless rejecting the idea of resurrection altogether. Otherwise why would he be deprived on the basis of rejection when all he has done is reject not the idea but the possibility that its authority derives from the Torah text? Why is he deprived of the Next World? Only if, in the minds of the rabbis, the two ideas are synonymous. If the argument is that only someone who accepts resurrection can experience life after death and one can only get to the stage of resurrection by achieving the afterlife first, then why not just use the same words? Why have two seemingly independent terms?

In a similar way, the famous Gemara about "reward and punishment" blurs the lines between resurrection and life after death. "Rabbi Yaakov said, 'There is not one command in the Torah that has its reward (written) by its side that is not connected with resurrection. In "Honor your father and your mother," it is written: "In order that your days will be lengthened and it will be good for you." In "Sending away (the mother bird from) the nest," it is written: "so that it will be good for you and you will have long days." So it happened that a father said to his son, "Climb up the tower and bring me the fledglings." He climbed up the tower and sent away the mother bird and took the babies, and on his return he fell and died. Where are his good days? Where is his long life? But "good for you" means in the world that is completely good. "Long days" means in the world that is forever long.' Maybe the situation was different and Rabbi Yaakov saw something happen but maybe he (the child or the father) had a sinful intention or maybe the ladder was rotten."[15] This debate about reward is an important one by itself, but the relevance to us here is that the term "reviving the dead," resurrection, is synonymous with the idea of reward coming in the World to Come—so that the distinction between these two terms is also not at all clear.

"Just as the womb receives in silence but delivers in lots of sounds, the grave that receives with lots of sounds should certainly deliver up with lots of sounds. Here is a reply to those who say there is no basis for resurrection in the Torah."[16] This too is a challenge not necessarily to those who doubt resurrection but rather to those who suggest that resurrection is not of Torah origin. Here it is not even that a quotation is being forced; only deductive logic is being used. Once again, the rabbis are eager to rebut the skeptics.

These variations of understanding are testimony to the variety of rabbinic thinking and to the openness of the editors of the Talmud. Some see resurrection as a procedure that is related to the advent of the Messiah. If that is the case, and the messianic era is a continuum of normal life on earth though on a higher plane, then possibly there may be humans still alive at the time of these transitional events who may not need to go through death and the afterlife before participating in the state of resurrection. "Until the dead come alive and then the Messiah the son of David will come."[17] A similar idea is expressed using Elijah as the precursor of the Messiah: "Until the dead come alive and Elijah comes."[18] This is made more explicit in the statement that "The Holy Spirit brings about resurrection and resurrection brings about Elijah, may he be remembered for good."[19]

That the idea of resurrection is used in a symbolic way is evidenced by the statement "He who wakes from sleep should say, 'Blessed are You YHVH Who brings the dead to life.'"[20] Of course a sleeping person does not die overnight and return to life in the morning. Similarly, "If a person sees his friend after thirty days he should say, 'Blessed is He Who has kept us alive to reach this time.' After twelve months he should say, 'Blessed is He Who revives the dead.'"[21] Thus "reviving the dead" can mean a sort of "miraculous" reappearance even though, clearly, no one actually died.

Once again, the variety and, equally so, the obscurity of rabbinic ideas leads to a position where it is all but impossible to know what is meant and certainly to talk as though there were just one single formulation of rabbinic opinion or of what we are supposed to believe.

5

There is another aspect to this discussion and that is the question of disembodied souls continuing to have a sort of human character after they leave the body on their "journey" back to God. There is a debate as to whether the souls of the departed know what is happening on earth.

> And do the dead really not know anything? It once happened with a scholar who gave money to the poor just before Rosh Hashanna in a year of drought and his wife fought with him and he went to sleep in the graveyard. He overheard two spirits talking to each other and one said to her friend, "Come let us pass through the world and hear from the other side of the 'division' what bad things are going to happen on earth." Her friend replied, "I cannot because I have been buried under a mat of sticks, but you go and come back and tell me." She went and passed through and returned. Her friend asked, "My friend, what have you heard?" She replied, "I have heard that whatever is sown in the first quarter (of the sowing season) will be destroyed by hail." He went and sowed in the second quarter. Everyone else's was destroyed but his was not.
>
> The following year he went and slept in the graveyard. He overheard the two spirits talking to each other and one said to her friend, "Come let us pass through the world and hear from the other side of the 'division' what bad things

are going to happen on earth." Her friend replied, "I have already told you that I cannot because I have been buried under a mat of sticks, but you go and come back and tell me." She went and passed through and returned. Her friend asked, "My friend, what have you heard?" She replied, "I have heard that whatever is sown in the second quarter will be swept away by floods." He went and sowed in the first quarter. Everyone else's was swept away but his was not.

His wife asked him, "How was it that last year everyone else's was destroyed and yours was not and this year everyone else's was swept away and yours was not?" He told her what had happened. Not long after there was a fight between this woman and her neighbor (the mother of the dead person). She said, "Look, I will show you that your daughter is buried under a mat."

The following year he went to sleep in the graveyard. He overheard two spirits talking to each other and one said to her friend, "Come let us pass through the world and hear from the other side of the 'division' what bad things are going to happen on earth." Her friend replied, "My friend, leave me alone; our words have been overheard by the living." So we see that the dead do know.[22]

This fascinating story confirms the rabbinic ambivalence about what happens after death. There is general agreement about the principle but no such unanimity about the modalities.

Relevant to this discussion is the tradition of saying *Kaddish* for the dead. According to one opinion this is to help the soul make the transition from this world to the next (others would emphasize that *Kaddish* is not a memorial prayer and it is the emphasis on human behavior on earth that matters; saying *Kaddish* is more for the living than the dead). But perhaps this too is an aspect of resurrection, that people in one way or another survive the cataclysm of death.

Maimonides, the supreme rationalist, rejects this altogether and puts these narratives down to human imagination.

6

Given this ambivalence and lack of precision, how are we to deal with the idea? What should we think? The term "reviving the dead" has two possible meanings: On the one hand it could simply mean the capacity of God or His agent, such as the prophet Elijah, to bring someone who has apparently died back to life.[23] A skeptic might describe this as resuscitation rather than resurrection but clearly the rabbis believed strongly in the Divine capacity to achieve the miraculous or the paranormal. It is indeed axiomatic that belief in a powerful, nonmaterial God implies the capacity to function beyond the bounds of material limitations.

It is possible to argue that the fact that the prayer asking God for rain, in the second blessing in the *Amidah*, that describes God as reviving the dead, strongly suggests that revival is figurative rather than literal. "We mention the 'greatness of rain' (*Mashiv HaRuach*, "He Who makes the wind blow and the rain fall") in (the blessing for) reviving the dead."[24] Rain bringing the world back to life is a common poetic and religious image. It is because of the greatness of God that we have a system of seasons that bring with them the various means of stimulating agricultural growth, which is what sustains humanity. In a sense the earth dies in winter. Such is the message of the myth about Persephone being taken down to the underworld during winter and being allowed up in the spring. The monotheistic response is that it is the greatness of God that controls our lives, not the coupling of gods.

Of course this need not mean that the rabbis actually thought that resurrection was no more than a figure of speech or the miraculous potential of God to do wonders. But given the inconclusiveness of their ideas, we can only surmise. Maimonides is so definite in his Principles of Faith: "I believe with complete conviction that there will be a revival of the dead at a time when it will be the will of the Creator, may His Name be blessed, and the awareness of Him will be established for eternity and for ever,"[25] yet why does he not include life after death among his list of Thirteen Principles? He leaves the issue of resurrection out of his philosophical work, his "Guide to the Perplexed," and gives it no prominence at all in his *Yad HaChazaka*. Yet when all said and done, it is clear that the concept of resurrection held a very special place in rabbinic thought.

The question is whether they meant it to be anything more than an assertion of the idea that God is capable of anything, even something illogical or that challenges our experience of the world, as does resurrection. Perhaps the emphasis that Christianity placed on the resurrection of its founder might have influenced the rabbis to redefine the concept in such a way as to make it clearly different from that. But it seems likely that the fact that they emphasize the error of denial rather than the merits of assertion indicates that they were primarily concerned with affirming Divine power against a rationalist's more restricted view of the universe.

If people actually affirm that resurrection is not possible, then they are making very definite assertions as to their perception of God and indeed about His limitations. The rabbis' understanding of God was that no human limitation should or could be applied and the "absurdity" of resurrection is a way of emphasizing the primacy of faith. It has been said that absurdity is a condition of faith. Resurrection, on the other hand, is a concept of the miraculous, not the absurd.

Belief in resurrection should not be seen as support for the idea that we will one day be reunited with our loved ones and be able to replicate the relationships we have had on earth. Attractive as this might be, it is in the realm of imagination because the recreation of our physical selves is simply beyond our capacity to understand. On the other hand, being resurrected within the spiritual existence of God is something that anyone who believes or experiences the presence of God within himself or herself knows is precisely what happens when we die. The myth is that the rabbis give any clear picture of what resurrection is or when or how it happens. Resurrection is in the realm of nonrational faith, not logic.

Notes

1. Talmud Bavli *Sanhedrin* 90b.
2. Talmud Bavli *Sanhedrin* 91a.
3. Ra'avad on Rambam *Hilchot Teshuvah* 3:7.
4. Genesis 25:8, 35:29, and 49:33.
5. 1 Samuel 2:6.
6. Ecclesiastes 3:19–21.
7. Ezekiel 37:1–14.
8. Talmud Bavli *Sanhedrin* 92b.
9. Daniel 12:2.
10. Daniel 12:12 and 13.
11. Genesis 4:3.
12. Mishna *Sanhedrin Chelek* 1 and 2.
13. Talmud Bavli *Shavuot* 39a.
14. Talmud Bavli *Sanhedrin* 90a.
15. Talmud Bavli *Kiddushin* 39b.
16. Talmud Bavli *Brachot* 16b.
17. Talmud Bavli *Sotah* 48b.
18. *Tosefta Sotah* 12:5.
19. Talmud Yerushalmi *Shekalim* 14:2.
20. Talmud Yerushalmi *Brachot* 4:7.
21. Talmud Bavli *Brachot* 58b.

22. Talmud Bavli *Brachot* 18a.
23. 1 Kings 17.
24. Talmud Bavli *Brachot* 5b.
25. Maimonides' Thirteen Principles of Faith, No. 13.

Chapter 7

Myth:
We Know Who
the Messiah Is

1

There is a lot of talk about the Messiah nowadays. Some Chassidim tell us to display stickers proclaiming "We want Moshiach now" and others tell us that the Rebbe of Lubavitch was the Mashiach and he will return. Christians tell us the Messiah has come and gone and will have a second coming, but most Jews (who actually think about it) are still waiting. For what or whom exactly are we supposed to be waiting?

If we examine the term *Mashiach*, messiah, as used in the Torah and in the Mishna, it simply means someone who is anointed. The word refers to someone appointed to a specific high position and confirmed by having oil poured out over his head. In the Torah this ceremony is applied only to a priest. The first time it is used is with reference to Aharon's appointment: "And you will pour oil on his head and you will anoint him,"[1] and then with regard to both Aharon and his sons: "And you will anoint Aharon and his sons."[2] Later on the term is applied to "the serving priest,"[3,4] and this is the main use of the word in the Mishna and the *Tosefta*. Actually the process of dedicating by pouring oil was not confined to people. The altar was anointed as indeed were various ceremonial objects.[5] Nevertheless the term came to be used to apply to several prominent appointments. There was the High Priest himself and then another priest who was appointed at times of war to go out into battle with the army. This way they protected, in a way, the main High Priest. This substitute priest was called the "anointed for war." Eventually the ceremony of anointing was adapted for use in designating the king.

The first reference to a king being anointed comes in the Book of Samuel when the prophet Samuel anoints Saul.[6] While Saul was still alive Samuel anointed David as his replacement.[7] Indeed, the phrase "the anointed of God" is used for the first time when David insists that Saul, though his enemy, should still be treated with respect.[8] Solomon is anointed to succeed David by both the High Priest Zadok and the prophet Nathan.[9] However, none of his successors to the throne of David were anointed. Rehoboam succeeded to his father's throne and then, of course, lost the ten northern tribes to Jeroboam and the new kingdom of Israel, but no member of the family was anointed. This has led some to suggest that anointing was reserved exclusively for the Davidic line and then only when there was either a break in the dynasty or a challenge to succession, yet in the breakaway northern kingdom Elisha is commanded by God to anoint Yehu to succeed Ahab.[10] Furthermore, in contradiction to the notion that the title of *Mashiach*, "the anointed," applies only to Jewish kings, the prophet Isaiah refers to Cyrus as God's anointed.[11] At this stage there is nothing unusual, nothing long term, nothing eschatological or miraculous about the concept of an anointed king.

It is from Isaiah that we first get the notion of some miraculous or unusual state in which the world will be a better place than it is now: "And in the future the mountain

of the house of God will be established as the main mountain and it will be more important than all hills and all the
nations will flow to it. And many nations will go, saying,
'Let us go up to the mountain of God to the house of the God
of Jacob and He will teach us His ways and we will go in His
paths because Torah will come from Zion and the word of
God from Jerusalem. And He will act as judge between the
nations and He will discipline them and they will beat their
swords into plowshares and their spears into pruning hooks.
No nation will fight another nation and they will no longer
learn to war.'"[12] This is the magnificent vision of a state to
which humanity should aspire and one which has become a
crucial element in traditional Jewish ideology—yet it is not
initially connected, necessarily, with any specific leader.

Isaiah does go on to talk about the emergence of a leader
who will bring about this state: "Therefore YHVH will give
you a sign. A young woman will conceive and give birth to
a son and will call him 'God is with us.' He will eat butter
and honey and through his own recognition he will reject
evil and choose good."[13]

Isaiah continues with his vision: "The people who are
walking in darkness have seen great light. To those who live
in darkness, bright light shall shine on them. You have made
the nation greater and increased its joy. They rejoice before
You like at harvest time or when they rejoice as they divide
their spoil. Because You have smashed the burden he was
carrying, the yoke on his shoulder, the staff that was used
to oppress him, like the day of Midian. For every thing
crushed in the whirlwind, every garment rolled in blood has
been burnt in consuming fire. For a son has been born for
us, a boy has been given and authority will fall on his shoul-
ders and he will be called 'wonderful, advisor, powerful god,
eternal father, prince of peace.' He will spread authority and
endless peace for the throne of David over his kingdom. To
prepare it and support it with justice and charity for now
and for ever. The concern of YHVH of hosts will do this."[14]

Isaiah goes on to reiterate that a new leadership will emerge for the House of David: "And a shoot will come out of the stock of Yishai and a growth will flourish from his roots. And the spirit of YHVH will rest on him, a spirit of wisdom and understanding, a spirit of counsel and greatness, a spirit of the knowledge of and the respect for YHVH. And his spirit will be one of respect for YHVH; he will not judge by (appearances) what his eyes see and he will not correct on the basis of what his ear hears (hearsay). He will judge the poor with justice and he will correct the humble of the earth straightforwardly; he will strike the earth with the staff of his mouth and with his lips he will put the wicked to death. Justice will be his clothing and honesty will cover his body. And the wolf will live with the sheep and the leopard will lie with the kid and a calf and a cub and a lamb together and a small boy will lead them. And the cow and the bear will feed while their children shall play together and the lion will eat straw like an ox. And a baby shall play by a snake's hole and by a scorpion's lair a child will (safely) place its hand. There will be no evil or corruption on My holy mountain for the earth will be full of knowledge of YHVH as water covers the sea."[15]

We are familiar with these quotes because they have for thousands of years been used by Christian theologians to prove that Isaiah was predicting the advent of a Christian Messiah. Traditional Jewish commentators took Isaiah to be referring to King Hezekiah, who brought about a great religious and social revival. Their arguments were supported by the fact that all prophets seemed to be concerned with a more immediate future for the Jewish people than events five hundred or more years ahead.

It is not until the postexilic prophet Malachi that we are given an expression of some wondrous state ahead that is to be ushered in by a mythical figure, someone who is already dead but will return to change the world. However, Malachi does not talk about a king; instead he says that God is sending the prophet Elijah: "Behold I am sending you Eliyahu the prophet before the coming of the day of YHVH, great and fearful. And he will return the hearts of fathers to their sons and sons to their fathers."[16]

The only other prophetic idea that is often linked to the messianic idea is that of Gog and MaGog (or Gog from Gog). This one or two characters (it varies) appear in only one place in the Bible, the Book of Ezekiel.[17] The context is a prophecy that the mighty king Gog will attack the Jewish people when they are resettled on their land. He will be defeated and buried in Israel and out of his defeat will come a period of peace and God's spiritual authority.

The expression that Ezekiel uses for this coming era (as does Isaiah) is "the end of days" but the Hebrew *Acharit HaYamim* does not necessarily mean the eschatological "end of days" but rather "after a period of time." Thus the actual text need not lead us to any specific conclusion. It is up to the Oral Tradition to convey what these ideas really meant in practice.

2

It is not surprising that after the exile of 586 B.C.E. and the loss of the independent monarchy, Jews would have longed for the return both of complete autonomy and of the reinstatement of their own monarchy. If they interpreted the Isaiah chapters as referring to a future leader they would certainly have expected such a leader to be temporal rather than ecclesiastical. They would have looked forward to independence under a strong king. Even the great triumphs of the Hasmoneans could not disguise the fact that the Jewish Second Commonwealth remained a client state and not a totally independent one. Of course, the failures of the later

Hasmoneans and their successors would also have reinforced the dream of a return to earlier leadership, particularly one identified with the spiritual tradition in the way King David, as author of the book of Psalms, was. By the time of the Mishna, the Jewish people were riven with internal dissension and subject to tremendous pressures, hardships, and often destruction by the Romans. The dreams of rescue, of freedom, would have increased and from the evidence of both the Dead Sea sects and Christianity we can feel how powerful this dream was.

Nevertheless the Mishna still uses the word *mashiach*, "messiah," predominantly to refer to a priest: "Who is the *mashiach*? He is only the priest who has been anointed with the anointing oil."[18] There, the political leader is called the *nasi* or the king. It is later that the idea of the *mashiach* is applied to a spiritual leader. Around the start of the Common Era, when different sects within Judaism were proclaiming the arrival of a "Teacher of Justice" or "Righteous Priest," many different ideologies developed.

Among the Jews of the mainstream rabbinic school there was disagreement about both the nature of the idea and whether it was something in which humans could be proactively involved. Rabbi Akiva, in the second century, proclaimed Bar Cochba the Messiah simply because he succeeded, temporarily, in throwing off Roman oppression. Clearly Akiva's concept was of a politically successful leader. Most of the other rabbis disagreed and instead of calling him Bar Cochba, "the Son a Star," they called him Bar Coziva, "the Son of a Lie": "Bar Coziva ruled as king for two-and-a-half years. He said to the rabbis, 'I am the Mashiach,'"[19] and: "The rabbis said to him, 'Akiva, grass will grow through your cheeks before the Son of David will come.'"[20] The debate and disagreement runs throughout the Talmud and in a way in which widely divergent views seem to have been more readily accepted than they are nowadays.

3

Focusing on the political aspect, it is interesting that there are two messianic leaders in the talmudic tradition: the Messiah the son of David and the Messiah the son of Joseph. "The *Mashiach* son of David is to be revealed to us quickly in our lifetime. God said to him, 'Ask me anything and I will grant it.' When he saw that the *Mashiach* son of Yosef was killed he said, 'The only thing I ask is to be allowed to live'"[21]

Given the political nature of the concept this is not really surprising. After the northern tribes split from Judah and Benjamin the two Joseph tribes, Ephraim and Menashe, were left out of the Judah-Benjamin alliance. Individuals from northern tribes may have been left behind or chose to reside in the south but both Menashe and Ephraim were part of the kingdom of the ten northern tribes. Menashe is actually called the tribe of Joseph,[22] but Menashe was also one of the tribes whose members stayed on the eastern side of the Jordan when Joshua crossed over.[23] Menashe and therefore Joseph came to be associated with the ten northern tribes, who adopted the name of Joseph as a sort of unifying code name. Despite the myth that the ten northern tribes conquered by the Assyrians in 722 B.C.E. disappeared, in fact they joined other exiled groups of Jews and when Assyria was conquered by Babylon, the probability is that many if not most joined with other exiled Jews and retained some of their northern traditions. Naturally, they would not have wanted to cede sovereignty to the southern tribes, so the idea of a messiah of the north was retained. By the time of the Talmud, we see that although the idea was still present, the supremacy of the Davidic line was generally accepted.

Apart from this disagreement there were plenty of others. One body of opinion held the view that the Isaiah pre-

dictions had been fulfilled and that there would be no new
messiah at all: "Rabbi Hillel said, 'There will not be a
mashiach for Israel because it was used up (eaten) at the
time of Hezekiah.' Rabbi Yosef said, 'May Rabbi Hillel's Master forgive him. When did Hezekiah live? During the First
Temple. Whereas Zecharia lived during the Second and he
said, "Rejoice Daughter of Zion, lift yourself up daughter of
Jerusalem because your king is coming, righteous and pure,
poor, riding on a donkey or on a mule (Zecharia 9).""[24] There
were also those who agreed that Isaiah and Ezekiel meant
characters nearer their day but that in practice things
worked out differently: "God originally intended that
Hezekiah would be the *mashiach* and that Sennacharib
would be Gog and Magog."[25]

4

There were two much more fundamental differences. One
body of opinion held that the great deliverance that the messiah would bring about would come when things got so bad
that only Divine intervention could rescue them: "In the lead-
up to the messiah rudeness will increase and prices will rise.
The vine will produce plenty but wine will be expensive and
the monarchy will become apostate and no one will give direction. The place of meeting will become a place of prostitution. The *Gallil* will be destroyed. The borders will be destroyed and the residents of the borderlands will have to go
round (begging) from city to city and no one will take pity.
The wise and the scribes will become corrupted and those
who fear sin will be rejected. Truth will become rare. Lads
will embarrass their elders and elders will rise before small
ones. A son will defile his father and a daughter will rebel
against her mother and the daughter-in-law against her
mother-in-law. A man's own household will become his enemy. The face of the generation will be like the face of a dog.

A son will not be embarrassed before his father. Who will we have to rely on? Only our Father in Heaven."[26] Another example of this position is: "The son of David will not come until all government has become apostate."[27]

Others took the view that humanity, by behaving in a positive way, could itself bring about this better state: "If Israel were to keep one *Shabbat*, the son of David would come immediately,"[28] and "Rabbi Chiya said, 'If all Israel were to repent one day the son of David would come immediately.'"[29]

Naturally there is also an attempt to keep both options open: "Rabbi Yochanan said, 'The son of David will only come in a generation that is completely guiltless or completely guilty.'"[30] Also, with a nod in the direction of the Joseph tradition (Ephraim being one of the sons of Joseph) and adding a reference to a new character in the role of Gog: "If (the generation) is not worthy then *Mashiach* the son of Ephraim will come but if they are worthy the son of David will come. A wicked king will arise called Amarillus. Bald with small eyes, leprous on his forehead, and his right ear closed."[31]

A third variation suggests that the concept is a spiritual one and dependent on the relationship between God's link with humanity through the soul and the time it would take for souls to fulfill their destiny and exert a positive influence on humanity: "The son of David will not come until all the souls in the bodies have been used up."[32]

The variety of traditions led some rabbis to sanction different views: "What is his name? The house of Rabbi Shila says 'Shiloh.' The house of Rabbi Yanai said 'Yanun' is his name. The house of Rabbi Chanina said 'Chanina.' And some say his name is Menachem Ben Hezekiah."[33] Notice how each rabbi finds a name that is reminiscent of his own. It is almost as though they are saying that a person's view of the messiah is colored by his own experience. On the other hand, Rav Huna tries to reconcile them all by suggesting they are simply different names for the same idea: "Rav Huna said he has seven names: Mashiach, Yenun, Tsidkeynu, Tsemach, David, Shiloh, Eliyahu."[34]

Many were concerned with trying to predict a specific date for deliverance: "The House of Elihu taught this world is (will last for) six thousand years; two thousand of chaos, two thousand of Torah, two thousand of Messiah."[35] This may have been one of the reasons that led Rabbi Yochanan to lay a curse on those who tried to predict the arrival of a, or the, messiah: "Rabbi Yochanan said, 'Let the bones rot of those who try to calculate the "end." Because people say that since the "end" came and he (the messiah) did not come, this means he will not come at all. But wait for him, as it says, "Happy are those who wait for him.""'[36] This position certainly resonates today.

6

The main issue that divided the rabbis seems to have been the nature of the messianic period. There was the issue of exactly who the messiah would be, the issue of when he would come and under what circumstances, and the question of what sort of world the messiah would usher in. There are many rabbinic statements about changes in the world order. Some were quoted in the previous chapter about "the Future to Come." These positions are represented by Rabbi Chiya: "Rabbi Chiya the son of Aba said in the name of Rabbi Yochanan, 'Whatever the prophets prophesied (about supernatural events) was for the messianic days but as far as the World to Come is concerned, "No eye has seen it apart from You God, something God has made for those who wait for Him."' And he disagrees with Shmuel who said that the only difference between this world and the messianic days is (that there will be no more) political oppression."[37] The position of Shmuel is the one that Maimonides selects as the basis of his conclusion that "the days of the messiah is this world and the world will continue to function normally, only the kingship will return to Israel. The early rabbis have already said that the only difference between this world and the messianic days will be government oppression."[38]

What conclusions can we draw from all this? First of all, a clear distinction emerges between the different rabbinic concepts and Christian messianism. Some saw the great prophecies as having already been fulfilled, but those who did not all expected to see a dramatic change in this world at the arrival of the messiah. They expected to see both political peace and a period of universal spirituality. This was why some rabbis, at least, were prepared to consider Bar Cochba a candidate for the title of Messiah, but were never likely to have been much impressed by the Nazarene.

There is no record in Jewish texts of the concept of a Second Coming, unless one wants to interpret the first coming as that of the Messiah the son of Joseph and the second as that of the Messiah the son of David. It is perhaps significant that the Gospels have Jesus' father named "Joseph." Perhaps this was in order to incorporate or impress those supporters of the northern messiah. The mainstream of Jewish thought has consistently held to the dream that the Son of David will one day arrive and usher in a great period of human interaction and spirituality.

The question remains exactly what it is to which we are required to adhere. Can the idea of waiting for the messiah be the same as the idea of waiting for God to intervene and improve life? All the different variations and nuances of rabbinic opinion are concerned more with the general state of human affairs than they are with the details. They all look toward a better world with greater spirituality, justice, fairness, and tolerance than the present one. This is, of course, why all past candidates for the title of Messiah, of any background, have failed to gain acceptance—because nothing changed tangibly and the messiah is a very tangible idea in Judaism. It is not relevant to see the dream of a better world as requiring a specific political system, monarchy as opposed to democracy, for example. The emphasis on King David is at least as important symbolically and nostalgically as it is historically.

The arguments are essentially over whether this better state of human affairs will come about as a result of Divine intervention or as a result of human endeavor. Traditionally the Orthodox world has tended to prefer the interventionist position, largely because of its emphasis on faith and the patient acceptance of the role of God in history without knowing how or when it would come about. This explains the aversion to Zionism among some groups, on the grounds that it is humans arrogating to themselves the role of God in history. The usual source for those who object to humans intervening in the return to Zion is the Gemara that says that Israel's exile was part of a special arrangement made by God and subject only to His intervention.[39] On the other hand, there is no reason why individuals should not see the hand of God working in many different ways.

It is also understandable that when political events put terrible pressure and suffering upon the Jews they would have been more likely to hope and pray for Divine delivery and salvation. Hence the expression *ikveta deMishicha*, "the footsteps of the Messiah," used in the Mishna to describe the difficult period that signals the coming of the change for the better. Similarly the expression *chevlei Mashiach*, "the birth pangs of the Messiah,"[40] indicate the difficulty of the process.

On the other hand, in times of peace and progress and material well-being, people might be more inclined to hope that humanity itself could help bring this dramatic change about. The essence of the idea of messianism is the optimism that the Divine order is committed to a better world. Since Noah's flood God has in effect given us the responsibility of improving ourselves and our world. This, together with the belief that God can and does intervene in human affairs, constitute important concepts in the Jewish spiritual world order. They emphasize both faith in God and an optimism about the future as well as a spur to human betterment.

Once again there is a difference between absolutely denying something and keeping an open mind. The attitude of the rabbis is strongly set against absolute denial, while allowing great freedom to explore and interpret. The clearest illustration of this is the variety of different concepts that Jews have to this very day about the details of messianism and who might be the Messiah. Just as Maimonides tells us that it is impossible to give positive attributes to God, so in this context it is easier to say what is not part of or included in the Jewish tradition than to come up with a single formulation of a concept with which everyone will agree. One can agree that a distillation of the ideas expressed produces an essential spirit of optimism, of dynamism directed toward improving society, combined with the acceptance of Divine intervention, to create a powerful element in the Jewish psyche.

Yet again, the rabbis virtually unanimously assent to a concept that is left unclarified and with multiple interpretations. The idea is allowed to float without specific conditions or limitations. It is a myth that there is one clearly defined formulation of exactly what will happen, on which all religious authorities can agree.

Notes

1. Exodus 29:7.
2. Exodus 30:30.
3. Leviticus 4:3.
4. *Tosefta Megillah* 1:18.
5. Exodus 40:9–15.
6. 1 Samuel 10:1.

7. 1 Samuel 16:13.
8. 1 Samuel 24:7.
9. 1 Kings 1:45.
10. 1 Kings 19:16.
11. Isaiah 45:1.
12. Isaiah 2:2–4.
13. Isaiah 7:14–15.
14. Isaiah 9:1–6.
15. Isaiah 11:1–9.
16. Malachi 3:23.
17. Ezekiel 38–39.
18. Mishna *Horyot* 3:4.
19. Talmud Bavli *Sanhedrin* 93b.
20. Talmud Yerushalmi *Taanit* 4:5.
21. Talmud Bavli *Succah* 62b.
22. Numbers 13:11.
23. Numbers 32:39.
24. Talmud Bavli *Sanhedrin* 99a.
25. Talmud Bavli *Sanhedrin* 94a.
26. *Mishna Sotah* 915.
27. Talmud Bavli *Sanhedrin* 97a.
28. Midrash Rabba *Shemot* 25.
29. Talmud Yerushalmi *Taanit* 1:64.
30. Talmud Bavli *Sanhedrin* 98b.
31. *Otsar* Midrashim 551.
32. Talmud Bavli *Yevamot* 63b.
33. Talmud Bavli *Sanhedrin* 98b.
34. Midrash *Mishlei* 19.
35. Talmud Bavli *Sanhedrin* 97b.
36. Ibid.
37. Talmud Bavli *Sanhedrin* 99a.
38. Maimonides' *Yad HaChazaka, Hilchut Teshuva* 9:10.
39. Talmud Bavli *Ketubot* 111a.
40. Ibid.

Chapter 8

Myth:
We Can See How We Are
Rewarded and Punished
for What We Do

1

One of the clearest messages of the Bible is that God rewards those who follow His ways and punishes those who do not. Yet to us humans there appears to be no reason or rhyme for so much that happens to us and around us. Terrible things happen to children and adults. Horrific tortures are applied to innocent people. Hideous disfigurement is inflicted even before birth, sometimes resulting from things such as nuclear fallout over which individuals have no direct control. As Jews we seem to have been particularly selected for death and destruction. Why? Is there some explanation?

Starting with Adam and Eve in the Garden of Eden and continuing with Cain's murder of Abel, God appears to punish those who disobey Him. Indeed, He destroyed all of mankind except for Noah and his family because His "spirit could not bear" the evil that His creatures were perpetrating: "And

God saw that the evil of man was increasing throughout the earth . . . And He was sorry that He had created man."[1] Yet, after the flood God decided that it is pointless to expect man to change his nature and that destruction is not the way to proceed.[2] Rather, humanity needed more specific guidance. In the beginning this guidance was generalized. After the flood came the first rules and regulations (apart from the original command to Adam not to eat from the tree of knowledge) that are the basis for the seven Noachide Laws. These laws were universals that in Jewish Law applied to all of humanity. They were given with the promise that God would seek out offenders and deal "personally" with them.[3] Slowly through the period of Abraham, Isaac, and Jacob, new, more specific instructions were given until finally the full measure of the Divine Covenant was revealed to Moses on Sinai and through him to the people of Israel.

The promises that were made to Abraham, Isaac, and Jacob, with regard to their seed and to the Land of Caanan, are seen as rewards for their dedication to God. But these rewards are specific: a land and a populous nation. Although the God-fearing fathers are rewarded in some respects, in others their lives are difficult and strewn with tests and trials. It is with the giving of the Torah that the direct connection between good behavior and benefits is made explicit. The best known expression of this comes in the Ten Commandments: "For I am YHVH your God, a God of principle, Who impacts the errors of fathers onto their children for three and four generations of those who hate Me,"[4] and "Honor your father and your mother so that your days will be lengthened on the earth that your God gives you."[5]

The promise of long days is repeated for other specific commands: "Send away the mother and then you may take the fledglings so that you will benefit and you will have long days,"[6] and "You should have complete and honest weights and complete and honest measures in order that your days shall be lengthened."[7] A lot has been read into the fact that these three issues—relationship with parents, nature, and commerce—have been selected specifically—as though these three issues are the three essential conditions of a balanced human society. "Long Life" could therefore mean not so much long life for individuals as effective survival for humanity. However, this promise of long life is not confined to these three items. There is an additional example: "Do not eat (blood) in order that it will be good for you and for your children after you."[8] This same commitment to benefit those who obey the Divine commandments is used in general as well: "And you should do that which is good and straight in the eyes of God in order that it should be good for you."[9]

2

The most familiar promise of reward is that which became the second paragraph of the *Shema*:

> And if you really pay attention to My commandments which I command you today, To love God your God and serve Him with all your hearts and all your being, then I will give rain to your land, the early rain and the late rain, and you will be able to gather in your corn, your wine, and your olive oil, and I will give grass for your cattle, and you will eat and be satisfied. Beware, in case your hearts are turned away, and you go after other gods and serve them and worship them, then God will be angry with you and close up the skies and there will be no rain, and the earth will not give produce, and you will disappear quickly from this good land that God is giving you, and you should take my words into your hearts and into your being, and you should tie them to your hands and as decoration between your eyes. And you should teach them to your children to talk about them when you are at home, when you travel, when you go to sleep, and when you wake up. And you should write them

on the doorposts of your house and your gate so that you
and your children will have long lives on the land, Which
God promised to give to your forefathers for as long as the
heavens are over the earth.[10]

This promise for better and for worse is repeated in
Deuteronomy.[11] A fuller, more graphic and dramatic statement of what will go wrong can be found in Leviticus.[12]

The question is whether this commitment to reward and
to punish is a national one rather than an individual one.
The promises to Abraham, Isaac, and Jacob were national
and the covenant on Sinai was a national one. This does not
mean that individuals were not automatically involved, but
that the real measure of obedience to the Divine plan lay in
the extent to which the nation obeyed and served God (or
not, as in the case of the golden calf). This national idea is
reinforced by the following quote, which indeed stresses the
peoplehood rather than individual recompense: "And if you
really listen to the voice of YHVH your God to keep and do
all His commandments that I command you today then God
will place you above all other nations of the earth and you
will receive all these blessings."[13]

There seems to be two clear issues here, the national
and the individual. The nation succeeds or falls on the basis
of its national decisions and its commitment to its heritage.
Individuals may get caught up in the fate of the people regardless of their personal merit. Similarly, the individual
may suffer as the result of what parents do, regardless of
his or her specific actions.

What exactly does the statement in Exodus about "visiting the sins of the fathers on the sons" mean? It certainly
is not a legal imperative. According to Jewish law, a person
alone has to pay judicially for his actions. This is reaffirmed
in the sentence in Deuteronomy, "Fathers will not die for
their children and children will not die for their fathers; a
person dies for his own misdeeds."[14] Thus the statement in

Exodus must be understood as meaning that actions bring about consequences. What parents do certainly impacts on their children, sometimes well beyond the immediate generation, but this is not a statement about reward and punishment on an individual level. The debate moves to the book of Ecclesiastes, where the issue is specifically and clearly stated: "The righteous and the wicked, God will judge,"[15] and "For every deed God will bring to justice, every hidden thing, for good or bad."[16]

So both as a nation and as individuals we are warned of almost a double jeopardy: If we do well, as individuals, the national disaster may overcome us regardless. And if we are evil, the credit of the wider community may save us. The rabbis sought to avoid this conclusion by seeing the real, true response as being on a very different level. They wanted individuals to feel that there was an immediate link between their actions and what happens to them.

3

By the time the Mishna discusses the issue, it is no longer a matter of doubt. God rewards and punishes people; the issue is how it actually works in practice. In affirming that individual actions matter and that they are judged, Rabbi Yehudah the Prince says, "Think of three things and you will not do wrong. Know what is above: an Eye that sees, an Ear that hears, and everything is recorded in a book."[17] Similarly, Rabbi Elazar said, "Know before Whom you labor and Who you are working for that will pay you for your work."[18] Rabbi Elazar adds the promise that it is God Who will reward.

The comprehensive statement comes from Rabbi Akiva, ironically the one person who, Moses points out, was apparently not rewarded for his good deeds, as he was tortured to death.[19] "He used to say everything has been given on loan and the net is spread for all human beings. The store is open and the shopkeeper gives credit. The register is open, the hand writes, and whoever wants to come and borrow may borrow. The agents go round collecting regularly and every day get their payment from a person whether he agrees or not. They have a legal authority and their case is just and everything is prepared for the banquet."[20] His contemporary, Rabbi Tarfon, expressed similar views: "The day is short, there is a lot to be done, the workers are lazy, and the Master is pressing (for the work to be done). He said you do not have to complete the work but you are not free to give it up. If you have learnt a lot of Torah you are given a lot of reward and you can rely on the Master to pay you for your work and know that the reward for the righteous is in the Future to Come."[21]

There are dissenting voices against these statements, though the dissent is about not the principle but the modalities. Antignos does not deny that there are rewards. He does, however, emphasize the idea that reward and punishment should not be the criterion by which we act. "Antignos from Socho received (the traditional authority) from Shimon HaTsadik. He used to say, 'Do not be like servants who serve their master in order to receive a reward, but be like servants who serve their master not to receive a reward and let the authority of Heaven be upon you.'"[22] Antignos clearly reflects an idealistic and even a philosophical position.

Another understanding seeks to emphasizes consequences: "He (Hillel) saw a skull floating on the water. He said to it, 'Because you drowned others you were drowned, and those who drowned you will be drowned.'"[23] In effect, this is a simple utilitarian statement. One's actions, says Hillel, are bound to lead to consequences. "Do as you would be done by" because in the way that a person deals, so will he be dealt with.

The most specific expression comes from Ben Azai: "Ben Azai said, 'Run to do even a small mitzvah (positive com-

mandment) and flee from an *avera* (negative command) because one mitzvah leads to another mitzvah and one *avera*
leads to another. For the reward for a mitzvah is a mitzvah
and the punishment for an *avera* is an *avera*."[24] In other
words, the pleasure one gets from doing good deeds, such as
the spiritual pleasure of keeping *Shabbat* or a festival, will
encourage him or her to repeat the act. The additional pleasure or sense of gratification one gets will in itself be sufficient reward. This feeling will continue to repeat itself as
the positive habits and actions are done again and again,
and the positive actions will be reinforced. Similarly, punishment becomes simply the absence of reward. So if one is
mean and uncaring, one deprives oneself of the pleasure one
might otherwise have had. If one does not keep a holy day
as a spiritual experience and does not have the pleasure and
the refreshment that come with the experience, then he or
she simply goes on living without these positive experiences
and as a consequence lives a lesser life, deprived of these
pleasures. This does not mean one lives a bad or useless life,
just that this spiritual dimension is missing.

This remains, rationally, the most persuasive of solutions,
avoiding some of the contradictions that have to be dealt
with otherwise. The fact remains that suffering does not
seem to be connected to actions at all. Pain, illness, loss,
and death seem not to be related at all to the way people
behave. Good and saintly people often suffer, whereas awful, selfish people appear to prosper. In response to this Rabbi
Yanai said, "We simply cannot explain (it is not in our hands
to explain) either why the wicked prosper or the righteous
suffer."[25]

4

Yet, the rabbis of the Talmud continue to be perplexed by
the problem of suffering: "Moshe asked God, 'Master of the

Universe, why are there righteous who have a good life and righteous who have a bad life, wicked people who prosper and wicked who suffer?' He said to Moshe, 'A righteous person who has a good life is a righteous son of a righteous father, a righteous person who has a bad life is a good son of a bad father, a wicked person who prospers is the bad son of a good father, and a wicked person who suffers is the bad son of a bad father.' Some say that this is what He answered: 'A righteous person who has a good life is a completely righteous person, a righteous person who has a bad life is an incompletely righteous person, a wicked person who prospers is not completely bad, and a wicked person who suffers is totally bad.'"[26]

The most common response is the suggestion that reward and punishment is not part of our present world but is a promise for the next one. In the context of life after death we have quoted Rabbi Yaakov: "Rabbi Yaakov said, 'There is not one command in the Torah that has its reward (written) by its side that is not connected with resurrection. In "Honor your father and your mother," it is written: "In order that your days will be lengthened and it will be good for you." In "Sending away the nest," it is written: "so that it will be good for you and you will have long days." So it happened that a father said to his son, "Climb up the tower and bring me the fledglings." He climbed up the tower and sent away the mother bird and took the babies, and on his return he fell and died. Where are his good days? Where is his long life? But "good for you" means in the world that is completely good. "Long days" means in the world that is forever long.'"[27] This is the dominant theme in the Gemara: "The reward for the righteous is in the Future to Come,"[28] and "There is no reward for (performing) *mitzvoth* in this world."[29]

Interestingly, there is a pragmatic response to this Gemara in *Kiddushin*, where the child falls and is killed. The Gemara continues: "Maybe the situation was differ-

ent and Rabbi Yaakov saw something happen, but maybe
he (the child or the father) had a sinful intention or maybe the ladder was rotten." The rabbis are loathe to just
put off the issue to the next world. They strongly believed
in consequences and that is why they try here to see if
the situation cannot be explained very simply in these
terms—so that indeed we are talking about consequences
again.

Yet the rabbis return again and again to the idea of reward and punishment being part of the next life. Nevertheless the position that reward and punishment are applied
only in the next world leaves open the question of why the
righteous suffer in this world. It is one thing to put off the
reward until a later time: it is quite another to come face-
to-face with serious suffering that seems to have no reason
or explanation.

The rabbis often used the concept of *yissurin*, which may
be translated long windedly as "the suffering imposed on
good people for no apparent reason." Of course, this is the
message of the biblical Book of Job. God is proud of his servant Job, but Satan—not a Christian Satan in conflict with
and opposing God, but one of His lesser agents whose function seems simply to have been to challenge, to put "the other
side of the story" (for this is one of the meanings of the word
"Satan": "another side")—wonders whether Job is good only
because he has it so good in life. God allows Satan to test
this by removing everything and doing all the evil he can to
Job, short of taking his life. Job survives the experience and
the three "comforters" who come to be with him. Despite their
encouragement, he refuses to curse God. In the end Satan
is defeated, good triumphs, and Job is restored to his former
state.

A good man suffers because of forces beyond his control
and, indeed, beyond the normal workings of this world. The
Book of Job is in itself a document that tries to answer this
perennial and perplexing problem. Of course, there is no an-

swer that satisfies the rational, human mind. Hence the statement that "Whomever God likes, He batters with suffering."[30] It is as though God shows an interest in someone only to test them. The testing is a sort of "act of love." This is reinforced by the experiences of Abraham, Isaac, and Jacob, who despite their close relationship and the Divine promises still endured difficult and tragic experiences in their lives.

The rabbis try to differentiate between the suffering that is caused by love, "He whom God loves, He corrects,"[31] and that which just seems random. Time and again, however, rabbinic opinion returns to the idea that when things go wrong a person should examine his ways. This does not necessarily mean that suffering is a consequence, but rather that improved behavior or higher standards can overcome or ameliorate the problem. Nevertheless, even suffering caused by Divine love is not welcomed.[32] All of this merely reinforces the fact that no explanation satisfies and that whatever criteria may be applied, the problem remains an intractable one.

5

In effect, trying to discover how God works, or what the criteria by which He runs human affairs are, is inevitably a fruitless exercise. It is logically impossible for a limited human being, no matter how exalted, to claim that he or she can know how God works. Attempts to suggest that one can explain (for example) the Holocaust in terms of the behavior of the Jews of Europe is, in my view, dangerous nonsense. This would mean that any human can know the mind of God and goes against everything the rabbis have said about the nature of God. It is true that the rabbis gave various reasons for the destruction of the Temples, but these were in situations where the Jews had clearly brought their fate upon their own heads by disregarding both the Torah and the messages of the prophets.

We cannot know why God acts in ways that defy logic. All sorts of spurious explanations are bound to fail. It is often suggested that people have allotted tasks in life, which some finish before others. The nonsense of this position is that it does not explain the death of a child at birth.

Some Jews have taken on board the idea that pain and suffering are good, but this not the approach of the rabbis or of the Torah. For them, suffering can teach lessons. Humans can turn a painful experience into one that teaches, but pain in itself is not all to be welcomed for its own sake.

In the end, we must seek satisfaction in the style of life we choose for ourselves. In this way, reward and punishment need to be divided into two different issues. The way we live our lives now must be based on what we consider to be the most appropriate and most beneficial. If we decide to act morally it must not be because we think we will benefit but because we believe it to be right. This is the position of Antignos. On the other level, how God organizes His world and repays those with whom He has a relationship is a matter of faith that cannot be dealt with logically.

Our lives are lived between two extremes. On the one hand we have responsibility and an obligation to act: "We do not rely on miracles."[33] On the other hand we are subject to forces beyond our own control. This is reflected in the Yiddish expression *bashert*, "fate, ordained from above." We tend to think that finding our life partners is in the hands of God.[34] But what about life in general? There are lovely stories told in the Talmud of Rabbi Akiva[35] or Nachum Ish Gamzu[36] dealing with bad "fate" in a positive way. Instead of despairing when something goes wrong, they say, "It is all for the best." "Fate" may appear initially to go against a person, but often we see only the short-term effect and fail to see the broader plan. Yet there are events that simply cannot be explained away. The possibility of being run over by a drunken driver is beyond our capacity to take precautions. One can hardly argue that being killed in a car would be "for the best."

Besides, our appeals to God may conflict with those of others. When we pray to God it is in the hope that what He considers best for us is also what we would like. But as we know, our requests often have dubious motives and ambivalent ends. Hence we are asked to "Do His will as though it were your will so that He may make your wishes His. And subordinate your desires before His in the hope that He may subordinate the requests of others to yours."[37] We see things through a narrow perspective and therefore both our desires and our judgments are limited. To expect God to conform to our standards is to limit God's role to that of a superman.

If one expects and hopes for a reward beyond the satisfaction of doing good and the pleasure derived from life itself, there is no guarantee that it will come about immediately. Reward is on two levels: a practical, this-worldly one that we can experience and recognize, and an intangible and purely spiritual one that we cannot conceive of in "this world" terms. The spiritual person does not seek reward as a condition of living a religious life. Rewards come from the life led itself. If there is to be something more, it is a bonus.

What about the evil people who seem to thrive? It is not a legitimate concern of religious people that others appear to have it better. "One's eyes should not look badly on others."[38] Neither will spiritually oriented people care if others have greater material rewards, because material rewards are not what they value above all else. Reward and punishment is more a priority of the spiritually challenged than it is of those who feel part of a much larger and transcendental world. Yet, for all of this, we often hear religious people tell us that things go wrong because we are not religious enough, or we have a false *mezzuzah*, or because we must have done something to deserve bad things. The myth is that any human, however pious, can know how God works.

Notes

1. Genesis 6:5, 6.
2. Genesis 8:21.
3. Genesis 9:5.
4. Exodus 20:5.
5. Exodus 20:12.
6. Deuteronomy 22:7.
7. Deuteronomy 25:15.
8. Deuteronomy 12:25.
9. Deuteronomy 6:18.
10. Deuteronomy 11:13.
11. Deuteronomy 7:12.
12. Leviticus 26.
13. Deuteronomy 28:1.
14. Deuteronomy 24:16.
15. Ecclesiastes 3:17.
16. Ecclesiastes 12:14.
17. Mishna *Avot* 2:1.
18. Mishna *Avot* 2:19.
19. Talmud Bavli *Menachot* 29b.
20. Mishna *Avot* 3:20.
21. Mishna *Avot* 2:20 and 21.
22. Mishna *Avot* 1:3.
23. Mishna *Avot* 2:8.
24. Mishna *Avot* 4:2.
25. Mishna *Avot* 4:19.
26. Talmud Bavli *Brachot* 7a.
27. Talmud Bavli *Kiddushin* 39b.
28. Mishna *Avot* 2:16.
29. Talmud Bavli *Kiddushin* 39b.
30. Talmud Bavli *Brachot* 5a.
31. Proverbs 3.
32. Talmud Bavli *Brachot* 5b.
33. Talmud Bavli *Pesachim* 64b.

34. Talmud Bavli *Sotah* 2a.
35. Talmud Bavli *Brachot* 60a.
36. Talmud Bavli *Taanit* 21a.
37. Mishna *Avot* 2:4.
38. Mishna *Avot* 5:16.

Chapter 9

Myth: Being Chosen Means Being Better

1

It is a favorite tool of anti-Semites to accuse the Jews of being arrogant and smug because they believe that they are better than everyone else—and, sadly, there are some Jews who actually believe that Judaism does confer upon them some sort of higher status. The Jews are indeed referred to in the Bible as a "special" people and God is described several times as having chosen the Children of Israel. The actual term "Chosen People" is a much later construction, but the idea itself needs to be examined for what it really is.

The Hebrew word for "to choose," *livchor*, with its root *bet chet resh* (*BHR*) usually means "to select" or "to make a choice." Choice usually means differentiating one object or person from others but not necessarily in a preferential way. Even when it expresses the preference of the chooser it need not convey any notion of the superiority of the chosen. The first time the word is used in the Torah it concerns the exercise of choice in a sexual context: "The 'sons of the judges' took wives from wherever they 'chose.'"[1] The sons of the judges (or perhaps the sons of gods) took their women wherever they felt like it and the implication is that they were being corrupt. They chose, they picked, and probably their choice was the wrong one, or at least motivated by corruption; the preference was not a morally superior one. Similarly Joshua is commanded to "choose" men to fight against Amalek.[2] The choice was to find fighting men as opposed, shall we say, to scholars—perhaps superior fighters, but not necessarily better people. The same Hebrew word is used about making the right choice in life by following the Divine commandments: "And you should 'choose' life."[3]

Certainly the word implies preference when it is used in the context of God selecting the city or place that He wants to have as His special sanctuary: "Only to the place that YHVH your God will choose from among your tribes to place His name there, to His presence you should seek and come there."[4] Six times in this chapter alone the word is used of God's selection of a place, and incidentally a tribe, in which it will be located. But it need not necessarily convey superiority rather than specification. Even the choice of the location confers no superior status on the tribe among whom it is set. Superiority can only be the result of superior human action.

2

Nevertheless, there is a clear statement of the special relationship God has with the Children of Israel. It is expressed first, in general, through Abraham, Isaac, and Jacob as a commitment to see their progeny installed in a land of their own, stretching from between the river Euphrates to the Mediterranean[5] (even though in practice this was never realized).

It was part of the Sinai covenant that God specifically made the statement "And if you really listen to My voice and keep My covenant you will be more special to Me than any other one of My nations on earth. And you will be My kingdom of priests and My holy nation."[6] The idea of a "kingdom of priests" is the crucial issue. Since early Judaism the priest played an important role as the repository and teacher of the tradition, and priests had certain benefits in terms of Temple sacrifices and tithes, but nowhere has it been suggested that priests were automatically superior to anyone else. It is not apologetics to emphasize that being given a role as a nation of priests does not confer superiority.

The Sinai covenant, which talks about this special relationship was certainly meant to be a two-way agreement and not intended to be an absolute guarantee of any preferential treatment regardless of good behavior. Indeed, after the episode of the golden calf God expressed the desire to destroy the people altogether and start again with Moses.[7] Thus the notion that "selection" confers automatic and permanent preference regardless of actions finds no basis in the Torah. Indeed, the repetition of curses and threats, particularly at the end of Leviticus, seems to turn the selection into more of a burden and a responsibility than a privilege: "And if you do not listen to Me and do not carry out these commands, and if you reject My statutes and if your souls are sickened by My laws so that you do not perform My commandments, and you break My covenant, I will do this to you. I will visit you with confusion and disease. . . ."[8] Before Moses died he reconfirmed the covenant in the following terms, "To get you to go through with the covenant of YHVH your God and the (concomitant) curse, which YHVH your God is making with you today."[9] That is, the good, the deal, comes with a curse as well. The speech continues: "If there is among you any man or woman or family or tribe whose heart turns away from YHVH our God to go and to serve the gods of those nations, if there is among you a decayed root or a rotten head. And when he hears the words of this curse he will bless himself inwardly, saying, 'Everything will go peacefully with me because I am following my heart,' to add pretense to his guilt. YHVH will not willingly forgive him for His anger and zealousness will burn against such a person and He will invoke all the curses written in this book and God will blot his name from under the heavens."[10] That is, any selection, any special relationship, is contingent on obedience and is reciprocal; it does not convey any automatic benefits. Not only is it not a reward, but the Torah emphasizes the moral failure of Israel: "And you should know that it is not because of your righteousness that YHVH your God gives this good land as an inheritance, for you are a stiff-necked people."[11]

The Torah does, however, emphasize the uniqueness of Israel in the sense that their remarkable system of law sets them apart: "And you should keep and perform (the Torah) for it is this that makes you wise and clever in the eyes of the nations, who, when they hear about all these laws, will say, 'This can only be a wise and clever great nation.' For which (other) great nation has God so close to it like YHVH our God (Who is there when) we call upon Him. And which (other) great nation has laws and statutes that are righteous like those of this Torah that I give you today."[12]

It is obvious that the selection of the Children of Israel was an opportunity and an obligation to set an example and to usher in a better moral order, rather than the granting of an automatic preference. Not only this, but failure to live up to the standards of the Torah would lead to even greater punishment than otherwise might have been the case. It would be more appropriate to talk about an "Obliged Nation "rather than a "Chosen" one.

Ba'alam was a pagan magician invited by the king of Moab to stem the advance of the invading Children of Israel by unconventional means rather than by force. In Ba'alam's speech about the Children of Israel, he pointed to some unusual features about the nation he was supposed to curse. "A nation that dwells alone"[13] does imply a certain difference that sets the people apart, but it does not necessarily imply any superiority. He does indeed praise "the tents of Jacob" and say that this people has God with it, and there is something remarkable about his prescience in describing the Jewish people as one that is set apart—alienated—from other peoples and unlike any other. It is virtually an accurate prediction of the next three thousand years of Jewish history. Still, this cannot mean that they are automatically superior. Certainly history attests to Jewish "otherness," but this seems to have been due as much to other peoples' reaction to Jews than to Jewish adherence to religious principles.

3

The Talmud develops the theme of Israel having a special relationship with God: "Rav Nachman bar Yitzchak said to Rav Chiya bar Abin, 'These tefillin that the Master of the Universe wears, what is written in them?' He replied, 'Who is like Your people Israel, a unique nation on earth?' (1 Chronicles 17). Can the Holy One Blessed Be He really praise Israel? Yes, because it is written: 'You have spoken for God this day,' and 'God has spoken for you this day.' (Deuteronomy 26:17–18). God says to Israel, 'You have made unique in this world. I will make you unique in this world. You have made Me unique as it says, "Hear Israel YHVH is our God YHVH is One," and I have made you unique in this world for it says, "Who is like Your people Israel, one nation on earth?"'"[14]

There is a reciprocal relationship. When Israel behaves according to the Divine wish, then the relationship with God is good; otherwise it is not. This is stated clearly in the Mishna's account of two miracles in the Bible: "'And when Moses raised his hands Israel won.' (Exodus 17:11) Can Moses' hands make war or can Moses' hands break a war? But it teaches you that for as long as Israel look upwards and submit their hearts to their Father in Heaven, then they are able to overcome and if not they would fall. Similarly when it says 'Make a model of a snake and put it on a banner and whoever is bitten sees it and lives.' (Numbers 21:8) Can a (model of a) snake kill or bring back to life? But it teaches you that for as long as Israel look upwards and submit hearts to their Father in Heaven, then they can be cured and if not they will be destroyed."[15] Thus the Mishna explicitly asserts that only correct behavior and a dedicated relationship with God can help. There is no automatic or failsafe formula that automatically protects. What applies to the group might also be said to apply to the individual, though there does appear to be some mystical connection between the people of Israel that transcends the individual Jew.

Given the Greek and Roman beliefs in their very special statuses, it is hardly surprising that the rabbis gave Israel some automatic preferences. If the political powers of the time could glory in their physical prowess and their cultural superiority, all that was left for the Jews to defend themselves with was spiritual superiority. If they were a small humiliated nation, they could find comfort in their "higher" calling. There is, after all, the famous Mishna in Sanhedrin: "All Israel has a part of the World to Come, as it says, 'And your people are all righteous, they will inherit the earth for ever, the growth of My plant, the work of My Hands, to be glorified.'" (Isaiah 60:21)[16]

Here is an explicit statement that every Jew has a place in the Next World, and yet the Mishna itself goes on to give a whole list of exclusions. Polemically, these exclusions deal with the heresies that were current at the time: The Sadducees were opposed to the Oral Law, the Christians claimed that the Old Testament had been superseded, and other sectarians cast aspersions on many of the theological positions that they claimed were later additions to the tradition of Moses. "And these are those who do not have a place in the Next World: One who says that resurrection is not mentioned in the Torah, that the Torah did not come from Heaven, and an Epicurean. Rabbi Akiva said, 'Someone who reads external books (either the apocrypha or heretical interpretations of the Torah—or, some suggest, Greek philosophical works). Someone who mutters over a wound, 'All the diseases I put on the Egyptians I will not place upon you for I am God who heals you.' (Rabbi Akiva suggests this is only if one spits as a magic spell before saying this phrase; others suggest it is treating God in a disrespectful way over trivial matters). Abba Shaul says, 'Also someone who utters God's Name by letters.'"[17] The list of exclusions goes on to name Jeroboam, Ahab, and Menashe as kings who corrupted Israel,;Bala'am, Doeg (the Edomite who betrayed the priests of Nob to Saul), Achitophel (King David's advisor), and Geychazi (Elisha's servant, who tried to take advantage of his position); the generation of the Flood; the generation of the Tower of Babel; the men of Sodom; the spies; the generation of the Wilderness; Korach and his supporters; the Ten Tribes; and "men of cities that have gone over to idolatry."

Of course, for each of these the Gemara contains debate and discussion as to what exactly they did wrong and why their crimes were so remarkable that they were set apart. But the range shows several interesting things: First, that the general exclusion applies to people who are supposed to have abandoned the Torah as the way of God or who behaved in a morally corrupt way. Second, the list includes both Jews and non-Jews, implying that everyone has the capability of getting to Heaven and everyone has the capability of behaving in such a way as to be excluded. Once again, the supposed preferential exclusivity of Israel does not stand up to scrutiny.

A parallel list of excluded people occurs in the Mishna: "Rabbi Elazar HaModai says, 'He who desecrates holy things and scorns the special days of the calendar and embarrasses his friend in public and who tries to undo the covenant with

Abraham (disguise circumcision) and who interprets the Torah in conflict with Halacha has no portion of the World to Come.'"[18] The combination of these two lists of exclusion leaves very few Jews! Therefore automatic preference seems confined to a very small group of good individuals rather than to a whole nation. It is a person's own behavior that counts.

4

The special status of the Jews is not an exclusive one, as emphasized by the attitude of the rabbis to the righteous of other nations: "The pious of the nations of the world have a place in the World to Come,"[19] or "The good of the nations of the world are the priests of God."[20] Surprisingly, given the attitude of most surrounding cultures and in particular the Graeco-Christian tradition of absolutes, the rabbis did not claim an absolute, universal truth for everyone. They did accept that others outside Judaism could both be good human beings and have a connection with God. Their opposition was primarily directed against pagans who had no code of morality.

There is a well known idea given great prominence in the mystical tradition that there are thirty-six good Jewish people for whom or because of whom the world is kept going by God: "Abaye said, 'The world will not be destroyed because there are at least thirty-six good people who enter the Divine presence.'"[21] There is also a version with forty-six good people and a debate as to how many of these are in Israel and how many in exile, and in a further expansion of this idea, "Rabbi Yehuda says, 'There are thirty pious non-Jews on whom the non-Jewish world depends.'"[22] Once again one sees how the rabbis were eager not to be exclusive. They wanted to emphasize the universality of mankind despite cultural differences. They did not want to fall into the trap of claiming that only Jews were "saved," unlike other competing religious systems.

In the Jerusalem Talmud there is a debate between Rabbi Akiva and Ben Azai. "Rabbi Akiva said, "'And you should love your neighbor as yourself"; this is the important principle of the Torah.' Ben Azai said, 'This is the book of the generations of mankind.'"[23] This appears to be an argument about whether loving one's neighbor is too restrictive. Perhaps it applies only to one's neighbor and not to all mankind, although Ben Azai wants a more universal principle that all of mankind is to be loved, not just one's neighbor. Ironically it is Rabbi Akiva who says in the Mishna, "Man is specially dear because he was created in the image. He was made aware of this special love because he was made in the image as it says, 'Because in the image of God He made man.'"[24] Here Rabbi Akiva emphasizes the universal principle that all of humanity is close to God, in the same way that Ben Azai does in the previous quotation. They agree on the basic universality. Rabbi Akiva in this context then goes on to talk about the special relationship with Israel and the importance of Torah. It is only by following the spiritual tracks to a relationship with God that one can sustain the special relationship, either as a human or as a Jew.

In other words, piety is not restricted to Jews. More importantly, a person's actions are what define a person as good or not good and as being close to or far from God. The accident of birth imposes obligations but not automatic superiority.

5

One is bound to wonder why it is that there are Jews—and not particularly religious ones at that—who make a great deal of this "Chosen People" business. On one level the Jewish people has indeed been remarkable. The very fact of its survival after two thousand years of horrific persecution is amazing enough. The reestablishment of a Jewish state after two thousand years of exile is also unprecedented in human history. The very high percentage of Jewish Nobel Prize winners and the very high representation of Jews in medicine, law, commerce, and entertainment throughout the Western world also point to something unusual.

What makes the Jews so special? Several peoples who have been exiled from their homelands have done well: East African Asians exiled by Idi Amin from Uganda soon rose in Britain to business and professional success beyond their numbers. Some minorities in America have recently leapfrogged others in achieving prosperity and a reputation for academic excellence. The dynamism that migration fosters often helps motivate people, particularly if a culture has a tradition of literacy. Jews, like the Chinese, have established commercial traditions that often depend on family connections spread out across different countries and continents.

My first position as a rabbi was in Glasgow, Scotland. At the turn of the twentieth century large numbers of Jews had arrived there, mainly from Lithuania. They soon established themselves in the city, and in the local schools Jewish children dominated academically. By the end of the century the Jews had become a comfortable, established community. They had moved into the more comfortable suburbs of the city and their children were, according to the heads of the schools in the city, just average in the schooling system— while the newer Asian immigrants were winning most of the prizes. This tends to support the idea that the need to establish oneself, the insecurity of being an outsider, is a powerful factor in encouraging initiative. One sees similar trends in the United States, with waves of upwardly mobile immigrants bringing a strong sense of identity, culture, and cohesion. Within Jewish communities around the world today, the newcomers are often the ones who are trying harder and working longer hours, desperate to succeed and establish themselves. A combination of factors helps keep Jews on their mettle, not least the insecurity, obvious or sublimated, that anti-Semitism generates even in America.

Yet Jews continue to assimilate in vast numbers. As they assimilate their specific or peculiar culture is lost and so also their recognizable differences. The epithet "Chosen People" then comes to be applied only to those who choose to stay. Who will survive? Certainly it was the Jewish religious traditions that kept the Jews identified and different throughout the exile. Within most Jewish communities it is religious commitment that seems to differentiate those who belong from those who do not. Of course there are those whose commitment is more cultural than religious, but numerically they are not significant.

Israel brings another dimension to the modern Jewish world. There, too, the *Kulturkampf* for survival pits the religious against the secular. There are many strongly committed Jews who are not religious, but this is not the same as a positive movement. It would be wonderful if secular Judaism could find a dynamic expression that would retain the vast numbers of disaffected Jews. Alas, there is no evidence of a serious alternative emerging in either Israel or the Diaspora. Expatriate secular Jews tend in the first generation to mix almost exclusively with other Israeli expatriates. If their children choose to marry into a Jewish Diaspora they tend to become absorbed into the local Jewish communities, but as often as not they marry out and have contact only with their Israeli family when they return to visit. Nationalism without some active religious or cultural component is not an effective guarantee of continuity.

It is the combination of Jewish traditions and external factors that makes the Jewish community so productive. If it abandons its traditions there is every reason to think that it would sink into mediocre anonymity: "When Israel performs the will of God no people or nation has any power over them."[25] Clearly, we have been failing.

There remains the charge of racism. If Judaism is a Chosen Religion then this sets it apart from all others, but the fact is that every religion is a sort of club that has its own criteria for entry—just as every country has its nationalization rules that must be followed if someone wants to become a citizen. The charge of racism is valid only if a group excludes another group on the basis of race, which is something a person can never change—but Judaism allows anyone from any race to convert (the conversion process is a form of application for citizenship). It is true that anyone born of a Jewish mother is automatically a Jew, but there is absolutely no racial condition or limitation whatsoever attached to conversion, only that the convert should be genuine.

The title "Chosen," when applied to the Jewish people, clearly means burdened with an obligation and a responsibility. It is true that we believe that being Jewish brings with it spiritual benefits as well, and perhaps we would rather talk about being a "blessed" people were it not for the fact that historically, given the fate of the Jews, this sounds rather strange. Yet throughout our history we have indeed considered ourselves privileged to have been party to a covenant with God that enables us, in theory, to have a special relationship with Him. But it certainly does not make a Jew a better person automatically and anyone who thinks that it does would be guilty both of misunderstanding the concept and of thinking in a way that goes against the whole spirit of Jewish teaching on humanity and God.

The myth persists that Jews, as the Chosen People, are in some way superior, and both Jews and non-Jews subscribe to this myth. In truth, Judaism offers opportunities; all the rest depends on individual effort.

Notes

1. Genesis 6:2.
2. Exodus 17:9.
3. Deuteronomy 13:19.
4. Deuteronomy 12.
5. Genesis 15:18.
6. Exodus 19:6.
7. Exodus 32:10.
8. Leviticus 26:14–16.
9. Deuteronomy 29:11.
10. Deuteronomy 29:17–19.
11. Deuteronomy 9:6.
12. Deuteronomy 4:6–8.
13. Numbers 23:9.
14. Talmud Bavli *Brachot* 6a.
15. Mishna *Rosh Hashana* 3:8.
16. Mishna *Sanhedrin* 10:1.
17. Mishna *Sanhedrin* 10:1, et seq.
18. Mishna *Avot* 3:15.
19. Tosefta *Sanhedrin* 13.
20. Tana DeBei Eliyahu Zutta 20.
21. Talmud Bavli *Sanhedrin* 97b.
22. Talmud Bavli *Chulin* 92a.
23. Talmud Yerushalmi *Nedarim* 9:4.
24. Mishna *Avot* 3:18.
25. Talmud Bavli *Ketubot* 66b.

Chapter 10

Myth: Prayer Is Meant to Be a Routine

1

Praying is boring! Prayer has become a problematic element in religious life today. The language of prayer itself seems artificial no matter what the language. Many people find it difficult to accept that prayers by so many apparently good and spiritual people have gone unanswered. One needs only to think of the Holocaust to wonder whether prayer can affect God's plans and why, despite prayer, such awful things happen. Lots of Jews find the synagogue rituals of prayer, no matter in which denomination, stultifying and uninspiring. Yet prayer is an integral part of the Jewish tradition.

In English, the word "pray" means "beg": "I pray you, give me something to eat" may be a little old-fashioned as a way of expression, but it conveys the meaning clearly. That praying equals begging or asking is in itself enough to put some people off. Of course, if we pray in English then naturally the restrictions of the English language will affect the way we think about the words we use, but in Hebrew the words used for prayer are so many and so varied that the impression ought to be quite different if we use the Hebrew language. Let us examine these words and see what conclusions we can make.

In the Torah, prayer is expressed with many words and in different ways. Abraham and Moses both use the word *tefilla* for prayer, and later on it will become the predominant word used to describe the way humans try to relate to or intercede with God. When Abraham tells Avimelech that Sarah is his sister, not his wife, in order to survive in an alien environment, Avimelech is visited by God in a dream and warned not to interfere with Sarah. God tells Avimelech that if he leaves Sarah alone, "He (Abraham) will pray for you and you will live."[1] The episode continues, "So Abraham prayed to God and God cured Avimelech."[2] The word used here is *tefilla*. It is an interesting aside that when Pharaoh is plagued earlier in Genesis for taking Sarah there is no mention of Abraham praying for him, whereas Avimelech, who according to the text is both moral and God-fearing, merits prayer. Anyway, here praying is clearly the equivalent of asking God for something. Similarly when Moses intercedes with God the same word, *tefilla*, is used: "And Moses prayed to God."[3]

Isaac uses a different word when appealing to God on behalf of Rivka. He uses the word *le'ater*, which is usually translated "to entreaty," and God responds with the same word: "And Isaac entreated with God about his wife . . . and God treated with him."[4] Moses also uses this word in appealing to God to remove one of the plagues: "And he appealed to God,"[5] after being asked to do so, using the same word, by Pharaoh. The fact that Pharaoh did not ask Moses to pray and that the word for prayer, *lehitpalel*, is not used says something about the word *tefilla* as a conduit between man and God: It requires a two-way interaction. If a person's mind is blocked, nothing gets through.

The first instance of a word that might possibly mean something more akin to meditation, for thinking about God or expressing inner thoughts rather than asking for something, is the word used of Isaac just before he meets Rebecca for the first time: "And Isaac went out to meditate in the field."[6] There the word use is *lasuach*, which is commonly understood to derive from the root that means "to speak"—but, as one would expect, there are other possibilities. This is the one chosen by the rabbis,[7] although Ibn Ezra goes for the more obvious root meaning, "plants"—thus Isaac went out, according to him, to look at his fields and see how the crops were growing.

It is also suggested that the phrase used of Judah when he "draws near" to Joseph to appeal for his brothers is related to prayer, though the word itself, *vayigash*, has no specific connotations of prayer in an etymological way. One might add the word *litsok*, "to cry out" as used regarding the Hebrew slaves, but I take this to be more an expression of pain than an appeal to God. On the other hand, Moses uses this word when he appeals to God on behalf of his sister Miriam: "And Moses cried out to God, saying, 'God please heal her, please.'"[8]

When Moses appeals to God after the golden calf episode, begging God not to destroy the people, he uses the word *vayechal*. Although translated as "And he appealed" (to the face of God)[9] it is the same word as "to begin," as for example in the sentence "Then they started calling in the name of God."[10] Similarly the word *lechanen*, "to try to find favor with God," is used by Moses: "And I tried to find favor with God at that time."[11] When Moses asks for something from God he also uses the word "please" as a form of request: "And Moses returned to God and said, 'Please,'"[12] or "And he said, 'if I can please You,'"[13] and as he does when Miriam is stricken with leprosy in the example mentioned above.

In addition to these unusual words, Moses most commonly communicates with God using the word *likro* "to call": "And he called on the name of God. As God passed by, he called."[14] Moses also regularly uses the word *lomar*, "to speak." What emerges from looking at the Torah are two levels of approach to God: asking for something, and, allied to it, begging for something urgently; or, by way of contrast, "expressing oneself to God" or communicating with God, as Daniel puts it later in the Bible: "He (Daniel) took it upon himself, thrice daily, to turn to Jerusalem and to say his blessings and to pray and to thank God."[15]

By the time of Daniel, living in exile in Babylon in the fifth century before the Common Era, a pattern of different elements emerges in the area of what we call "prayer." There are the ritual blessings, the *brachot*, blessings that are referred to in the Torah such as "And you shall eat and be satisfied and thank the Lord your God,"[16] as well as those made over the First Fruits and the tithes.[17] There is the biblical process of praising and thanking God, such as Samuel's mother rejoicing in his birth and the Book of Psalms. This very powerful tradition was essential to Jewish spiritual life, but in the pre-Ezra world there is nothing specified or legislated as "official" prayer and the Levites singing over the sacrifices in the Temple is the only record of a formal function for singing the praises of the Lord. There is the reading of the *Shema*, referred to as an obligation in the Torah, as a statement of commitment, but this is not what we mean by prayer. Finally, there is the obligation to read from the Torah, but before Ezra this too was not a feature of regular community activity, and nothing has yet officially been instituted as an act of communal worship called "prayer."

2

The Midrash extends the list of words used to describe prayer to ten: "Rabbi Yochanan said, 'There are ten words that are used (to mean) prayer: to open oneself up, to cry, to groan, to exalt, to engage, to importune, to call, to fall down before, to express oneself, to appeal."[18] In effect, however, the word *tefilla* came to be used overwhelmingly throughout the later books of the Bible and beyond. The process was obviously a complex one with many different facets and aspects.

The word *lehitpalel*, "to pray," is a reflexive verb based on the root *PLL*, or *PALAL*. If the word *lefalel* means "to express," as in "Pinheas stood on his feet and spoke" [19] Then *lehitpalel* means to "express oneself." That is, on one level it means to express one's inner feelings, but it is used in various other, different ways in the Torah. In addition to its use as a way of appealing to God it is also used as an expression of hope, of a deep desire that lies beneath surface in the way that Jacob did not dare hope that he would see his son Joseph again: "I did not imagine (express the hope) that I would see your face again." [20] The word used there is *filallti*, a word also used for "judges," (*felillim*).[21] Thus the reflexive version, *lehitfalel*, would mean "to judge oneself," which is another dimension of prayer: self-examination. Prayer is an opportunity to look in on oneself.

According to many authorities, there is an obligation, implicit in the Torah, to pray to God in a very personal and unstructured way. It is more than just the thanking of God for the good things that happen. As Maimonides puts it, "It is a positive commandment to pray every day, as it says, 'And you will serve the Lord your God.' By tradition they learnt that this service is prayer. Because it says, 'And you will serve Him with all your hearts. The Wise men said, "What is the service that is done with the heart? This is prayer."'" He goes on to say, "If a person was used to appeal and to ask or if he (or she; the obligation applies equally to women) found it difficult to express himself he should speak according to his ability and at whatever time he is able to. And so the number of prayers was according to each person's ability. Some would pray only once a day and others would pray lots of times. They would pray toward the Temple in any place that he was. And this was the way it was from the times of Moses our teacher until Ezra."[22] In effect prayer was and remains a Torah imperative, a personal obligation to relate to God, not necessarily to ask for anything but as the word itself implies to stand before God, to judge oneself and to express one's inner feelings and thoughts.

The Babylonian exile introduced a new dimension. There the synagogue—or to be more precise the Study Center—functioned as the community focal point, replacing the Temple. As there was no sacrificial system in Exile, studying it became a substitute for performing it. In addition, according to Maimonides, the influence of the alien languages led to the loss of Hebrew as a natural means of expression and indeed the deterioration of linguistic expression in general. Some form of community prayer began as an addition to study, and authority for this innovation was found by asserting that Abraham, Isaac, and Jacob had each begun the custom of praying formally to God at different times of the day: "Abraham instituted the morning prayer, as it says, 'And Abraham got up early in the morning to go to the place where he stood,' and 'standing' can only mean prayer, as it says, 'And Phineas stood up and prayed.' Isaac instituted the afternoon prayer because it says, 'Isaac went out to speak in the field toward evening,' and talking can only mean prayer, as it says, 'A prayer of a poor man as he faints and before God he pours out his speech.' And Jacob instituted the evening prayer, as it says, 'And he approached the place,' and 'approach' can only mean prayer, as it says, 'And now do not pray for this people and do not raise (your voice) for them in song and prayer and do not approach me.'"[23]

There is no reference in the Bible to official prayers at these three times of the day and so one must suppose that the tradition was meant to refer to informal and personal prayer at this stage. It was on the return from Babylon that Ezra adopted the new ideas of community service and study and prayer and retained them even though the Temple service was restored. The synagogue in Judea became a center both for education and for prayer. By tradition, the prophets had instituted the system of the *Mishmar* and the *Maamad*.[24] The land of Israel was divided into zones, whose local communities sent their priests and Levites to Jerusalem for a two-week period to stand by and participate in the Temple service. At the same time, the local community gathered in the synagogue to study what was going on in Jerusalem and to pray. This was, of course, a brilliant method of educating the masses and involving them in the religious system, but there is no necessary connection made between the *Maamad* and prayer.

In addition to introducing the regular weekly reading of the Torah in synagogues in the fourth century before the Common Era, Ezra is credited (by Maimonides at least) with having instituted the three-times-a-day prayer system that ran parallel with the Temple service.[25] Maimonides suggests that the Babylonian exile led to Jews forgetting both the language of personal prayer and indeed the art of self-expression. Ezra's innovation seems to have been the basis of the clashes between the Sadducees and the Pharisees. The Sadducees objected to these Pharisaic innovations and argued that they would detract from the mystique and authority of the Temple. The rabbis argued that these were necessary devices to ensure that education reached everyone and was not just the preserve of the priesthood. Regardless, these prayer services still seem to have been informal and optional and were designed to assist with the performance of the individual obligation to pray. Community service still revolved around the Temple. Thus for the first two Temples of Jewish history, prayer was a personal expression, in any language at any time, with guidance but no compulsory structure or formulation. The lack of structure is reflected both in the later establishment of the text of the eighteen benedictions known as the *Amidah* or indeed as *Tefilla*, "prayer," in later legal terminology, and in the debate as to how many services were obligatory during the course of each day.

3

When the Second Temple was destroyed, there was an existing alternative: the synagogue, which functioned as an educational center and had a prayer system that with minor modification could replace the sacrificial system as the community act of worship. It was then that prayer acquired a dual function. It was still a medium of individual self-expression, but now became also the medium of communal cohesion. It was officially decreed that prayer would substitute for the two "eternal" community sacrifices of Dawn and Afternoon.[26] There was still some debate about the evening prayer,[27] but Rabbi Gamliel squashed any opposition over this issue and declared the evening prayer "an obligation."[28] In addition there was the twice-a-day reading (notice the word "reading," for it applied to the text of the Torah) of the *Shema*, to which the rabbis added the paragraphs and their before and after blessings. Extracts from the Book of Psalms were added before the *Shema* in the morning service to praise God, following Daniel's formulation that one should praise God before asking for anything.

The text of the eighteen blessings that we call the *Amidah*, the prayer said standing, began to be formalized in the years immediately following the destruction of the Temple, by the rabbis at Yavneh. It was based on earlier compilations and came to be known as, simply, "The Prayer." It is a magnificent piece of literature, its poetry creating a simple series of rhythms and alliterations that makes it easy to learn by heart and at the same time creates a sense of excitement and climax. This is lost when the prayers are translated into another language. For example the opening blessing goes "Our God and God of our Fathers, the God of Abraham, the God of Isaac, the God of Jacob." In English the word "God," has a hard sound, and the frequent repetition sounds staccato and uncomfortable, but the Hebrew is *Eloheynu, vElohey avoteynu, Elohey Avraham, Elohey*

Yitschak, vElohey Yaacov. The sound of the *El* is soft, and there is a flow of lullaby-like sweetness and soft *vav* sounds rather than hard consonants. This poetic rhythm and song runs right through the *Amidah*, which is why it is so easy to memorize (and also to gabble through).

At a time when there were no printing presses, written texts were at a premium. Very few had access to the printed word, so the oral skills were essential. We see in the Talmud how memory tricks, phrases that contain a sequence of letters reminding one of the topics, are found throughout the text. So prayer was formulated to be easy to remember and to contain virtually the complete gamut of personal and national issues that one might want to raise or "discuss" with God. The *Amidah* was designed as a menu of ideas and concerns that would enable a person to be selective and focus on what was particularly appropriate at any one moment. That one could insert one's own requests at appropriate stages also reinforced the possibility that the individual was meant to interact with the text. The design was for personal prayer to be integrated into the community service for those unable or incapable of making up their own or improvising. Not everyone had or has that capacity. It was understood that however hard a person tried it would be all but impossible to concentrate on every word of the *Amidah*.

There is an old story, which I heard from my father, of a wonder-rabbi coming into a town and the locals asking the rabbi of the town whether he had some test to see if the visitor was genuine. He replied, "Ask him if he has a secret method of concentrating on the *Amidah* from start to finish. If he says he has, then you'll know he is a fake."

4

Given the communal nature of the new prayer structure it became increasingly difficult to combine personal prayer with communal prayer. The rabbis were very definite in wanting prayer to be a positive spiritual experience: "One should not get up to pray in a state of sadness nor laziness nor laughter nor idle talk nor lightheartedness nor empty words but in a state of (the) joyful (desire to carry out a) Divine command."[29] This is perfectly illustrated by Rabbi Akiva's "problem." When he went up to pray (as the representative of the community) he finished first so as not to trouble them by taking a long time. But when he prayed for himself he started first in one corner of the synagogue and after everyone had left could be found still lost in prayer in the opposite corner.[30] The rabbis developed a new term, *iyun tefilla*, "looking deeply into prayer," to contrast it with conventional or routine performance.

They understood that genuine prayer is a difficult and fraught process: "Four things require (Divine) support: Torah, good deeds, prayer, and earning a living."[31] Nevertheless they still required prayer to be a personal, reflective, and focused process, as Rabbi Eliezer said, "If a person makes his prayer routine, his prayer will not be accepted."[32] On the other hand prayer was and is the ultimate way of getting closer to God: "If only a person would pray all day long."[33]

The rabbis were also eager to emphasize that individuals could add their own petitions into the established structure of the *Amidah*. It is now incorporated into the *Shulchan Aruch*, the Code of Jewish Law, that one may add one's own personal requests into any of middle blessings of the *Amidah*.[34] They did not specify the language or the phraseology, merely suggesting that it not go on for too long.

The two types of prayer, personal and communal, should have stayed separate and complementary but increasingly became fused. The skills and methodology of personal prayer became subsumed under and integrated into communal prayer. The result is that while individual rabbis composed beautiful poems and prayers they did not alter the character of praying. Until the mystics began making their innovations, particularly the school of Isaac Luria, the Arizal, in sixteenth-century Safed, the art of private prayer was all but lost. Only hints remain, such as the Mishna in *Brachot*: "One should only stand to prayer when one is in a serious mood. The early pious men used to wait one hour before praying in order to focus their minds on their Father in Heaven."[35] The prayer experience for these pious men was so profound that it required hours of preparation beforehand, and raised them to such a level that they needed time to "wind down" afterwards. What did they do? What were their methods? We can only guess, but clearly there was more to prayer than just reciting some set phrases.

5

Time and circumstances have brought us to the present state in which prayer has lost its luster and the individual no longer dares to be innovative or personal. Despite the dramatic attempts of the kabbalists of Safed in the seventeenth century and the early Chassidim, little can be found nowadays of creative, spiritual prayer that has roots in the Jewish traditions of meditation and *dveykut* (adherence), the art of getting closer to God (with the possible exception of some Chassidim, particularly in Jerusalem).

This does not mean that we cannot experiment. The Torah obligation to pray to God remains in force. Although the rabbis encouraged individuals to add their own prayers within the existing structures, they did not in any way forbid people from developing their own prayers and their own devotional or meditational exercises. We can still do this. It can be done within the service structure by focusing on specific lines and words in the way, one supposes, that Rabbi

Akiva did. It can be done by arranging periods of preparation before or after prayer the way the early Chassidim did. And it can be done by creating one's own private prayers and services at times that suit or at times that are meaningful to the individual. We have in general lost this skill but there is no reason or restriction why we should not try to regain what was lost and restore personal *tefilla* to its original purposes of talking privately to God; revealing one's inner secrets, fears, and aspirations; and at the same time examining ourselves and judging, not to convict or find guilty but to encourage and move on.

There is another feature of prayer that we have lost. This is self-analysis and the opening up of one's inner thoughts by using prayer as a way of having a conversation with God. Nowadays we have become used to opening up only to psychiatrists or counselors, but in earlier times, speaking to God fulfilled this function. Expressing one's innermost thoughts, fears, agonies, and even hatreds is one of the most important healing qualities of prayer because it helps a person recognize what is really going on inside his or her mind. The process of opening up to God, in addition to being therapeutic, helps a person come to his or her own conclusions about certain types of problems and issues. In this way, talking to God can evoke a response: One can realize very clearly the right course of action is once one has recognized honestly and openly what the problem is.

The biblical law of confession was required before a sacrifice could become effective as a means of atonement. But this confession was made not to another human but directly to God. One had to actually give expression to what one had done wrong, in this way recognizing the problem rather than sublimating it. Opening up completely to another person was looked at as both making oneself vulnerable and an act of self-humiliation, but talking openly to God was seen as a way of healing and recovery.

6

There still remains the rabbinic instruction to pray as part of a *minyan*, the ten needed to make up a community, and to identify with a community to balance the solipsism of individuality. The double need to be part of a community and at the same time not to neglect one's personal spirituality is the essence of the Torah experience. However, we have allowed the synagogue to become the focal point of both community activity and prayer and this, to my mind, is a mistake. We are now conditioned to think of prayer and synagogue as being almost synonymous. Yet for many, synagogue is a stultifying and unspiritual experience. It has become a social arena in which the participants are there not to pray but to talk, to see and be seen. To make matters worse, the service often goes on for too long and becomes something of an ordeal rather than a spiritually concentrated and uplifting experience.

"There were no happier days than the sixteenth day of Av and Yom Kippur because on those days the daughters of Jerusalem used to go out in white garments . . . with music into the vineyards and they would say, 'Young man open your eyes and see what you should choose.'"[36] It was part of an ancient tradition that on these two days young men and women were encouraged to go out to choose marriage partners. Isn't it strange that this should happen on Yom Kippur? That indeed a good measure of the day would be spent not in the Temple or the synagogue but outside in the vineyards? It tells us something about how attitudes have changed. Similarly, the reason that on Festivals we call up only five people to read from the Torah and not seven is in order to have more time to be at home eating and drinking and rejoicing. The Talmud itself says, in the context of the number of people called to the Torah, that on Festivals "We come (to the Temple or the synagogue) later and we leave earlier."[37] Rabbi Moshe Isserles, in his notes on the *Shulchan Aruch*, says that services on Festivals should be shorter than on *Shabbat* in order to increase the joy of the day![38] The reality nowadays is that most Festival services take longer than those of a normal *Shabbat*.

Fashions in music change as well. Cantorial singing pleases some but is not everyone's favorite. Tastes in Jewish music vary too, by background and age as much as anything else. Can it be said that any one musical tradition is "right?" It is a shame if the desire to keep traditions recorded or to preserve historical experiences gets in the way of attempts to find satisfying ways of praying as a community and as individuals.

Although the format for communal prayer has been established, the room for variety and individuality is still great and must be emphasized rather than hidden as though it was in some way subversive. This is true of the major traditions, Ashkenazi and Sephardi, which, while sharing the same basic structures, have lots of different traditions and forms. It is equally true of the Chassidic traditions, each one having its own particular style and customs, and the non-Chassidic strains. Just as no two people will agree on a range of political issues, the same goes for prayer and services. We must avoid the impression that there is only one format. Only by releasing creativity can prayer be more meaningful and exciting.

It is a measure of the variety of Jewish life that there are so many different types and alternatives. In big cities there are choices; otherwise one has to be creative. Sadly, it is only in very large concentrations of Jews that one can encounter these alternatives. But just as it is important not to neglect individual prayer, so too it is important to make community prayer an important and uplifting experience. Unfortunately there is not enough spiritual creativity going on in our communities at this moment.

It is a myth to believe that there is only one style of

prayer, it is a myth to think that there is only one form of reacting to a service, and it is certainly a myth to think that prayer in Judaism is a dry ritual, devoid of spiritual excitement. Where you find this excitement is dependent on who you are, what you feel, and where you live.

Notes

1. Genesis 20:7.
2. Genesis 20:17.
3. Numbers 11:2.
4. Genesis 25:21.
5. Exodus 8:26.
6. Genesis 24:63.
7. Talmud Bavli *Brachot* 26b.
8. Numbers 12:13.
9. Exodus 32:11.
10. Genesis 4:26.
11. Deuteronomy 3:23.
12. Exodus 32:31.
13. Exodus 34:9.
14. Exodus 34:5–6.
15. Daniel 6:11.
16. Deuteronomy 11:15.
17. Deuteronomy 26.
18. Midrash Rabba Deuteronomy 2:1.
19. Psalms 106:30.
20. Genesis 48:11.
21. Exodus 21:22.
22. Maimonides' *Yad HaChazaka Hilchot Tefilla* 1 and 3.
23. Talmud Bavli *Brachot* 26b.
24. See, for example, Mishna *Taanit* 2:6–7.
25. Maimonides' *Yad HaChazaka Hilchot Tefilla* 2.
26. Talmud Bavli *Brachot* 26b.
27. Talmud Bavli *Brachot* 27b.

28. Talmud Bavli *Brachot* 27b.
29. Talmud Bavli *Brachot* 31a.
30. Talmud Bavli *Brachot* 36a.
31. Talmud Bavli *Brachot* 32b.
32. Talmud Bavli *Brachot* 31a.
33. Talmud Yerushalmi *Shabbat* 1:2.
34. *Shulchan Aruch Orach Chayim* 119.
35. Mishna *Brachot* 5.
36. Mishna *Taanit* 4:8.
37. Talmud Bavli *Megillah* 23a (Rashi: "To rejoice on Yom Tov").
38. *Shulchan Aruch Orach Chayim* 529:1.

Chapter 11

Myth:
Women Are Treated
the Same Way As Men

1

Women, in general, have suffered discrimination and poor treatment in virtually every society around the world for as long as history has been recorded. Of course not every woman feels herself to be hard done by, but a lot do. All sorts of theories have been suggested as to why this has been the case, from child-rearing to division of labor to inherent dominant genes. The question that needs to be answered as far as Judaism is concerned is not whether some Jewish men may have treated some women badly (you bet they have) but to discover how the Jewish tradition has, over the years, dealt with the role of women.

The Bible is usually blamed for giving Divine authority to an inferior role for women. God Himself is a "He." Adam, the male, was created first and Eve came second. Adam was ordained the master and Eve was told to be subservient to him.

But a closer examination of the situation shows it is not

quite so simple. In the first chapter of Genesis there are two interesting features that go some way toward balancing the cliche. The first reference to God acting in the universe is in the second verse. After God has decided to create, the world is described as being "chaos," *tohu vavohu*, and the "Spirit of God was hovering over the deep." The verb for "hovering," *merachephet*, is a female-ending verb—so the "Spirit of God" is in the female form. Just as later in Jewish literature the word used for God's presence, the *Shechina* (literally, "the Dwelling Place of God"), is a feminine verb, so here reference to God is in the feminine. There is nothing "humiliating" or secondary in having God described in the feminine form.

It is true that the most common verbs applied to God are masculine, but in many languages the masculine form includes the feminine. The plural "they," in English, does not differentiate between male and female. In French or Hebrew there are different words for "they" male and "they" female, but only the male "they" can be used for both. By itself this may be seen as an example of male domination. However, the fact that the Torah has no problem using the feminine to describe God is to my mind significant: There is no stigma attached.

We are familiar with the story of woman being made out of the rib of man in the second chapter of Genesis, but we too often ignore the first chapter. There it states unequivocally, in verse 27, that "God made man in His image, in the image of God He created him, male and female He created them." This same formulation is repeated after the episode in the Garden of Eden, too.[1] The name "man" is used for humanity in general, but both male and female were created by God at the same time.

The retelling of the acts of creation in the second chapter functions as a supplementary narrative, which is common throughout the Torah. In both narrative and legal instructions a principle is established, followed by details;

or a story is told first through the actual events and then through someone describing what happened.[2] The same process is at work here. The principle in the first chapter of the Bible is that the elements, the ingredients of creation, receive Divine sanction. The second chapter describes the mechanics and how the created world works. For instance, it explains that agriculture requires either the natural cycle that brings rain, or man to work the ground and irrigate. The first chapter describes the creation of male and female, in which they are simultaneous and equal. In the second chapter, the Bible describes their interaction and the relationship between them, which may not always be ideal.

Man cannot find spiritual or emotional companionship from the animal kingdom. Humans need more than physical gratification. It is only with someone drawn from opposite the heart that the human race, which depends on the family, can develop and function effectively. The ribcage symbolizes the seat of the heart and the heart symbolizes emotions. The law of the tefillin, or phylacteries, requires one part of the tefillin to be placed on the head to symbolize the submission of the intellect to Torah (which is encapsulated in the texts inside the "house"), and the other on the upper arm against the ribcage to symbolize the submission of the emotions. Eve's coming from the rib symbolizes emotional love. This is the basis of their relationship, the marriage of contrasts.

The episode of the snake in the Garden of Eden illustrates how disobedience to God causes distortions and corruption. Before humans disobeyed God, nakedness was not considered a problem. Disobedience shows that anything can be misused and turned into a means of domination or distortion. This is not intrinsic. There is nothing wrong in being naked; it is, unfortunately, dependent on how humans use or misuse nakedness that it can be something "bad" as opposed to natural.

After the fruit is eaten and God issues His punishment comes the fateful line to Eve, "You shall desire your husband and he will rule over you."[3] To our ears this sounds very much as though God is condemning Eve to a subservient role, but ironically exactly the same formulation of words is used later referring to Cain after he has been rejected by God: "Sin will lie crouching at your door; you will desire it and it will rule over you."[4] In other words, dependence is not a necessary or natural state of affairs. Dependency is something that we may bring upon ourselves.

Sadly, just as mankind continued to disobey God, so too mankind continued to disregard the integrity of the "other." Whether it is male or female, weak or strong, people rather than God seem to need to find ways to dominate and subjugate. This why the ideal state posited as the messianic period is one without "oppression," where according to Maimon-ides each person will be able to fill his or her potential to the fullest without being oppressed or subjugated by those in power.[5] The ideal relationship is one based on love and respect where the two partners complement each other. In such a relationship there is no room for superiority or dominance. The Bible in this early narrative is describing, not prescribing.

Males, however, did come to dominate, though of course one cannot lay the blame on Judaism by itself for this. Japanese culture, for example, can hardly be said to have come from the rabbis! The question is whether the Bible regarded it as a necessary or an accidental phenomenon, the result of abuse of the system rather than its fulfillment or the natural order of things. The example of the Fathers shows the different aspects of this issue. Abraham and Sarah are described as both having accumulated "souls" in Haran together,[6] which the rabbis take to illustrate their partnership in spreading the monotheistic tradition. Over the issue of Hagar, Abraham is commanded by God to listen to Sarah and to accept her way of understanding the situation.[7] It is the woman who makes the crucial decision about inheritance and who will continue the spiritual tradition, in the cases of both Sara and Rebecca. Rebecca has no qualms about defying her husband over the inheritance[8] (although one cannot deny that it is the male who passes on the blessing and the property). The question of naming children also shows the role of the wife[9] although in Benjamin's case the husband overrules his wife's choice.[10]

The mention of such personalities in the Torah as Naama,[11] Timna the concubine,[12] and Sarach Bat Asher[13] without amplification of their achievements or explanation as to why they are there indicates that these were well-known and established female figures about whom a great deal of oral tradition must have revolved. Despite the fact that Miriam is punished for her "rebellion" against Moses, she is still referred to as a prophetess[14] and leads the community in response to the miracle of the Red Sea (the assumption that she led only women is not necessarily supported either by the text or by traditional commentators). It may be argued that this is dredging for crumbs and that she and the later prophetesses Deborah[15] and Hulda[16] are exceptions. However, the fact that these exceptions did exist and gained fame shows a different perspective to the totally male agenda. The fact that Tamar could even plead her case to Judah [17] at all, against a background of total male domination, does indicate a degree of understanding and sympathy with those individuals who were able to break the mold.

What emerges from the biblical tradition is that in all areas of appointment, males maintained a monopoly—the kingship was a male preserve (except when Jezebel's daughter Athalia took over the throne of Judea by force) and so was the priesthood—but in areas not subject to appointment and dependent entirely on personal qualities, such as prophecy, one does find, albeit in limited numbers, female leadership emerging.

2

What was the real position of a woman in early Judaism? It is no accident that the Code of Hammurabi and other legal documents of the pre-Sinaitic era in the Middle East did indeed differentiate in judicial terms between freemen and slaves and between men and women: The punishment for civil offenses against one was different from the punishment meted out to the other. In Torah law, however, there was never any such distinction. Civil crimes were prosecuted equally and in cases where compensation is paid it was usually greater when paid to women, as in the case of the obligation to feed and clothe a woman.[18] The whole concept of compensation for "shame," which the rabbis develop according to the principle that it all depends on the status of the victim, allowed for all sorts of applications that could (though might not necessarily) be applied to benefit women. The attitude of the Torah to rape is surprisingly sensitive. Given the context that intercourse was the method of marriage and that virgin brides had a higher "value" on the marriage market, rape was regarded as a serious violation, and compared to murder.[19]

On the other hand, in matters of property control was vested overwhelmingly in the male. Tribal allocation went according to the males. The seventy elders were all males. The priesthood was male. Still, it is interesting that the Torah allowed the daughters of Zelophchad to inherit their father's property when there were no males.[20] Similarly, the Book of Job has him dividing his property among his daughters as well as his sons. This, after all, was not legal in Europe until the nineteenth century (with the exception of royalty due to political considerations and even then only under exceptional circumstances and as a sort of national guardianship). Rabbeynu Yaacov Ben Asher gives a fascinating answer in the seventeenth century to a question about inheritance when he says that one should not follow the prevailing non-Jewish custom of passing on one's property only to the male; one has an obligation to make provision for all of one's children.[21]

The greatest problems that Jewish law left unmodified were the question of a woman's ability to give evidence in court and marriage and divorce laws. No doubt the reason for not subjecting a woman to public cross-examination was to protect women from public scrutiny and to protect their privacy. It was not because of lack of reliability, since under some circumstances the testimony of even a single woman would be accepted.[22] Not only that, but in fact a woman could act as a judge.[23] The explanation often given for this is that in Jewish Law the litigants can choose to be judged by individuals and may "accept" a woman as a judge. Whatever the reason, female reliability is established.

If the intention of excluding women from giving court testimony in general was that of protecting women on the basis of the phrase "All the glory of a king's daughter is inside,"[24] then one might be able to abide the theory. In practice however, it has led to women's exclusion from a great deal of Jewish life and has given them an inferior status, de facto if not de jure, in Jewish courts.

Even more problematic is the fact that a woman cannot give a divorce and is dependent on the male. It is true that there are circumstances under which she can insist that the *Beth Din* arrange for a divorce and that in principle she can refuse to receive a divorce, but in practice divorces have been a constant bone of contention over the years. We do not need to reiterate here the extent to which this has been used by men to blackmail so many unfortunate women. It is true that steps are being taken now to deal with this by means of prenuptial agreements and occasionally annulment, but to this day women are very often still at a distinct disadvantage.

Although technically women must be willing to receive a bill of divorce, there are in practice a range of devices open to unscrupulous husbands to evade this that are not open to women. An example is the notorious *heter meah rabbanim*, "permission from a hundred rabbis," device of getting a hundred "rabbis" (actually, any male will do) to permit a man to remarry. This device was originally intended for overruling a special rabbinic decree (Rabbeynu Gershom's decree against polygamy was such a rabbinic innovation that could under extreme circumstances be set aside), but it has been used exclusively in the area of allowing a man whose wife refuses to divorce him to remarry. Those few rabbis in the Orthodox world who try to ameliorate the situation usually find themselves in a minority.

3

What exactly was the attitude of the rabbis to women? What did they really think? The first thing that is obvious is that there are different voices that might have reflected different social and political environments. The Talmud, after all, was a compilation of views of rabbis covering a time span of a thousand years. It reflected different environments and cultures from India to Italy. Its protagonists were rich and poor, aristocratic and humble, and of course there would always have been different attitudes and arguments even within one society.

On the one hand we can find opinions that are condescending and humiliating, but on the other hand that indicate a high degree of respect and approbation. They tended to think of women as having a different nature from men: "A man seeks (sex) with his mouth, a woman with her heart."[25] But this difference did not necessarily mean something negative. Of course there are very "sexist" attitudes, such as: "A man does not want to have daughters."[26] A well known and oft repeated negative view is "Women have a light mind,"[27] which supposedly explains why two women should not be alone with one man. It is also used to explain that women are more likely to reveal secrets under torture to Roman oppressors.[28] Another very negative view is of a woman's sexuality: "A woman prefers one *kav* (a small amount to live off) with immorality than nine *kavs* and separation (from immorality)."[29] There are other negative attitudes to be found throughout the Talmud.

Against these attitudes one can find quite different expressions such as: "Women have been given greater understanding by God than men,"[30] "Women take better care of guests than men,"[31] and "Women are more merciful than men."[32] The fact is that attitudes are bound to differ and it is a pointless exercise to catalogue examples claiming women to be on a higher level than men or to have greater success in appealing to God or in upholding the religion. The acid test lies not in personal opinions but in legislation.

On a general legal level the very fact that biblical and postbiblical law allowed a man to have more than one wife (whereas a woman was restricted to one man) created a whole area of female disadvantage that was ameliorated somewhat only by Rabbeynu Gershom's ban on polygamy a thousand years ago. However, this ban did not affect the Islamic Jewish communities (in practice the movement of most Sephardi communities to the new Jewish State of Israel after 1948 effectively ended polygamy altogether).

Technically, adultery was defined simply in terms of intercourse between a man and only a woman that he was forbidden to marry, not a "free" one. It has taken time for rabbinic opinion to come around to the view that adultery may be understood on different levels, involving deceit and betrayal as well as contractual violations. Instead of thinking only in terms of intercourse it can now be seen in terms of betrayal.

The rabbis declared that "Women, slaves, and minors were free from the obligation to carry out those ritual commandments related to time."[33] Logically this humiliating

coupling of women with minors and slaves is taken to mean
that since they are all subject to more immediate human
authority than the Divine, they are not in a position to act
freely and set other priorities. Women were subject to their
husbands in the way that slaves were subject to their mas-
ters. This is why the Talmud says that a woman is less
obliged to carry out the command to "Honor your mother
and your father," because she is subject to her husband and
therefore less free.[34] On the other hand, a divorced or wid-
owed woman was reinstated in terms of her obligations to
her parents, as we shall see.

If the issue was simply one of freedom to act, free from
the restraint of either a husband or society, then women of
independent means or those who chose to remain independent should have been allowed to do as they pleased. Indeed
one opinion was that women may opt to do those commandments; they are not obliged to do if they choose to do so.[35]
Yet in general rabbinic opinion was against adding to one's
obligations. They preferred to see laws as being Divine obligations that tested one's obedience and submission rather
than opportunities to assert one's religious interest. The
debate between Rabbi Yossi and Rabbi Shimon, who allow
women the right to do something they are not obliged to,
and Rabbi Yehuda, who objects, is one that continues through
the posttalmudic authorities. On the other hand the rabbis
emphasized the equality of the mother and the father as far
as obligations to a child were concerned: "Mother and Father are equal."[36] The Talmud Yerushalmi takes this further:
"The same applies to a man as it does to a woman. A man
has the means to carry out his obligations but a woman does
not because she is under someone else. But if she is wid-
owed or divorced then she is just like the man who has the
means."[37]

It does appear that the rabbis were sensitive to the position of independent women and women of independent
means. They insisted that an important woman should re-

cline on Passover just like a man.[38] Indeed the rabbis hint at the possibility of women opting to put on tefillin, something related to time by talking of Saul's daughter Michal,[39] a princess and with no children, deciding to do this, and also of the wife of the prophet Jonah. Similarly with regard to sitting in a *succah* they use the story of Queen Helene, who frequented rabbinic circles, to illustrate a woman's right to do more than was required by law.[40]

What becomes clear is that women of substance were able to manage a great deal independently, in talmudic times and beyond. Cursory study of *ketubot* (marriage documents) in both Ashkenazi and Sephardi traditions shows that wealthy women were able to lay down strict conditions for preserving their independent wealth as well as for deciding on issues such as where they would live, children, concubines, and marital obligations. Sadly, as always "money answers everything,"[41] and there seem to be two standards, one for the rich and one for the poor—something that should be unheard of in a religious tradition.

The debate about whether a woman should study Torah shows the polarized attitudes that have prevailed for so long. The debate between Ben Azai and Rabbi Eliezer as to whether one may teach Torah to a woman (Ben Azai says one should but Rabbi Eliezer feared she would abuse the knowledge)[42] highlights the two camps in talmudic and rabbinic thinking on women. One assigns women an inferior role due to both a lower level of obligation and a lower level of commitment to Torah learning and accepts this as the inevitable lot. The other offers ways for those who want to educate themselves, to enrich themselves, and to rise within the community. A similar difference of opinion applies to the rabbinic attitudes toward peasants. They too were subject to disdain and ostracism because of their ignorance and lack of education—but this is little comfort.

Another factor that mitigated against the woman's position in society was the synagogual system, which developed in the working place as a male study center at a time when the home was the true center of practical Jewish living. The synagogue, therefore, was by force of circumstances a male preserve, rather like the gentlemen's clubs that were so popular in the upper echelons of society in the English-speaking world. Nevertheless in practice the home was always considered the primary location for religious behavior. To this day, the greater the commitment, the more important the role of the home is. Time and again the rabbis emphasize the role of the woman as the center of home life.[43]

The rabbis saw the importance of defining roles. Their emphasis on the home as the center for rearing and educating children and for supporting the husband in his study meant that they genuinely wanted to assert that the primary role of women was indeed to take care of the home and children. The problem was that no provision was made for the exception—perhaps because the exceptions then were so few. Yet it is clear historically that women always have escaped the home, either out of the necessity of earning money or because of compulsion by conquering societies. The rabbis, as good religious conservatives, wanted to preserve their vision of the ideal even as it was being eroded.

4

It is true that there are other examples of "discrimination" in the tradition, not confined to women. Priests and Levites are given preference over other males and there is a whole slew of mainly biblical laws that apply only to them. Indeed the female *Cohen* had rights well beyond and far more beneficial than those that applied to the "ordinary" male or female Jew. The learned person was given benefits that did not apply to the ignoramus, the judiciary was given special rights, and the political leadership had rights that did not apply to the ordinary person. Even the Hebrew slave had an array of special rights that extended to an obligation on his master to set him up in business (or at least to provision him when he left to manage on his own). Nevertheless, two wrongs do not make a right.

The Mishna in *Horyot* establishes a series of priorities in discussing whom the community should support or save first: "A man comes before a woman to be kept alive (for example if two are drowning and only one can be saved), to return lost property to. A woman comes before a man to be clothed, to be freed from captivity. But where both may be sexually attacked a man should be freed first."[44] One's outrage at this clear bias may be assuaged, though not totally extinguished, by continuing in the Mishna: "A *Cohen* comes before a *Levi*, a *Levi* comes before an *Israel*, an *Israel* comes before a *mamzer* (a Jewish child of an illegal intercourse), a *mamzer* comes before a *netin* (a convert under false pretenses), a *netin* over a new convert, and a convert over a freed slave. When does this apply? When they are equal (in their level of Torah knowledge). But if the *mamzer* is a learned man and the high priest is an ignoramus, then the learned *mamzer* comes before an ignorant high priest."

These generalizations underline the real priority: There are differences in social standing and position, but the over-riding consideration is Torah. This is why, amazingly, despite the emphasis in the Ten Commandments on honoring one's father and mother, respect for one's teacher takes priority in Halacha (unless, of course, one's father is one's teacher as well). Thus a learned woman would certainly leapfrog the others in the list of priorities. One needs to understand this attitude to Torah to see why so many remarks sound antifeminist. It is because a woman then, like the *am ha'aretz*, the peasant, was not educated and was not trained to value study. It was not her fault; it was the result of the system.

One cannot take the rabbis totally out of their historical and social context. The genius of the rabbis was in making alterations to suit changing circumstances. Certainly they accepted that the Torah was given within a specific time and cultural context: "The Torah speaks in a language of humans (that humans at the time would understand)."[45] This "explains" the acceptance of slavery in general and of selling children into slavery (something the later rabbis forbade) and the right of fathers to betroth their underage children. All of these are issues that eventually fell into disrepute, even if it took thousands of years to do so. The fact that the Torah introduces protective and qualifying legislation to ensure civil and marital rights for women,[46] well ahead of its time, is remarkable.

The rabbis were able to differentiate between laws that were obligations and laws that were optional. For those that were optional (for example: you did not have to have a slave, you did not have to sell a child, you did not have to suspect your wife) the rabbis could simply remove the option. One could simply not act and the rabbis could simply prevent people from exercising their options. This was a device they were happy to use instead of trying to find ways of changing laws.

Nevertheless they did take several steps to protect women and to improve their lot,[47] well ahead of the times. The laws of the *ketubah*, the marriage document, were designed among other things to protect women from the abandonment of divorce by ensuring that they had some financial independence, and by insisting that heirs stand by commitments to both wives and daughters. This was a tremendous step because otherwise a divorced woman would be left penniless, with her only option to go back to her father's home to live the existence of a drudge. Women whose husbands had disappeared (a very common problem then) were allowed to remarry on the evidence of one witness, and some allowed it on the basis of hearsay or the testimony of a male slave, a woman, or a female slave.[48] The famous case of the woman suspected of adultery, the *sotah*, was altered by Rabbi

Yochanan Ben Zakkai because he felt that the level of male morality was such that men ought not to have preference over women.[49]

Despite this, the rabbis were clearly aware and reinforced the common assumption of male superiority. A woman could not be called up to read from the Torah, not because any law forbade it but because it was considered beneath the dignity of a man to have a woman represent him.[50] Similarly a woman was capable, legally, of making certain blessings on behalf of a man, but it was considered shameful if a man was so ignorant as to need his wife to bless for him.[51] It is troubling to read Maimonides' attitudes toward women even if one does set them against the dominant Muslim society influencing his thinking. It is not until Maimonides that one finds a categorical legal (as opposed to midrashic) statement that a woman cannot be appointed to a public position[52]— but notice that he has to go back to the precedent of a king for support.

5

The interesting question is how we, in the twentieth century, tackle the obvious gap that exists between female expectations and rabbinic flexibility. In principle there is a lot to be said for the role definition that makes homemaking a priority. Particularly in view of changing circumstances and attitudes in society, family life and values need reinforcing. But the problem with strengthening family life is that it makes it more difficult for those women (or men, for that matter) who choose to break conventional patterns in their own ways of living or choose not to have a family.

This recalls to the question of whether a woman who is not a homemaker ought to take on male rituals. There is enough weight of halachic opinion to support this option, more so than if a man decided to become the homemaker.

Similarly there are enough precedents for learned women being consulted on and indeed teaching halachic issues. It is probable that women will increasingly turn to women for information and advice on religious issues.

The argument over whether a woman can use the title of "rabbi" is a smoke screen because the title has been devalued anyway and no longer conforms to the talmudic *semicha* ordination, which ceased two thousand years ago. Very few rabbis nowadays are halachic authorities. Most of the functions they perform can be done just as well by a layman. The only halachic issues are those of representation: Only someone absolutely obligated can act on behalf of someone else obligated in the same way. This creates a problem for women performing for men, particularly in the synagogue. Similarly, the problem of women acting as witnesses in the public arena affects areas such as marriage.

There are solutions or at least ways of dealing with most of these issues halachically, as indeed there are with regard to marital and divorce problems. A major stumbling block is "process." Halachic authority cannot and will not allow itself to be pressured or harassed into decisions that it has difficulty adjusting to anyway. This is the conservative nature of religious authority. Worse, the secular world is perceived as being corrupt and lacking in morality, influenced by self-indulgence and materialism. Secular values are perceived as transient, unstable, and not a reliable basis for change. The growing demographic strength of Orthodoxy and its self-perception as the bulwark against reformation and assimilation make its leadership reluctant and resistant to change.

Under these circumstances the way forward is to increase female study and expertise and to establish female norms and forms of prayer. In this way "facts" are created or changed. If the rabbis can say, "If only a person could pray all day long,"[53] this certainly allowed for freedom to create one's own praying format in addition to the established structures. There is no reason, given the Torah obligation, that this should not equally apply to women. It is true that it is possible to campaign for women to perform various ritual functions within an Orthodox framework, such as reading the *Megillah* on Purim or saying various blessings at the *Shabbat* table, but every one of these issues in a sense demeans the female by forcing her to battle for recognition.

I am not enthusiastic about tinkering with existing structures of synagogal prayer. Each variation of synagogal activity meets a need of one section of the Jewish community even as it disappoints a much larger group. I strongly believe that there are many avenues and different types of praying experiences. There should be room for a female framework and female forms of prayer emerging parallel with the male structures. Diversity and creativity can only be healthy. This, after all, is hinted at in Miriam's song that is parallel to Moses'. Furthermore creativity, albeit without altering the superstructure, was how the kabbalists of Safed generated new modalities of prayer in their day. How wonderful it would be to experience different forms of spirituality.

Women are increasingly exploring new and different ways of expressing themselves spiritually. Inevitably establishments resist change, particularly if the change is perceived as coming from a cultural context that is inimical to its values. But the drive for women to demand more of a voice in religious affairs is as much a result of genuine spirituality as it is of political agitation—and this must be recognized.

As Hillel puts it, "In a place where there are no one (*ish*), strive to be someone."[54] Yes I have translated the word *ish*, normally taken to be "man," into "person." This is a perfect example, on a very minor scale, of what can be done. In the sacrificial system the word *ish*, "man," is used to include women as well. Why not then translate it as "person?" Where there is a will there is often a way.

The myth is that women are treated equally. In too many cases they are not, but this is a problem of male attitudes rather than inherent in the religious system.

Notes

1. Genesis 5:1.
2. Genesis 24.
3. Genesis 3:16.
4. Genesis 4:7.
5. Maimonides' *Yad HaChazaka Hilchot Teshuva* 9:2.
6. Genesis 12:5.
7. Genesis 21:12.
8. Genesis 27:6.
9. Genesis 29:32 et passim.
10. Genesis 35:18.
11. Genesis 4:22.
12. Genesis 36:12.
13. Numbers 26:46.
14. Exodus 15:20.
15. Judges 4:5.
16. 2 Kings 24:14.
17. Genesis 38.
18. Mishna *Horyot* 13:1, Maimonides' *Yad HaChazaka Matanot LeEvyonim* 8.
19. Deuteronomy 19:16.
20. Numbers 27:7.
21. *Tur Shulchan Aruch Choshen Mishpat* 282.
22. Talmud Bavli *Yevamot* 39b.
23. *Tosafot Niddah* 50a.
24. Psalms 45:14.
25. Talmud Bavli *Eiruvin* 100b.
26. Midrash *Tanchuma Chaye Sarah* 3.
27. Talmud Bavli *Kiddushin* 80b.
28. Talmud Bavli *Shabbat* 33b.

29. Mishna *Sotah* 3, Talmud Bavli *Ketubot* 62b.

30. Talmud Bavli *Nida* 45b.

31. Talmud Bavli *Brachot* 10b.

32. Talmud Bavli *Megillah* 14b.

33. Mishna *Kiddushin* 1.

34. Talmud Bavli *Kiddushin* 29a.

35. Talmud Bavli *Eiruvin* 96b.

36. Mishna *Keritut* 6:9.

37. Talmud Yerushalmi *Kiddushin* 1:7.

38. Talmud Bavli *Pesachim* 108a.

39. Talmud Bavli *Eiruvin* 91a.

40. Talmud Bavli *Succah* 2b.

41. Ecclesiastes 10:19.

42. Talmud Bavli *Sotah* 20a.

43. Talmud Bavli *Shabbat* 118b.

44. Mishna *Horyot* 3:8.

45. Talmud Bavli *Brachot* 31b.

46. Exodus 21:10.

47. For a fuller treatment see Judith Hauptman, *Rereading the Rabbis* (Westview).

48. Mishna *Yevamot* 16:7.

49. Talmud Bavli *Sotah* 47a.

50. Talmud Bavli *Megillah* 23b.

51. Talmud Bavli *Brachot* 20b.

52. Maimonides' *Yad HaChazaka Melachim* 1:5.

53. Talmud Bavli *Brachot* 21a.

54. *Avot* 2:5.

Chapter 12

Myth: Judaism Discourages Conversion

1

It is not easy to become a Jew. Is this because Judaism does not welcome conversion or is it because individual Jews do not like converts? Why do so many rabbis make it so difficult to convert? Is it because they are suspicious of the convert's motives? Or is it simply out of xenophobia?

The structure and nature of the Jewish people has gone through several changes over the millennia. Despite the fact that Noah and his family were saved and he himself "walked with God" he is not regarded as the founding father of Judaism. That honor is traditionally held to belong to Abraham. Abraham's covenant with God was sealed or confirmed through circumcision,[1] and Abraham circumcised not just himself and Ishmael but also "All the men of his household, born in the house and those bought for money from outsiders, they were circumcised with him."[2] It appears to have been the norm that joining a household or a tribe meant joining the tribal religion too. From Abraham onwards through his grandsons tribal loyalty seems to have been crucial, with men importing wives from a variety of external tribes, some more approved of than others.[3]

Conquest followed by circumcision, in those early days, was the only way to join the Tribes of Israel. It might have been obvious to the men of Shechem that if they wanted to ally themselves with the Sons of Jacob they would have to adopt their customs, yet the only law they discussed was circumcision.[4] When the Children of Israel left Egypt they were joined by "a mixed multitude,"[5] but there is no indication that they were "converted" in any recognizable way and we know from the Book of Joshua that no one was obliged to become circumcised in the forty years they wandered in the wilderness. Similarly, the "son of an Israelite woman and he was the son of an Egyptian man," who was punished for cursing, may have automatically been a member through his mother, but again there is an absence of detail.[6] There are similar lacunae as to what happened with Jethro and his tribe—whether they joined or simply allied themselves to the Children of Israel[7] and whether Miriam's complaint against Moses' wife being black was because of her affiliation or because of how Moses was treating her.[8]

The Torah does lay down laws forbidding intermarriage with the seven Canaanite tribes as well as the men of Ammon and Moab, but this interdiction is not applied universally against all peoples or even against the female members of the two latter tribes. Ruth the Moabitess abandoned her idolatrous people and her expression of faith is taken, to this day, as the paradigm of genuine conversion. However, with her, too, the sources omit any mention of a formal ceremony of conversion. Did King David and King Solomon convert their non-Jewish wives and concubines? Again the text remains silent. The case of the woman captured in war who was brought home and went through a period of mourning prior to becoming a full wife[9] may indicate a general process of conversion, but it would be difficult to extrapolate from this special case that there was an established conversion procedure.

It was Ezra who clearly forbade intermarriage between Jews and non-Jews.[10] Nevertheless, even after Ezra there was some ambiguity as to what exactly a *ger* was because the word now meant both "a convert" and "a stranger." It is clear that the biblical term *ger*, meaning "stranger," did not necessarily apply to a convert. There were two kinds of "strangers": the *ger toshav*, a stranger who lived amongst the Jews and abandoned idolatry, and the *ger tsedek*, the convert.[11] The Gemara debates whether the *ger toshav* was obliged simply to abandon idolatry or to also keep the Seven Noachide Commandments, or more.[12] Maimonides in his code accepts the Seven Noachide laws as defining the *ger toshav*.[13] After the destruction of the Temple and the Exile, the concept of the *ger toshav* was abandoned.[14] Many of the fifty-six times the word is used in the Torah do not have relevance to conversion. The five times that we are commanded to remember what it was like to be *gerim*, strangers, in the land of Egypt are certainly not to be taken as describing us as having been converts to the Egyptian religion. No other idea is repeated as often as this one of being sensitive and understanding of the position of the outsider, whether a passing visitor, a resident, or a convert.

The Canaanite slave who became his master's property had to go through circumcision and obey those commands of the Torah that were not related to time. As soon as he was freed, he became automatically a full member of the Jewish community. The Talmud records that Rabbi Eliezer entered a synagogue and found they needed one more person to make up the *minyan*, so he freed his slave on the spot.[15]

But other ambiguities remained. The Samaritans claimed that they were Jewish, but some authorities insisted they were non-Jewish while others were prepared to accept them without conversion. The Samaritans, often called Cutheans in the Talmud, were the inhabitants of the Northern Kingdom who had been brought in by the Assyrians to replace the Ten Northern Jewish tribes who had had been exiled in 722 B.C.E. They adopted many Jewish customs and may have been joined by returning remnants of exiled Jews. Initially they fought the return of the Babylonian Jews but later seem to have accommodated themselves to coexistence. Their status remained an ongoing issue. One opinion says that "A Cuthi is a complete Jew,"[16] and another says that a Cuthi is a complete non-Jew![17]

2

At this biblical and early post-biblical stage, there is no indication of any objection or hesitation in accepting converts. The turning point seems to have been the result of the forcible Hasmonean conversion of some of the neighboring tribes. They became known as *gerei ayarot*, "lion converts," who only did so out of fear. The term actually originated with regard to the Samaritans[18] but it was adapted to cover anyone who converted out of fear and came within a category of suspect converts. "Whether they are lion converts, dream converts, or Mordecai and Esther converts they are only converts if they convert now (not for ulterior motives). Rabbi Yitschak bar Shmuel bar Marta said in the name of Shmuel that the law goes according to those who say they are converts."[19] It is hardly surprising that the rabbis of the Talmud might have had their doubts about forced conversions. After all, the Idumeans were converted by the early Hasmoneans and Herod was descended from them. Given that he assassinated the last of the Hasmoneans and established his own dynasty, it is hardly surprising that his ancestry would have been held against him.

Nevertheless converts were welcomed into the fold and achieved the highest positions in Jewish religious life. Shemaya and Avtalyon, the teachers of Hillel and Shammai, were either converts or descended from converts. According to one opinion, they were descended from Haman.[20] Onkelos, who wrote the authoritative Aramaic translation and interpretation of the Torah, was a convert and "gloried" in the title Onkelos the Convert.[21] There are suggestions that Rabbi Akiva and Rabbi Meir were converts or the children of converts. Rav Shmuel bar Yehuda is confident enough to point out that he is a convert in the context of a debate about the function of a convert on a court of law.[22] "A convert who studies Torah is considered as important as the High Priest."[23] They clearly were held in the highest esteem if their conversion was out of genuine conviction. "God loves converts" says a popular Midrash.[24] Another says: "When a possible convert comes to you, you should stretch out your hands to bring him under the protection (the wings) of the Shechina."[25]

Ironically, we see in the different attitudes of Hillel and Shammai toward converts an indication of different philosophies: "It once happened that a non-Jew came to Shammai and said to him, 'How many Torahs do you have?' He replied, 'Two, a written Torah and an oral Torah.' He said, 'I believe you about the written Torah but I do not believe you about the oral Torah. Convert me on condition that you only teach me the written Torah.' He attacked him and threw him out aggressively. He came to Hillel and he converted him. (Hillel then sets about convincing him to trust Hillel to teach him both the written and the oral Torah, so Hillel was using a stratagem to bring him into Judaism.) Again it happened that a non-Jew came to Shamai and said, 'Convert me on condition that you can teach me all the Torah while I stand on one leg.' He threw him out by pushing him with the builder's plane he had been holding. He came to Hillel and he converted him. He said, 'What is hateful to you do not do to your friend. This is (the essence of) the Torah; all the rest is commentary. Go and learn.'"[26] These and other examples the Talmud goes on to give there illustrate different approaches. Shammai clearly feels that the non-Jew is unserious and disrespectful. He owes it, out of respect for the Torah, not to tolerate this frivolity. He is willing to take in converts but only on his terms. Hillel is much more flexible. He seems to be looking for any excuse to rope in as many converts as possible. He recognizes that it takes time for the fullness of the Jewish experience to become appreciated and that patience will pay dividends.

This difference was not confined to Hillel and Shammai. The most often quoted anticonvert opinion is that of Rabbi Chelbo, who says, 'Converts are as bad for Israel as a disease.'[27] There were stories of converts with dual loyalties betraying Jews to the Romans.[28] Still, the overwhelming body of opinion was positive and supportive even to the point of suggesting that giving up idolatry was enough to give a person the right to call himself a Jew: "Whoever rejects idol worship is called a Jew."[29]

There was, as well, a philosophical debate. One might be inclined to say that someone who chooses to become Jewish, and voluntarily comes to recognize the greatness of its spiritual tradition, should be on a higher level than someone who by accident of birth is automatically Jewish and does not necessarily have to affirm his or her belief at any time. On the other hand, the rabbinic tendency was to argue that simple acceptance of Judaism as an act of commitment to God was a greater form of obedience to the Divine and superior to rationally coming to the conclusion that Judaism was "right." The latter, after all, is following his or her own mind rather than accepting a superior One. This is what is behind the phrase "Greater is the person who is commanded (obliged) and does, rather than the person who is not commanded and (chooses) to do."[30] They used this argument in regard to the issue of whether or not women who are not commanded to perform certain rituals should volunteer to do them, but it was used also to argue that there was no reason to accept converts since they were not obliged to take on the more onerous obligations of Jewish Law.

Despite these arguments there is exhaustive literature and halachic decisions about converts in the Talmud covering virtually every area of law and ritual. Can a convert use the format of blessings "Our God and God of our fathers?" Does a convert have the obligation to honor his parents? Can he be disqualified as a witness by a relative from before his conversion? If he had children before conversion what is their status? Does he now have an obligation to have more children? Who inherits from a childless convert? There are laws that restrict the role of a convert: A convert can become a judge but cannot be appointed to a position of tax collector so as not to be put in the position of having to enforce collection (with all the animosity that surrounds it). One is forbidden to remind a convert of his origins. The rabbis understood human nature and wanted to protect converts from the inevitable slights to which they would be subjected by the thoughtlessness of ordinary folk.

The historical situation is that conversion in the "golden" period of the Roman Empire was common. This is evidenced by the fact that the rabbis established both a ritual procedure as well as a recommended approach. They taught that when a convert comes to be converted (under the conditions of later Roman persecution), "they say, 'What reason have you found to want to convert? Do you not know that Israel nowadays is sad, pressured, tortured, and confused, and awful things happen to them?' If he says, 'I know and I am not worthy,' they receive him immediately and inform him of some of the least important commandments and some of the most important commandments and they tell him about the "sin" (of not giving) gleanings, forgotten produce, and the corner of the field (to be left for the poor) and tithes for the poor and they inform him of the punishment for (not doing) the commandments and they tell him, 'Before you arrived at this level you could eat fats without being punished with being cut off; if you would have broken *Shabbat* you would not be stoned.' But just as they tell him about the punishments for disobeying commandments so they inform him about the rewards: 'Know that the World to Come is only for the righteous and for Israel nowadays since they cannot cope with either too much good or too much punishment.' But they should not press too much upon him and they should not be too strict on him. If he accepts all this, they circumcise him right away . . . and submerge him (in a *mikvah*) and two elders stand above and recite some light commandments and some serious ones. He dips under and comes up and he becomes a complete Jew.[31] This text is the basis of the formulation given in the *Shulchan Aruch*[32] for accepting converts, with the added requirement of a *Beth Din* of three to oversee the procedure.

3

If a great rabbi like Hillel was very eager to convert and was even prepared to use subterfuge to encourage converts to join, what led to the modern state of affairs wherein conversion is looked on somewhat askance by many and is certainly not encouraged as an active policy? It cannot be simply because Judaism allows other religious and moral standards for non-Jews, requiring of them only the basic Seven Noachide Commandments, so that therefore there is no religious requirement for conversion to Judaism. It cannot be because Judaism is not an absolutist religion: "We are right and everyone else is wrong." Christianity is so strongly missionary because one of its cardinal beliefs is that only through its messiah can a person be saved, but such a position is not the Jewish one. All of these conditions applied at Hillel's time too, but they did not stop him from having his more lenient and open attitude.

Leaving aside the internal evidence, we know historically that the Jews were avid converters in the post-Maccabee era. Monotheism was recognized by an increasing number of Greeks and Romans as a far more preferable religion than the Graeco-Roman traditions revolving around the rather sordid goings-on of the gods. The exchanges in the Talmud involving Roman matrons or Roman officers indicates that a lot of dialogue and crossing over was taking place reaching the highest levels. Licinius, who for a while ruled jointly with Constantine in the third century, belonged to a family that had converts to Judaism. One is tempted to fantasize on the fate of the Jews had he, rather than Constantine, won the battle of Adrianople in 323, for following it, the Council of Nicea in 325 established Christianity as the religion of the Roman Empire and forbade Jews to convert non-Jews on pain of death. Despite a brief period of respite under Julian ("The Apostate" for Christians, but a "good guy" for the Jews) it became virtually impossible for Jews to convert. Not only were Jews forbidden to proselytize but someone who did convert was likely to be put to death himself. In 1222, Robert of Reading, a student at Oxford, converted out of love for a Jewish girl. He was burnt at the stake. Thus in effect the Jews abandoned the process and turned in on themselves. Although the records show that individuals did continue converting to Judaism in small numbers, it was very much a low-key business and kept as quiet as possible so as not to offend the Christian authorities.

What emerges from the text of the conversion process as used in the *Shulchan Aruch* is an awareness of the poor and downtrodden state of the Jewish people and a feeling that no one in their right mind would willingly become a Jew. This reflected the reality of Roman, Christian, and even the less harsh Muslim hegemony. Nevertheless it is in-teresting that nowhere does the law require absolute and immediate obedience to the whole body of law as a condition of acceptance. The emphasis does indeed seem to be on genuine conversion for ideological rather than social motives.

After the Enlightenment in Europe and the freedom of belief that was accorded non-Christian communities in the last century, when circumstances began to change and conversion to Judaism was no longer an act of folly, a new set of problems arose. The opening up of society led to the possibility of social conversion, converting to marry or to mix with Jews without a strictly religious motivation. This was something that the rabbis had not considered since the time of Esther and Mordecai.[33] The battle of Ashkenazi rabbis against the leniency of Reform led them to take very strict measures against social conversion, arguing that conversion for an ulterior motive was unacceptable. In general, in Diaspora communities, the Orthodox world makes it difficult to convert in general and almost impossible if marriage is seen as a motive. Yet the Gemara I quoted above, referring to forced converts, starts out like this: "A man who converted for (to marry) a woman or a woman who converts for a man . . . is not counted as a convert, says Rabbi Nechemia. . . . Rabbi Yitschak bar Shmuel . . . says that the law is that they are converts."[34]

So what happened? Why are the Courts of Law much stricter now? Why do they demand much stricter standards of religious behavior than the letter of the law demands? Certainly the rabbis are not inclined to turn Judaism into a proselytizing religion and many even look askance at the dramatic efforts of Chabad Lubavitch to bring assimilated Jews back into the fold. It seems that the old antipathy to conversion, a legacy of the pre-enlightenment era, lingers. It is also true that the gulf that anti-Semitism and the Holocaust created in Eastern Europe have reinforced an earlier reluctance to deal with non-Jews on religious matters, and biases that assume that every non-Jew is fundamentally antipathetic to Jews. In addition there is the polemic against Reform Judaism, where matters were made more complex by Reform's changing the religious criteria for defining a Jew and accepting a patrilineal criterion. Orthodoxy, in response to what it sees as a challenge to its authority, is trying to define itself more rigidly and exclusively. Of course, Orthodoxy is not monolithic. There are Chassidic groups that are much more enthusiastic about accepting converts than others. Despite the disagreements and differences of policy, no religious authority has ever suggested that genuine converts are other than absolute Jews and no kind of racial or national limitation has ever been applied to conversion.

4

The State Of Israel, for all its blessings, has created a range of new problems in the area of Jewish identity. First, definitions of who is a Jew became confused with the intervention of purely secular authorities, the Knesset (the Israeli Parliament), and the Supreme Court, in drafting legislation. Because Israel wanted to protect Jews wherever they were, they instituted the Law of Return, which gave Jews wherever they were automatic citizenship in the Jewish State as a protective measure. Never again would a Jew be in danger because there was no country willing to take him or her in. This laudable principle led to a widening of the definition of a Jew beyond traditional religious legal limitations. According to Jewish law a person's mother has to be Jewish as a condition of recognition. According to the Law of Return, one grandparent was sufficient. Given the criteria that the Nazis used for defining Jewish identity, one can understand why Israel would expand its definitions for the purpose of offering refuge.

From the point of view of religious identity, however, this has proved a major source of conflict. Many came to Israel under a law of Jewish return who were not Jewish by either religious definition or religious practice. One might argue that this influx has strengthened the Jewish State and thus Judaism itself, which has flourished there. It is even suggested that a return to a policy of encouraging converts might help strengthen Diaspora communities as well. But the two-thousand-year subconscious sublimation of resentment of the outsider and the need to protect inner integrity as a defense mechanism cannot easily be jettisoned, and when large numbers of incoming "Jews" are practicing members of Christian churches, tensions are naturally bound to emerge.

If the State decides for the purpose of its "Law of Return" how to define a Jew, why should a religious person who accepts religious definitions care? Interestingly, there was a case in Israel in the 1950s in which a Jew who converted to Catholicism and became a monk wanted to be accepted as a Jew under the Law of Return. Brother Daniel was rejected by the Supreme Court even though it might have been argued halachically that he was technically still a Jew. There have been other examples of secular law and religious law diverging in Israel. One common reason for opposition to defining Jewishness secularly is that the lines defining Jews in a Jewish state would become blurred. There would be "Jewish" Jews and "non-Jewish" Jews! This danger was behind the original decision of Israel's first Prime Minister, the secular David Ben Gurion, to make matters of personal status subject to Jewish Law. It is indeed a shame to have a dual-class society, but in fact this already exists. There are many Israelis whose status is religiously questionable. This becomes a problem only when a religious partner wants to marry one of suspect lineage, but rarely have these problems been insurmountable. They are no different from those experienced in the Disapora by Jews of different denominations wanting to marry.

5

Another relevant issue is that the State of Israel has revived the earlier historical situation whereby someone coming from the outside into a Jewish community could be considered

Jewish by absorption. This was behind the lenience of the late Chief Rabbi Goren's belief that converts in Israel would be influenced automatically by living in a Jewish State. He therefore made a policy of being supportive and lenient with potential converts who were going to live in Israel. Many Orthodox rabbis disagreed with his position, thinking that he was being taken advantage of.

The issue remains an important one because of the current immigration of Ethiopians, whose Jewishness is challenged, and thousands of Russians, who were avowedly atheists or Christian. The political pendulum has beenconstantly swinging, so that policies of facilitating conversion in Israel one year are capable of being changed the next. Generally, Israeli rabbis take a more relaxed attitude to conversion or to accommodating problems than their Diaspora colleagues. They have tended to be much more accommodating to possible converts who intend to stay and integrate into Israeli society. Rabbi Goren used to include the condition in some of his conversions that it was applicable only if the person stayed in Israel. Many rabbis have questioned whether one can make such a conversion "on condition." The trouble was that some individuals converted in Israel and then moved out, raising questions about the original procedure and challenging the different-standard approach.

The modern division of Judaism into different sects with widely varying attitudes to Jewish Law has created another problem in Israel. In the Diaspora each sect is entitled and free to set its own standards and criteria for conversion. Israel's concordat with the Orthodox parties has made Halacha the standard for Judaism, and conversions not performed halachically are not accepted. Of course, this does not mean, as some Reform rabbis like to suggest, that the Orthodox do not recognize them as Jews—the criterion is whether one's mother is Jewish, regardless of the current state of one's commitment—but it does mean that they do not accept Reform rabbis, Reform conversions, and the Reform definitions of who a Jew is.

This is only a problem in Israel, and in effect it is a political rather than a religious one. The Orthodox rabbinate controls a large and important empire, with its concomitant patronage. They do not want outsiders muscling in on their patch. The problem with religious issues in Israel is that more often than not, they are political. This is the downside of State and Religion co-habitation. The battle for religious, halachic recognition, is one that large numbers of immigrants to Israel have endured, from the Yemenite Jews to the Beta Israel of India and the Ethiopians and many Russians. In the end, means are usually found to deal with the problems, admittedly after long bureaucratic wrangling. These examples emphasize that despite the political dishonesty of the United Nations in its (now rescinded) declaration that Zionism is racism, there is absolutely no racist element in Jewish Law whatsoever. There is no limitation on anyone from any race joining Judaism; the condition is simply one of commitment.

None of this directly affects the condition of conversion. Genuine conversion is a "noble state." It is based on the example of Ruth, from whom the ideal Jewish King was descended. It is a heritage that rabbis were proud to proclaim: "God loves converts very much."[35] The notion that Judaism does not like converts may have some visceral reality in individual minds, but for Judaism as a system, it is another myth.

Notes

1. Genesis 17:10.
2. Genesis 17:27.
3. Genesis 28:9 and Genesis 38.
4. Genesis 34.

5. Exodus 12:38.
6. Leviticus 24:10.
7. Numbers 10:29.
8. Numbers 12:1.
9. Deuteronomy 21:10.
10. Ezra 9:13.
11. Talmud Bavli *Yevamot* 48b.
12. Talmud Bavli *Avoda Zara* 54b.
13. Maimonides' *Yad HaChazaka Issurei Biya* 14:7.
14. Talmud Bavli *Erchin* 29a.
15. Talmud Bavli *Brachot* 47b.
16. Talmud Yerushalmi *Brachot* 7:1.
17. Talmud Yerushalmi *Demai* 6:1.
18. 2 Kings 17:24.
19. Talmud Bavli *Yevamot* 24b.
20. Talmud Bavli *Sanhedrin* 96b.
21. Talmud Bavli *Megillah* 3a and *Avoda Zara* 11a.
22. Talmud Bavli *Yevamot* 101b.
23. Midrash *Tanchuma Vayakhel* 8.
24. Midrash *Tehillim* 146:8.
25. Midrash Rabba *Vayikra* 2:8.
26. Talmud Bavli *Shabbat* 31a.
27. Talmud Bavli *Yevamot* 47b.
28. Talmud Bavli *Shabbat* 33b.
29. Talmud Bavli *Megillah* 13a.
30. Talmud Bavli *Kiddushin* 31a and *Bava Kamma* 38a.
31. Talmud Bavli *Yevamot* 47a.
32. *Shulchan Aruch Yoreh Deah* 268:1.
33. See note 19.
34. Talmud Bavli *Yevamot* 24b.
35. Midrash *Tehillim* 146:8.

Chapter 13

Myth: Jews Should Live in Israel

1

If Israel is the Promised Land of the Jews and any Jew who so desires can go and stay there, why are not all Jews (at least those who are committed to Judaism) living in Israel?

The Land of Israel plays a crucial part in Jewish thinking and Jewish history. From Abraham onward there is a special relationship between the land and the people: "On that day God made an agreement with Abram, saying, 'I will give your children this land from the river of Egypt to the great river, the river Euphrates.'"[1] This agreement incorporated in it the exile in Egypt: "You should surely know that your children will be strangers in a land that is not theirs, and they will serve them and they will oppress them for four hundred years."[2] If one part happened as promised we might reasonably expect the other part to be fulfilled too. The agreement did not give Abraham immediate rights; he had to enter into treaties with the Philistines[3] and buy land from the Hittites to bury his wife Sarah.[4] The promise of the land seems to have been an expression of intent rather than an effective transfer. In practice, the exact terms of the territorial promise were never fulfilled—unless of course Ishmael is included. After all, God did talk about the "seed" of Abraham without specifying anyone in particular, in which case certainly the seed of Abraham has done much better than this.

The Torah itself is heavily focused on Israel. The whole narrative leads up to the ultimate goal of settling in the land, and many laws are specifically related to the Land of Israel. There is a specific command to conquer the land: "And you should take over the land and live in it because I have given the land to you as an inheritance."[5] There is a range of agricultural laws that were given in the wilderness in preparation for settlement in Israel. There are laws about when one can start to eat the produce of fruit trees: "When you come into the land and you plant fruit trees,"[6] and laws about how much one leaves for the poor, "Speak to the Children of Israel and say to them, 'When you come into the land which I am giving you and you reap the harvest.'"[7] There is the command relating to the seventh-year release: "When you come into the land that I am going to give you and the land will rest, a rest for God,"[8] and the jubilee after seven seven-year cycles. Later there is the law regarding the first fruits "When it will be that you come into the land that YHVH your God is going to give to you as an inheritance and you will take it over and dwell in it, you will bring the first fruits to God."[9] There are special laws relating to cities in the Land of Israel, both with regard to buying and selling property and with regard to who can settle and where.

The laws that apply specifically to Israel were not just about land and agriculture. Civil law was integrated into the actual land: "And God spoke to Moses, saying, 'Speak to the children of Israel and say to them, "When you cross the river Jordan into the land of Canaan, you should set aside cities of refuge."'"[10] The cities of refuge were an important part of the penal system and although some were to be set aside outside the borders of the land, the system would only take effect when the first cities were established in Israel. The tribal inheritance system that carried with it a range of laws about inheritance and transfer, short-term and long-term, was based exclusively on the territory of the Jewish state: "Command the Children of Israel and say to them, 'When you come into the land of Canaan this is the land that will fall to you as an inheritance.'"[11]

If settlement in the land of Israel was so important, one might think that the Torah would require everyone who came out of Egypt to go and settle in the Land of Israel. Yet even then, tribes who asked for permission to stay in Trans-Jordania were allowed to stay. The tribes of Reuben and Gad, later joined by part of Menashe, were allowed to remain on the lush cattle-rearing plains of Gilead provided their warriors helped in the conquest of Canaan.[12] That is, in principle, living outside the Land of Israel can hardly have been contrary to the Divine Will, though certainly it was not the ideal. The number of cities of refuge across the Jordan was out of proportion to the population and more numerous than those in the main sector. The feeling must have been that further away from the core of the Jewish people, standards were bound to decline. Nevertheless, Moses, with God's sanction, agreed; the ideal was not an absolute.

2

In Jewish law, the conquest and the sanctification of the land had both theological and practical ramifications. If certain laws applied to the produce of the land, the boundaries had to be defined. If settlement was in any way related to the holiness of the land, from whence did this holiness derive? The rabbis debated this issue in depth. The holiness of the land derived first of all from the invasion of Joshua[13] roughly three thousand two hundred years before, and there was a second consecration under Ezra seven hundred years later, when he established the new Jewish settlement under the auspices of the Persian Empire.[14] There is a long-running debate as to whether the sanctification of the land under Joshua was a permanent one and applied ever after or whether it was a temporary sanctification and it took the second settlement under Ezra to establish permanence.

After the Babylonian exile was, possibly, the only period in which no Jews lived in Israel at all. The Assyrians had already destroyed the Northern Kingdom in 722 B.C.E. and the Babylonians took away the upper and skilled classes in the two conquests of Judea in 597 and 586 B.C.E. They left the poor behind under the Babylonian governor-appointee, Gedalia. Gedalia was assassinated by a rival and the remnant population fled to Egypt, fearing reprisals. Perhaps the significance of the Fast of Gedalia after Rosh Hashanna is to record not just Jewish internecine wrangling and the murder of a good man but also the only time that there were no Jews at all in the Land of Israel.

The question of the sanctity of the borders was relevant primarily for issues of agriculture and tithes, but it was also important for all of those commandments that applied to the Land of Israel, the agricultural laws, the Festivals, and the calendar. Before the universal calendars were fixed by calculation, dates and times were fixed by sighting the moon and fixing the time of the new month. Once the *Beth Din* or the Sanhedrin agreed on the time, bonfires were lit to carry the message throughout Israel and then on to the Diaspora (until internal sectarianism led opponents to destroy the system by creating "false alarms").[15] Israel was vital not just because of the Temple and its service on behalf of all Jews wherever they lived, but also because of its importance as the only authority for deciding issues of the calendar, which would affect the practice and the cohesion of the overall Jewish community. After the Babylonian exile the majority of Jews no longer lived in Israel. Babylon, then

Egypt, and later Rome held greater numbers, but until the calendar was fixed, Israel retained its centrality in this sphere.

The main rivalry for authority throughout the talmudic period was between Babylon and Israel (or Judea, Palestine, or Jerusalem; the names were often interchangeable). This competition was based on the issue of who could best protect and nurture Torah study and affiliation. While the Temple was still functioning there was no question but that religious authority was vested in the Temple and in the courts surrounding it. However, the Babylonian academies became more and more powerful and exercised an increasing amount of halachic autonomy and decision-making. During the Temple period and the century afterwards the academies of Jerusalem were still elite: Hillel moved from Babylon to Israel to study and eventually become the spiritual head of the community. It was only after Rabbi Yehuda the Prince and the decline of Jerusalem Jewry following the Bar Cochba revolution that the Babylonian community moved from an inferior to a superior position religiously and academically with its powerful *yeshivot* at Sura, Pumbedita, Machoza, and Nehardea. The position of Exilarch (*Resh Galuta*) was a venerable one that traced its history back to the first exile and paralleled the *Nasi*, the head of the Jerusalem community. Both traced their lineage to King David and there are even examples of Rabbi Yehuda HaNasi in Israel deferring to Rav Huna the Exilarch in Babylon.

The Babylonian community slowly overtook the declining Palestinian communities and grew in authority during the first five hundred years of the millennium—so much so that the Babylonian Talmud was accepted as the major source text over the Yerushalmi, which had been completed much earlier but was less comprehensive. This digression is to set the scene to explain the tension and conflict that is found in the Talmud over the issue of whether or not settling in Israel is an obligation, a requirement of Jewish Law.

3

Quite apart from the agricultural laws that logically and with textual authority apply only to the Land of Israel, there are a series of laws in the Talmud that emphasize the importance of living in Israel: "Everybody (in a man's household) can be made to go up to the Land of Israel but not everyone can be made to leave. Everybody (in a man's household) can be made to up to the Land of Israel but not everyone can be made to leave. The same thing applies to males as it does to females."[16]

The Gemara expands on this: "If he wants to go up (to Israel) and she does not, he can force her to go up with him; otherwise she forfeits her marriage settlement (ketubah). If she wants to go up and he does not, he is forced to go up and if he does not want to he is forced to divorce her but he must pay her settlement. If she wants to leave (Israel) and he does not, we force her not to leave but if not she is divorced without a settlement. If he wants to leave and she does not, he is forced to stay and if not he is forced to divorce her and she is given her settlement."[17]

Interestingly, Maimonides understands the implication of this Mishna's statement about "everyone in a man's household," to mean that "A slave who wants to go up to live in Israel (one assumes for religious reasons) can force his master to go up with him."[18] The commentators on the Gemara argue about whether this is a Jewish or a non-Jewish slave. A slave had obligations to keep Torah commandments that were not related to time, but this obligation applied only in the land of Israel—hence the Mishna: "If one sells a slave to a non-Jew or to a Jew who lives outside the and of Israel, the slave automatically goes free."[19]

The rabbis declared that the land outside Israel was ritually impure.[20] The official reason given was that the dead were generally buried at random, so there was no way of knowing what ground was ritually pure and what was not.

It has been suggested that this was an economic measure to protect the potteries of Israel from foreign competition.[21] (Restrictive practices and trade barriers were as much a part of the economic realities of two thousand years ago as they are today), but it is probable that this was a way of differentiating between Israel and the Diaspora, underlining the special status of Israel with regard to vessels used for ritual purposes and, indeed, burial. There is a very ancient tradition of either sending bodies for burial in Israel, where one is buried directly into the ground without a coffin, or placing some soil from Israel in the coffin of those buried outside of Israel.

In addition to the legal issues, of which these are no more than a few samples, there are many rabbinic exhortations concerning the importance of living in Israel: "Living in Israel is as important as all of the other commandments in the Torah,"[22] "A person should always live in the Land of Israel, even in a city where most of the inhabitants are idol worshippers, rather than outside Israel, even in a city where most of the inhabitants are Jewish, because whoever lives in Israel it is as though they have a God and whoever lives outside Israel it is as though they have no God,"[23] "Rabbi Abahu said, 'Even a Canaanite maidservant who lives in the Land of Israel is guaranteed to have a place in the World to Come,'"[24] "Whoever walks four *amot* (paces) in the Land of Israel is guaranteed a place in the Next World,"[25] "Whoever is buried in the Land of Israel it is as though they were buried underneath the altar (in the Temple)." This is just a selection of statements to be found in the Talmud about the importance of the Land of Israel.

There is even a suggestion that "The air of the Land of Israel makes a person wiser."[26] In fact the rabbis of Israel thought themselves in general to be brighter and sharper intellectually than the Babylonians, whom they criticized for wearing fancy clothes to bolster up their images.[27] They also thought their relationship with other rabbis was far superior to those of the "barbaric" Babylonians.[28] The hyperbolic wording of these statements shows the strength of feelings on this issue.

The Babylonians countered with their own statements: Rabbi Yehuda said, 'Whoever goes up to Israel from Babylon goes against a positive command,'"[29] and "Rabbi Yehuda said, 'It is forbidden to leave Babylon to go up to other lands.'"[30] Nevertheless, the fact that prayers were directed toward Israel and that special prayers for Israel were part of the universal format of the *Amidah* prayer show the paramount place of the Land of Israel in Jewish ritual and thinking—this, of course, even before the Exile made the return to Zion perhaps the most important feature of Jewish life in the Diaspora. One has only to read the poetry of Yehuda HaLevy or follow the dramatic pilgrimage of Nachmanides to realize how essential the dream of returning to Zion was for the Jews of all communities during the long dark exile.

4

The miraculous reestablishment of the State of Israel in this century has raised the question of whether there is a religious obligation to return to settle in Israel. Halachically the authorities are divided. Maimonides does not include the issue in his list of the biblical commands, *Sefer HaMitzvot*. Nachmanides, the Ramban, includes the obligation to live in Israel as one of the 613 Torah commands. In his additional notes to Maimonides' list he says, "We were commanded to inherit the land that God gave our fathers, to Abraham, to Isaac, and to Jacob, and we should not leave it to any other one of the nations or leave it abandoned. . . . This is a command that applies to all generations and every individual is obliged to try to carry out this command, even nowadays in exile.[31]

In his commentary on the Torah, Nachmanides says, "'And you will inherit the land and dwell upon it for I have given it to you as an inheritance.' It is my opinion that this is a positive command that they were commanded to settle in the Land of Israel and to take it over because it was given to them." However, Rashi understands this to mean that they should drive out the inhabitants. It means, according to him, that if you are able to you will live there and if not you will not be able to carry this out.[32] Going even further, Nachmanides says that all the commandments of the Torah were given to be kept in Israel. The only obligation to keep them outside Israel is in order that they should not be forgotten.[33]

It is fair to say that most authorities do not believe there is a religious obligation to settle in Israel, important as it may be. There is a strong body of opinion that believes that it is wrong to go up in any force, based on the talmudic tradition that God made three binding vows at the moment of exile: "One was that Israel would not return to the land by force, one was that the Holy One Blessed Be He made Israel swear that they would not rebel against the Nations of the World, and one was that God made the nations swear that they would not oppress Israel more than necessary."[34] This is the source for those Chassidism who object to Zionism, not just on the grounds that the movement is a secular one but that setting up a Jewish state ahead of the Messiah goes against the will of God.

Nevertheless, throughout the time of the Diaspora Jews kept trying, albeit in small numbers, to settle in Israel. The small numbers simply reflected economic and political realities: The land was hardly able to sustain the few settlers it had. The small Jewish communities of Jerusalem and Safed were poor and exposed. The Ottomon Empire was not well disposed to a massive influx of Europeans. The episode of the seventeenth-century false messiah Shabbetai Zvi shows both the eagerness of European Jews to pick up and move and, equally, the reluctance of Turkish powers to permit an invasion.

In the nineteenth century the campaign to resettle in Israel grew in strength primarily because pressure brought to bear by Western European powers began to force open, however unpredictably, the gates of Palestine. The movement to settle in Israel was a movement that benefited from a rise in nationalistic sentiment. There were outstanding Orthodox rabbis who supported those movements, like the Hovevei Zion, who actively worked to send youngsters to Israel despite the hardships imposed by Turkish rule. Men like Rabbi Samuel Moholiver of Bialystock (1824–1898), who was associated with Hovevei Zion; his successor Yitzchak Reines; Shmuel Yaacov Rabinowitz; and many others who stood apart from affiliation to any specific movement supported and encouraged the return to Zion.

Most Orthodox rabbis opposed the political movement that became known as Zionism not so much for halachic reasons as religious ones. Zionism, as people like Herzl envisioned it and as the majority of its early activists such as Lilienblum, Pinsker, and Mandelstamm believed, would replace the old religious values associated with ghetto life, attitudes that characterized the Exile. Herzl's "Jewish State," written during the Dreyfuss manifestation of anti-Semitism in France, sought to "solve the Jewish problem" rather than enhance Jewish religion or culture. Most—though not all— of the original philosophers of Zionism certainly saw Zionism as an alternative to Judaism. This was one of the reasons why many voted for the British government's 1903 proposal to offer the Zionists a home in Uganda. There were indeed conflicting voices like that of Ahad Ha'am, who argued for the centrality of Jewishness in Zionism, but his heirs in the Revisionist movement were, for most of the century, outvoted. Hence the famous debate between Ben Gurion, the first Prime Minister, and Hadassah over whether Zionism requires one to settle in Israel. Ben Gurion argued that living in Israel was the fulfillment of the Zionist dream (regardless of whether one lived as a Jew or not). For him Zionism rather than Judaism was the supreme ideal. This upset the many supporters of Zionism who lived in America and had no intention of moving away from the United States, however strongly they supported a Jewish State.

Religious Zionism sought to combine both the idealism and the practical nationalism of Zionism with a commitment to Judaism. Out of this came the insistence that a "good Jew, a good Zionist" can live only in Israel. If during the two thousand years of exile more Jews did not go to Israel, it was not because they were not required to; it was because they could not because of political or economic realities. Now that the situation had changed, there was no reason why a Jew who wanted to adhere to the Jewish religion should not go to live in Israel. Certainly the reconquest of the West Bank after the Six Day War in 1967 gave an added religious dimension to settlement on land that had been more integral to historical Jewish settlement in Israel than many parts of the new Jewish State.

I would argue that Israel has been the powerhouse behind the post-Holocaust revival of Judaism and even with the present *kulturkampf* between Orthodox and non-Orthodox there is more Torah learning and academic scholarship in Israel than in the rest of the Jewish world combined. The fact, however, is that it is impossible to claim, unchallenged, that Jewish Law requires settlement in Israel. It may encourage it. It may be that only in Israel can one fulfill all the Torah commandments available to us. But throughout Jewish history many Jews have lived outside Israel. Once again, the variety and difference of opinion within Halacha make one absolute statement impossible.

Without doubt the Land of Israel is vital to Jewish religious life. It is one of the "Three strands that cannot easily be broken."[35] It is, together with God and Torah, what defines the Jewish people and the Jewish religion. In prayer,

in study, and in practice it is central. However the issue of
whether one has an obligation, as opposed to a desire, to
settle in Israel is another matter. The Zionist myth is that
Judaism will not survive outside Israel. Important though
Israel is in the resurgence of Jewish life, this extreme position is another example of mythic thought.

Notes

1. Genesis 15:18.
2. Genesis 15:13.
3. Genesis 21:27.
4. Genesis 23:17.
5. Numbers 33:53.
6. Leviticus 19:23.
7. Leviticus 23:10.
8. Leviticus 25:2.
9. Deuteronomy 26:1.
10. Numbers 35:9.
11. Numbers 34:2.
12. Numbers 32.
13. Talmud Bavli *Chagigah* 3b, et al.
14. Talmud Bavli *Yevamot* 82b.
15. Mishna *Rosh Hashanna* 2:2–3.
16. Mishna *Ketubot* 13.
17. Talmud Bavli *Ketubot* 110b.
18. Maimonides' *Yad HaChazaka Hilchot Avadim* 8:10.
19. Mishna *Gittin* 4:6.
20. Talmud Bavli *Shabbat* 14b.
21. Louis Finkelstein, *The Pharisees.*
22. *Tosefta Avoda Zara, Sifri* on Deuteronomy 12:29.
23. Talmud Bavli *Ketubot* 110b.
24. Talmud Bavli *Ketubot* 111a.
25. Ibid.
26. Talmud Bavli *Bava Batra* 158b.

27. Talmud Bavli *Shabbat* 145b.
28. Talmud Bavli *Sanhedrin* 24a.
29. Talmud Bavli *Ketubot* 110b.
30. Talmud Bavli *Ketubot* 111a.
31. Addition 4 to Maimonides' *Sefer HaMitzvot*.
32. Nachmanides' Commentary on Numbers 33:53.
33. Nachmanides' Commentary on Leviticus 18:25.
34. Talmud Bavli *Ketubot* 111a.
35. Ecclesiastes 4:12.

Chapter 14

Myth:
Jews Should
Be Governed
by a Theocracy

1

Do religious Jews want Israel to be a theocracy, ruled by God? What is a theocracy? Could a Jewish religious state not be a democracy or some other form of government? Of course, we would have to define democracy. "One person, one vote" was certainly not practiced by the Greeks, who excluded a whole lot of people from a say in government, and there are many different types and forms of democracy practiced around the world today. By common assent, democracy, meaning that every citizen has an equal vote, is an imperfect system. However, no one has yet come up with a better alternative. Without getting into detail, the issue is whether people in general can have a say in how they are governed as opposed to having to accept decisions handed down either by absolute rulers or by religious leadership.

The first example of governance that the Children of Israel had was Moses. The uniqueness of Moses lay in his special relationship with God: "If there is a prophet, I make Myself known to him in a vision, I speak to him in a dream. Not so My servant Moses; he is the most trustworthy in My Household. Mouth to mouth I speak to him and in a vision that is not a riddle and he can see an image of God."[1] He was the undoubted—if not the undisputed leader—of the Children of Israel. If the narrative of the exodus confirms one thing, it is that no leadership ever goes unchallenged. It also shows the difficulties of government and of handling a restive population. More than once Moses asks for permission to retire or even die (to be blotted out of God's book).

However, Moses does not govern alone. His brother Aharon was his mouthpiece: "Aharon your brother the Levite, I know he can speak . . . And you will speak to him and put words into his mouth and I will be with your mouth and with his I will teach you what to do."[2] It is also clear that there was already, in Egypt, a form of Jewish leadership by elders because Moses is told, "Go and gather together the elders of Israel."[3] Perhaps Moses felt that he had to take over completely from old forms of governance because later in Exodus Jethro, Moses' father-in-law, sees that Moses is exhausting himself and suggests delegation to "officers over thousands, officers over hundreds, officers over fifties, and officers over tens. And they are to judge the people regularly and anything that is too difficult, they bring to Moses and anything small they can judge."[4]

The actual appointment of seventy elders who are inspired by God does not occur until later in the Torah.[5] There is some ambiguity about the actual timing. It is an accepted tradition in the Talmud that when Moses came down from Sinai he taught the Torah to the elders. Were these the original ones or the later appointed ones? Either way there must have been some leadership role for the elders. According to the Midrash the transmission of the Torah went like this: "Moses learnt from God (literally 'The Greatness'). In came Aharon and Moses taught him his study. Aharon moved and sat to the left of Moses and two his sons came in and Moses taught them their study. Then they moved and Elazar sat to the right of Moses and Itamar to the left of Aharon. . . . Then the elders came in and Moses taught them and then all the people came in and Moses taught them."[6] This was the hierarchy that existed as the first system of governance.

The first test of the overall system came when Joshua fought his battle against Amalek. The religious leadership was in no position to lead the warriors into battle, so Moses sent his general out to fight and sat overlooking the fray to show his involvement. He had Aharon on one side and Chur on the other and they supported hum during the course of the battle, in which his hands pointing up to God signified the moral dimension to the battle. This incident indicates that below Moses there were three levels of leadership: Aharon, representing the priesthood and the spiritual heritage; Chur, the representative of the elders and the political assistant; and Joshua, the military leader.[7]

When Moses went up Sinai he left Aharon and Chur and the elders in charge.[8] Chur is never heard of again. The Talmud suggests he tried to stop the people who wanted to make the golden calf and was assassinated.[9]

There is a clear command to establish a judiciary[10] and to have a court of appeal with a dual role for the priesthood and a chief judge.[11] In Deuteronomy there is the controversial command about appointing a king: "When you come into the land that YHVH your God is giving to you and you inherit it and live in it and if you say I will appoint a king over me like all the other nations around me. You may indeed appoint a king whom YHVH your God will choose. From amongst your brothers you should appoint a king. You may not appoint a stranger who is not your brother. But he should not have too many horses and not take the people back to Egypt to get even more horses because YHVH your God has said you will not return again this way. And he should not have too many wives so that they will not turn his heart, or too much silver and gold. And when he sits upon the throne of his kingdom he should write a copy of this Torah on a book before the priests and the Levites. And it should be with him and he should read from it all his days so that he learns to fear YHVH his God and to keep all the words of this Torah and these laws to keep them. So that his heart does not rise above his brothers to turn away from the commandments right or left."[12] The constitution, the Torah, is above any individual and not even the king is above the law (although later the rabbis compromised and agreed that the king was in a special position).[13]

This is a very important principle, remarkable in the fact that it is so far in advance of its time. In fact, the issue of whether the king is above the law was famously challenged by King Yannai in conflict with Simon ben Shetach.[14] The aggressive behavior of the king and the passivity of the other rabbis led to a decision that the king was indeed above the law and the rabbis sought to explain the principle of Deuteronomy as applying only to the Davidic line. This of course hints at what the importance of the return of a descendant of King David meant to the Jewish people, dreaming of an honest and spiritual leadership and why messianism seemed so dependent on the reinstatement of the Davidic dynasty.

Rabbi Nehorai claims that this law was simply a concession to the complaints of the people whereas Rabbi Yossi sees this as a positive command that is a requirement.[15] Maimonides takes this to be one of the positive commands of the Torah.

2

The Torah presents a range of governing possibilities: The priesthood, the prophet, the Judge, and elders. In fact, Moses appointed Joshua to succeed him without appointing him as king. If kingship was the natural state the Torah required, one may wonder Moses did not choose it. Joshua gave way to a series of leaders called "the Judges," who were leaders of different tribal groupings and rarely commanded the loyalty of all the children of Israel. Famous names such as Samson, Jephtah, Gideon, Ehud, and Devorah seem to have had different qualities and strengths but none was able to unite the people or to get them to follow the Torah of Moses, until Samuel finally emerges as a generally accepted Judge. Throughout this period the priesthood seems to have been ineffectual. Eli, Samuel's mentor, was the great exception of course, but his sons seemed to have lost moral authority.[16]

When the people come to Samuel asking for a king he is strongly opposed. He sees this as an example of preference for military leadership over spiritual leadership: "And it was bad in the eyes of Samuel when the people said, 'Give us a king to judge us.' And Samuel prayed to God. And God said to Samuel, 'Listen to the voice of the people and to what they are saying to you. It is not you that they are rejecting but Me.'"[17] Whether because of their motives or because of his disagreement with the idea, Samuel does not take the appointment of a king, initially, as a religious requirement.

Nevertheless, from Saul and then David onward, the favored form of government was the king, with the priesthood as a hereditary aristocracy given charge of the Temple and, in theory, educating and judging the masses. Yet the role of the priesthood as the fount of spiritual authority seems to have passed rapidly to the prophets. The classic example is Nathan's assault on King David after he took Bathsheba from Uriah the Hittite.[18] One wonders why the priests did not intervene. If it was because Nathan was inspired by God one is bound to wonder why no priest merited this communication directly from God. One can understand the role of Elijah and Elisha in the Northern Kingdoms because the Northern breakaway from the Jerusalem priesthood would

have weakened the place of priests in the hierarchy. Nevertheless the priests as well as the prophets who emerged exercised different forms of spiritual authority. The Priesthood
was the voice of "organized," established religion, while the
prophet was not appointed or elected or voted into office,
but emerged solely on the basis of his or her own personality and talents. They were the charismatic voice of God and
spirituality. One might guess that the prophet was a prod-
uct of the mystical tradition, in contrast with the priesthood,
which stuck closely to a constitution that guaranteed it
privileges of tithes and sacrifices. Certainly in both cases
they were under the political power of the king, in both the
North and the South.

The Torah also includes the *Urim* and the *Thummim*,
the Jewish equivalent of the Oracle of Delphi, in the equa-
tion of leadership. The stones engraved with the names of
the tribes on the breastplate worn by the High Priest could
be consulted on a range of issues. The stones would highlight certain letters that the priest would interpret for the
king. The *Urim* and the *Thummim* disappeared during the
First Temple times and so did not play a part in the thinking of the rabbis as to how political leadership should develop. Similarly, the loss of prophecy later on also took the
prophet out of the picture of governance.

3

The last Judean kings and their families were exiled to
Babylon, where their positions gave them authority and led
to the office of Exilarch. Zerubavel, who was from the royal
family, led the initial return to Judea, but there is no
evidence that he was declared a king. We can only guess as
to whether this was because the Persians did not want
to raise hopes of complete independence or whether the
Jews themselves felt that it was time to move beyond the

manifestly incompetent leadership system that had led them to exile.

Ezra, the mastermind behind the reestablishment of the Second Commonwealth, is considered almost as great as Moses: "Ezra was fit to have had the Torah given through him had not Moses come before him."[19] The testimony of the books of Ezra and Nechemia evidence his remarkable job of reinstating the rule of Torah and renewing the credibility of the priesthood. The Talmud credits him with a series of innovations, among them the establishment of the Sanhedrin (to be accurate the name "Sanhedrin" did not appear till the time of Greek influence later on; the more accurate term would be *Beth Din HaGadol*) as the judicial authority of the community.[20]

The Sanhedrin, sitting in the "hewed stone chamber" of the Temple, fixed times and dates for the community throughout the Diaspora as well as in Israel. From this moment on the Sanhedrin became the model for Jewish governance. It was essentially a meritocracy: One had to earn one's place by study and achievement. It is true that it was a self-perpetuating body, but the moral and legal requirements of the Torah were there as an objective test and standard for entry. Indeed the Talmud sees the Sanhedrin as originating with Moses, existing at the time of King David[21] and Mordecai and Esther.[22] This underscores the importance that the rabbis attached to the institution. It judged, in theory, king and priest, rabbi and commoner.[23]

The Sanhedrin was the nominal authority, throughout the Second Temple, though the government changed. Internally the battle between Sadduccee and Pharisee meant that there were constant power struggles, while Alexander the Great brought the Jewish state under Greek domination. During the post-Alexander battle between the Ptolemies and the Seleucids, the priests and the Sanhedrin constantly called on outside powers to intervene in their internal battles. The High Priesthood became the senior position and gave its holder the virtual power of local king. Even within the priesthood itself rival clans battled for political supremacy. When, as with the Hasmoneans, a period of autonomy was allowed, the Jewish king played one party against the other, but as the later Hasmonean kings battled between themselves and spent more time ingratiating themselves with the Romans, the Sanhedrin took over more and more of the internal workings of the Jewish religion. After the destruction of the Second Temple and the transfer to Yavneh, the Sanhedrin was the undisputed source of Jewish authority for almost two hundred years.

The actual leadership, as opposed to the judiciary, of the Jerusalem community was divided between Zugot, Pairs, the head of the *Beth Din* and the Academy, and the Prince, the head of the community. A similar pattern existed in Babylon. That is, over and above the judiciary there were titular heads, the equivalent of a President. But already, under this system, local communities had forms of local government administered by officials either appointed or elected. There were the *gabbaei tsedaka*, whose job it was to collect and distribute charity,[24] sometimes appointed by the *Beth Din* and sometimes locally. There were the Seven Good Men of a City, who functioned to make crucial decisions like shutting down a synagogue.[25] They were appointed by the citizens of the city,[26] a clear indication of the rights of citizens to determine who would represent them, although there is no indication whether the citizens of a city were defined on the basis of residence or property ownership. It would make sense to suggest that thirty-day residence gave a person rights since this is the period required for fixing a *mezuzah* on one's living quarters and being eligible for local poor support. The clearest evidence of popular involvement in public appointments is in the statement "One does not appoint a *parnass* (official) unless one consults the community."[27] Here there is a very clear precedent for political consultation and indeed for some sort of democracy in appointments. Local citizens also had the right to fix market prices, weights and measures, and workers' wages and the right to impose their decisions.[28] The language used implies that all the citizens shared in the decision-making process.

There is one remarkable incident that cannot be passed over and this is the vote to depose Rabbi Gamliel as head of the academy. There are three different versions in the Talmud of how Rabbi Gamliel humiliated Rabbi Yehoshua on the issue of when Yom Kippur fell and whether the evening service was obligatory or voluntary. In both cases Rabbi Yehoshua deferred to Rabbi Gamliel but the humiliation continued. Rabbi Akiva led a revolt that deposed Rabbi Gamliel and replaced him, temporarily, with Rabbi Elazar ben Azariah.[29] However sacrosanct the religious leadership was, it could be challenged. Admittedly this was a challenge of peers and not democracy in the sense that we understand it, but it says something very clear about the nature of the government.

4

Sadly, throughout the Second Commonwealth outsiders interfered with Jewish affairs and internal divisions gave government a bad name. This is reflected in the different attitudes in the Mishna to *reshut*, the ruling power. Shemaya said, "Love work, hate authority, and have nothing to do with the ruling power."[30] Clearly Shemaya is referring to Roman rule here although his words might equally apply to a puppet Jewish regime, of which there were many in the two centuries on either side of the Common Era. Rabbi Gamliel, living some two hundred years after Shemaya, said, "Be careful of the ruling power because they only come close to a person at a time when it benefits them; they appear friendly when they can benefit but they will not stand by a person when he is in need,"[31] a bitter comment on the experience he must have had as head of the Jewish community, dealing with local Roman officials. On the other hand stands the opinion of Rabbi Chanina, an officer of the priesthood: "Pray for the welfare of the ruling power, for without fear of them a man would swallow up his neighbor alive,"[32] a cynical opinion of human nature preempting Hobbes's comment fifteen hundred years later that men are "nasty and brutish."

With the breakdown of the Jerusalem community during the third and fourth centuries and the dispersion of more and more Jews to new centers in the Diaspora, the governing of Jewish communities became more local and more varied. Medieval rabbinic responsa show that it was assumed that citizens of a town, or members of a Jewish community, had a say in the running of their own affairs. Even though the basis in the Talmud is tenuous, there is evidence both of the principal of "No taxation without representation" and of the right of citizens to have a say in their government even if they had no property or assets. In Christian Europe the Jews belonged to either the King or the Church. Often they were given control of their internal affairs with the proviso that they supplied money to their "owners" in exchange for a respite from persecution. To whom the king delegated this internal authority varied from time to time and from place to place. The most famous and most powerful example, for a time, was in Eastern Europe. The Vaad Arbaa Aratzot of sixteenth-century Poland had both rabbinic and lay representation, as did many of the administrative committees that were established throughout Europe to manage Jewish affairs.

In the eighteenth century, emancipation created a new set of circumstances. In various stages Jews began to be treated as citizens of their states. Their communities were governed by state-decreed organizations like the Consistoire in France, which became the pattern for those countries through which Napolean had traveled. Under Islam, persecution was less harsh. Jews were officially *dhimmis*; second-class citizens like Christians and other non-Muslims, they too were subject to the varying whims of their overlords and governance varied. Privileged Jews like the Duke of Naxos ran their own affairs and those of the communities under their care. Others were less fortunate. The Ottomans allowed a great deal of internal independence to each religious minority under the overall control of the Empire. Over the past two hundred years Jews have lived under a whole range of different political and economic regimes, some more tolerant than others, some more cruel. The guiding principle has been "The Law of the Land (on civil matters) is the Law."[33] No single pattern of government has achieved unanimous approval. All halachic experts have agreed that a Jew choosing to live in a land and under a legal system has an obligation to obey the law of the land. The only way out is emigration.

It is not possible to say that any one form of economic theory or fiscal policy is a "Jewish" policy. We can see clearly from the Torah that consultation in one form or another is required and we can see that there are obligations on the citizenry. Obligations exist as religious imperatives on the community to take responsibility for the poor and the disadvantaged, and on those who have to help those who have not. These obligations are enforceable. Any form of policy that does not include this within its area of concern would be failing in its duty. Which type of fiscal system best ensures this is open to debate. Capitalism may place the emphasis on individual freedom to accumulate wealth, but most capitalist systems still subsidize and support to varying degrees welfare, health, and education for the weaker members of its society. Conversely, those Marxist systems that supposedly put the people before financial success have often tended to provide less well in the long run for their citizens because their fiscal policies failed to generate the wealth needed for government welfare. The broader moral imperatives of Judaism allow flexibility to explore different policies and systems of government. The requirement of Torah is to subject them to constant analysis and scrutiny.

5

There are two models at which we should look in considering a religiously approved form of government. Throughout the period of exile, Jewish thinkers (and even Napoleon) have returned to the model of the Sanhedrin as the ideal system of government. The historical desire to see the House of David restored as part of a messianic Golden Era did not negate the idea of the Sanhedrin as the constitutional means of government. The Davidic line was a magnificent symbol of leadership that combined military strength and power with the capacity to sing and write psalms in praise of God—the ideal combination. It was also the symbol of a period in which there was no foreign oppression or *shibud malchuyot*, "domination by alien nations." There was still room in a messianic world for an Elijah to solve problems or for a Sanhedrin to administer the rules and deal with daily issues.

The Talmud describes the Sanhedrin in these idealistic terms: "Rabbi Yochanan said one does not appoint on the Sanhedrin anyone who is not a man of wisdom, of fine appearance, of height, of age, familiar with magic, and speaking seventy languages so that the Sanhedrin does not have to rely on interpreters."[34] The reasoning is clear: the members should be in a position to evaluate evidence without the personal nuances that a translator might give and without the tricks that clever illusionists might use to persuade or delude. The members would be independent and of such ideal character and free from any human frailty that pure justice would prevail. The ideal is of absolute independence of mind. The realistic likelihood of this is minimal. After all, Shimon ben Shetach, quoted above, could not find such a

Sanhedrin strong enough to stand up to King Yanai. Nevertheless, in examining the possibility one should bear in mind that the Sanhedrin then and in the theoretical future could not function in a vacuum. "Experts" were consulted to testify in a way very similar to the select committees and hearings that are a major part of congressional, senatorial, and parliamentary life nowadays. Just as a rabbi giving advice on medical issues calls on the latest expert medical knowledge, so too a government would be expected to call on economists and industrialists to advise on legislation.

When people talk about theocracy they can intend different things. Literally it can mean "the rule of God," but the Torah and its development have already taken us into a situation where the development of Halacha has become a human process, albeit within ordained guidelines as the story of Achinai's Oven,[35] quoted in an earlier chapter, indicates. The Sanhedrin would classify as "the rule of rabbis" rather than of God, something many find as frightening as the rule of God. Of course, there is a difference between "the rule of rabbis" and the rule of democratic institutions given rabbinic guidance. In the end it depends on the package, and the history of Jewish self-government is such that accommodations are always possible. Just as the *Beth Din* had tremendous leeway to impose punishments or to desist from applying them, from detention to the death penalty, so too the *Beth Din* could negotiate different forms of advisory and consultative bodies with varying functions. It is wrong to suggest that there is no room for democratic institutions in Judaism—just as it is incorrect to suggest that Judaism has nothing to contribute to political decision making.

On a practical level the Jewish model would be a country run according to Jewish Law, which could easily accommodate civil and spiritual issues that are the day-to-day business of any legal system. The current Israeli system is a dual-track one. Officially Israeli law is an amalgam of Ottoman, British Mandate, Jewish, and hybrid law but citizens can choose a parallel system of judges applying only Torah law. Both systems are manned by government appointees. Over and above the judiciary sits the Knesset. The role of a democratically elected parliament would be to function as they do in most Western democracies, and the Sanhedrin could function both as an upper house subjecting legislation to scrutiny based on spiritual considerations and as a court of higher appeal.

The second example for a modern style of government is, surprisingly, a constitutional monarchy. The rabbis experienced absolute monarchs and sought to justify their authority. Originally, according to the Torah the king was subject to Jewish Law and not above it, but as circumstances changed so too did their attitude. They allowed the king to be above the law in his responsibility for maintaining Law and Order:[36] "Rabbi Joseph said, 'They only said this of the kings of Israel (the Northern apostate kingdom) but the kings of the David House both judge and are judged.'"[37] In one of the discussions on the principle of "The Law of the Kingdom is the Law," the Rashbam (replacing Rashi's commentary) says, "All taxes, impositions and custom charges instituted by kings for the running of their kingdom are the law because the members of the kingdom willingly accept them upon themselves to obey the laws of the king and his statutes. Therefore it is an absolute law."[38] In deciding how to run his country a king could choose the details of the form of government that he felt appropriate. His absolute power extended, ironically, to imposing a form of government that could even limit his own constitutional power. There is no reason why a king should not decide that democracy, for example, is the most appropriate way to run his country.

In other words, it is possible to see a model for government that takes the spiritual as its guiding imperative without it being tarred with the brush of theocracy, which implies no useful role either for lay men and women or for democracy. We are still evolving our ideas of the ideal form of government. In the West there are plenty of arguments still to be decided on voting systems and on effective governance.

The point of this is to emphasize that traditional Jewish models still have something useful and positive to contribute to the debate and are still relevant as possible forms of government. They could incorporate many of the ideas we admire in present systems, while adding dimensions that many of feel are sadly absent. The checks and balances of the Sanhedrin model would avoid the extreme of secularism and amorality on the one hand and Khomeniism on the other.

Meanwhile, unfortunately, there is such animosity between and within different religious groups—not to mention the gap in Israel between the religious and the secular—that there is little likelihood of this situation becoming more than academic in our lifetime. One can hardly envision the gamut of Chassidic groups coming together under one authority, let alone the rest! Nevertheless, as with the Messiah the Jewish tradition encourages us to think, to believe, to plan, and to hope for a better form of government as well as for a better and more equitable form of society. The myth is that there is one specific form of government that can be said to be Divinely ordained.

Notes

1. Numbers 12:6–8.
2. Exodus 4:14.
3. Exodus 3:16.
4. Exodus 18:25–26.
5. Numbers 11:24.
6. Talmud Bavli *Eiruvin* 54b.
7. Exodus 17:10.
8. Exodus 24:14.
9. Talmud Bavli *Sanhedrin* 7a.

10. Deuteronomy 16:18.
11. Deuteronomy 17:8–9.
12. Deuteronomy 17:14–20.
13. Talmud Bavli *Sanhedrin* 18a.
14. Talmud Bavli *Sanhedrin* 19a
15. Talmud Bavli *Sanhedrin* 20b.
16. 1 Samuel 2.
17. 1 Samuel 8:6–7.
18. 2 Samuel 12.
19. Talmud Bavli *Sanhedrin* 21b.
20. Talmud Yerushalmi *Megillah* 4:1.
21. Talmud Bavli *Brachot* 4a.
22. Talmud Bavli *Megillah* 16b.
23. Talmud Bavli *Yoma* 19a.
24. Talmud Bavli *Pesachim* 49a.
25. Talmud Bavli *Megillah* 21a.
26. Ibid. and Talmud Bava *Metziah* 106a.
27. Talmud Bavli *Brachot* 55a.
28. *Tosefta Bava Metzia* 11:23.
29. *Tosefta Bava Metzia* 27b.
30. Mishna *Avot* 1:10.
31. Mishna *Avot* 2:3.
32. Mishna *Avot* 3:2.
33. Talmud Bavli *Gittin* 10b.
34. Talmud Bavli *Menachot* 65a.
35. Talmud Bavli *Bava Metzia* 59b.
36. Mishna *Sanhedrin* 4.
37. Talmud Bavli *Sanhedrin* 19a.
38. Talmud Bavli *Bava Batra* 54b, Rashbam loc. cit.

Chapter 15

Myth:
Sex and Religion Do
Not Go Together

1

Sex is good. So religious people can't really approve, can they? Growing up in a Christian world and in a world that also contains very strong reactions against its values, we are inevitably influenced by the attitudes of the dominant culture. Nowhere is this more evident than in matters of sexuality. The ideal Catholic person is the celibate Pope. The Dalai Llama is single too. In Judaism our leaders are expected, indeed required, to be married and have children. Why the difference?

The Christian attitudes are very much influenced by the story of the fall of man and Original Sin. Adam and Eve disobey God.[1] They eat from the fruit of the tree forbidden by God. It is an interesting assumption that the fruit was an apple. The text does not say so—but in Latin an apple is *malum* and, similarly, evil is *malum* too. Perhaps that is where the idea came from. The Jewish tradition suggests a fig, because they covered themselves with fig leaves (D. H. Lawrence would appreciate the relevance of that given his use of the fig as a sexual symbol). Alternatively it suggests the vine, given the dramatic impact its fruit can have on people behaving in an irrational and degrading way. The Talmud also proposes corn as the fruit because it is the very basis of the human diet.[2] Whatever the fruit was, the act of disobedience led to Adam and Eve realizing that they were naked.

Before Adam and Eve disobeyed God, the Torah says, "And they were both naked and they were not ashamed."[3] Afterwards it says that Adam excused himself: "And he said, 'I heard Your voice in the garden and I was frightened because I was naked and I hid.' And He (God) said, 'Who told you that you are naked? Did you eat from the tree I commanded you not to eat from?'"[4] Was it the eating of the fruit or the act of disobeying God that transformed man? The Jewish tradition sees this as the "first sin" but not as "Original Sin." The difference is that Original Sin causes humanity henceforth to exist in a state of sin from which only Grace can rescue it. Human beings are seen as essentially evil, by nature, from birth. For Judaism this incident in the Torah was one example of how humans can and do disobey God and find themselves more limited as a result, not freer as they might think. Obedience to God helps humanity fulfill its potential and make the world a better place. Disobedience leads to domination, corruption, and the realization that a good and natural process such as sexuality can be used as a weapon of exploitation and inhumanity. It was this realization, that anything can be abused and that sexuality is perhaps the primal tool of abuse, that made man ashamed of his nakedness.

The original scheme of creation put human beings in a special position. They were given a garden to tend and to protect and one simple instruction, but that was not enough to keep them on the "straight and narrow." They failed and were exiled and had to cope with a harsher reality. In this situation, man had already discovered that companionship meant more than simply physical gratification. He might have found that among the animals who passed before him and whom he named,[5] but he did not. It is immediately after this that God decides than man needs a companion. The companion is symbolically taken from the ribcage, which protects the heart. This asserts the fact that sexuality is only one dimension of the male-female relationship. The phrase "support alongside him"[6] reiterates the relationship rather than simply the means of procreation. It is crucial that the word for sexual union is "knowledge."[7] Knowledge of a person is far more than simply knowing how to do something.

2

Is sexuality seen as something bad or negative in the Torah? Not in itself; however, its abuse is a major theme: "The sons of the judges (or however one wants to translate the ambiguous Hebrew) took the daughters of man as they chose."[8] What was wrong, it appears, was the act of choosing wherever men felt like it, an act of selfish gratification and domination rather than willing partnership. That this attitude continued after the Flood is evidenced by the incident in which Abraham, fearing for his life because of Sarah's beauty, tries to protect himself by saying that she is his sister.[9] It must have been common, at that time, to kill a man to take his wife. The real issue that the Torah emphasizes is that the abuse of sexuality was perhaps the major underlying evil of pagan society. We know from archeological evidence that many of the things the Torah specifically outlaws—Temple prostitution, sex with animals, and giving oneself to whoever comes along as a religious rite—were common features of contemporary society. This atmosphere that prevailed among the Canaanite tribes was the reason for their being driven and replaced: "It is not because of your righteousness or your honest hearts that you are going to inherit their land. But it is because of the wickedness of these nations."[10] The list of forbidden sexual acts in the Torah is prefaced by this introduction: "Do not behave like the Egyptians amongst whom you lived and do not follow the behavior of the land of Canaan where I am bringing you. Do not follow their laws."[11]

Despite the list of forbidden marriages, nowhere is there any suggestion that celibacy is acceptable or that marriage is in any way a concession. Not only that, but the Torah actually specifies the legal obligations of marriage, which include sexual activity (of course, there are other aspects to a marriage relationship but these are far more difficult to legislate). The three obligations of marriage are "food, clothing, and sex."[12]

If the Torah did not see man as basically evil and sexually corrupt, how did the Torah view human behavior? Was man seen as essentially good or evil? Despite the repeated failure of mankind to live the sort of life of which God approved and despite God's repeated disappointment with mankind, nowhere is man described as evil from birth. However, there is something called the *yetzer*, the "inclination," that seems to be the cause of evil rather than man himself. It is as though man is neutral but is led by this inclination to do "bad" things: "And God saw that the evil of man was increasing on earth and that the inclination of the thoughts of his heart were only bad all the day."[13] We can only guess at the intention of the original test. "Heart" is usually the code word for emotions, with "head" being the code for intellect. Thus it is the tendency of emotion to mislead mankind that is to blame. Does this tendency come inborn as a sort of instinct? The Torah says that after the Flood, "God said in His heart, 'I will not continue to curse the ground any more because of man, for the inclination in the heart of man is bad from his youth.'"[14] The tendency does not come with birth but from youth. Humans learn to abuse and misuse from a very early age. It almost sounds Freudian.

When man is created the first record uses the word *vayivra*, "And He created."[15] The second time, the word used is *vayitzer*, "And He fashioned," and the word has two letters *yud* in it. The rabbis use this to make the homiletic point that God created man with two inclinations, a good one and a bad one. [16] However, the so-called "bad" one is not completely bad: "Without the bad inclination a man would never get married or build a house or plant a vineyard."[17] To support the idea that the evil inclination is not inbuilt, they said, "The evil inclination starts as a guest and afterwards becomes the owner of the house."[18] The two are in a state of constant competition for control. Man is caught up in this struggle and has to find ways of enabling the good inclination to triumph. "A person should always excite his good inclination against the bad one,"[19] and the rabbis give advice along the lines of studying Torah and keeping oneself busy.

The rabbis were very much aware of the power of temptation: "There are two things a person really deeply desires: sex and theft."[20] There seems to be a solution for someone who has difficulty coping: "If a man feels that his inclination is getting too strong for him he should go to a place where no one recognizes him and dress in black and cover himself in black and do what his heart desires and not desecrate the name of heaven in public."[21] The commentators disagree as to whether this was meant literally and he could act on it (Rashi) or whether the point was to find a way of delaying and cooling off (*Tosafot*). Either way, the rabbis recognize the difficulties of the constant battle with sexual urges but do not suggest that it is an evil that is intrinsic.

The attitude to sin in general is less harsh in the biblical tradition than it is in others. There is no "state" of sin into which one falls, only habits. The words used for sin all indicate an action that takes one off the straight and narrow: *avera* (to pass by), *cheyt* (to miss the mark), *avon* (to mistake), or *pesha* (to fall short). The implication is that one can easily correct the error by getting it right or stepping back on the track. This is the function of *teshuva*, "repentance," which literally means "to return." Nowadays this is a process that, broadly speaking, anyone can do at anytime. There is no need for priestly intervention. In the past there was a procedure that involved first putting right anything wrong done either to another person or to God. This would be followed by a confession, a private and personal statement to God accepting and specifying what one had done wrong. These procedures were required before one could proceed with the sacrifice of atonement, which was a ritual confirmation and penalty.

The general term for sexual misdemeanor is *gilui arayot*, "revealing nudity" or "that which should not be revealed." It seems there is no odium attached to the act of sex itself but rather to the effect it has when it used wrongly (interestingly, there is no special word for incest). To reveal what is hidden can be a good and necessary process under some circumstances, but it can also be a negative one. Some things need uncovering; others do not. This dual use of a word is an important feature of the Hebrew language. The word for "holy," *KaDoSH*, is also the word for a prostitute, *KaDeSH*.[22] The word "to sin," *CHeT*, is also the word used for cleansing the altar or other vessels.[23] The word for "kindness," *CHeSeD* is also the word for corruption.[24] There are other examples but these specifically in the sexual context emphasize that it is not the act of sex that is wrong but the misuse of it. The context is what decides the morality of an act.

The mood of the Torah on sexual matters seems to us nowadays to be remarkably tolerant. The incident of Judah and Tamar is primarily concerned with the honesty of Tamar rather than with the behavior of Judah,[25] and there is no direct suggestion that Judah was wrong. On the other hand Joseph is admired for not giving in to Potiphar's wife's entreaties,[26] but this is because she was a married woman and the issue was more of betrayal than of sexuality.

The Torah even makes certain concessions to the sexual urge. In battle a man may face all kinds of temptations and the law of the beautiful captive allowed a man to take a woman home (there is a debate among the authorities as to whether or not he was allowed to give in to his urges in the heat of battle).[27] One might wonder at the relaxed approach of the Bible to the story of Esther. She is forced to enter the competition to find a wife for Ahasuerus and becomes the queen of a non-Jewish monarch. Some rabbis have her being taken forcibly; others suggest it was a plan devised by Mordecai. The Talmud has a fascinating range of opinions about what she ate (kosher or vegetarian) and about whether or not she continued to sleep with both Mordecai and with Ahasuerus.[28] This uncensored discussion says a great deal about the relaxed and positive attitude of the Jewish tradition toward sexuality.

3

The biblical laws of marriage require, as we have mentioned, a man to provide for his wife sexually: "Her maintenance, her clothing, and her sexual satisfaction"[29] are required and grounds for compelling a husband to divorce if not met. Of course, one can point to a great deal of inequality in sexual matters. The male could have more than one wife. The master could give his female servants for procreation. The father could betroth his underage daughter. The permission to divorce[30] could be seen both as an advantage and as a disadvantage to women. It was an advantage in that it might free her from an unhappy marriage, but it might be a disadvantage in removing her from financial and social security. In some circles a divorcee was forced back into her parents' house and kept in a position of virtual slavery. This is why the rabbis later sought to ensure that divorcees had some financial security. Nevertheless, divorce is inscribed in Jewish law and approved as a way of avoiding hatred and tension. Any odium attached to divorce has been absorbed from non-Jewish society. The qualification of not taking back a divorced wife after she remarries [31] could be seen as a way of trying to prevent the frivolous use of divorce. My aim here is not to try to explain away anything that seems problematic to our twentieth-century conventions but simply to underline the very different attitude that the Torah evinces toward sexuality at a time before external values came to be imposed on Jewish thinking.

The Torah and the rabbis set down very strict rules about with whom one could have sex. It is possible to come up with theories to explain them, just as people try with the dietary laws. There are historical and utilitarian explanations. There are mystical and rational ones. In the end they are part and parcel of the unique Jewish experience that by its own account is beyond human logic. In order to reinforce these laws in what is an extremely delicate, not to say passionate area, they set down additional rules to act as buffers, such as not being alone with someone one could not marry and not even touching, let alone kissing, those with whom intercourse is barred.[32] Sex with an unmarried woman or someone eligible for marriage was seen in biblical times to be in itself a quasi act of marriage; if one did not complete the process there were penalties. Premarital sex was forbidden both because it would have devalued the woman on the marriage market and because it might have threatened the system of early betrothal that applied commonly in earlier times. We may find these ideas strange but they still hold sway in many parts of the world to this day, and death is often meted out to those who infringe these conventions.

In addition to limiting whom one can marry, the Torah also forbids intercourse during a woman's period.[33] This had the practical effect of preventing sex before marriage since one could have sex only after going to the Mikvah, the ritual pool, something confined to married women. But it also had the effect of strengthening sexual excitement within marriage by creating monthly periods of abstinence that heightened attraction and desire within marriage itself. One is reluctant to suggest that this was the utilitarian reason for the law, but it certainly is an effect. All of these negative regulations were intended simply to shift the emphasis in a positive way onto married life and sex within marriage.

4

The Talmud looks at sex within marriage from two angles. Everyone agrees that there is a positive command to reproduce. The schools of Hillel and Shammai argue about when one can be said to have fulfilled this command: with a boy and a girl or two boys.[34] There is also disagreement as to whether the obligation applies only to men or also to women. Everyone agrees that sex is a requirement and that there is something lacking in a person who is not married and has not participated in intercourse. The Mishna discusses the obligation of sex this way: "The amount required (to fulfill the Torah obligation to have sex with one's wife) is: for men of leisure, every day; laborers, twice a week; donkey drivers (who travel limited distances), once a week; camel drivers (who are away for longer stretches), once in thirty days; and sailors, once in six months according to Rabbi Eliezer."[35]

There is disagreement about the attitude one should take toward sexuality, hardly surprising given the inevitable influence of Greek thought. Some rabbis took the view that draws from the Stoic school: The world has two substances, spirit and matter. Spirit is superior and matter is inferior. Anything material is inevitably a handmaiden of the spirit. Sexuality therefore is a necessary procedure for reproduction but something that should be regarded as a necessity rather than a pleasure. This approach is best illustrated by this conversation: "They asked Imma Shalom, 'Why are your children so good-looking?' She replied, '(My husband) does not talk with me (a euphemism for sex) at the beginning of the night or at the end but in the middle, and when he talks he reveals a *tephach* (of nakedness) and then covers a *tephach* and he behaves as though an evil spirit was forcing him.'"[36] This very Stoic approach sees intercourse as a requirement to be taken seriously and with the objective of satisfying one's wife. It is not the basis for the myth that Orthodox Jews make love through a hole in a sheet (the only time I have ever come across this custom was in a film by a Mexican Catholic). Of course, nowadays we might be inclined to think that self-control and partial detachment is good advice for prolonging lovemaking. How the rabbis conducted themselves during intercourse was even considered part of Torah education. Rabbi Kahana crept under the bed of Rav Shemaya and heard him talk and laugh before he had intercourse. When he remonstrated he replied, "It is Torah and I have a duty to learn."[37] The question of modesty was very important: "One should not have intercourse by day, or in front of children."[38] But there is no dispute about the importance of pleasing one's wife: "It is forbidden to force one's wife even if it is for a *mitzvah* (of reproduction)."[39]

The other point of view regards sexuality as a Divine gift and pleasure, to be indulged in with enthusiasm (as well as moderation). The Gemara quotes Rabbi Yochanan as saying, "Whatever a man wants to do with his wife he may do," which is elsewhere qualified that of course this must be with her consent. There is even a sort of Epicurean strain in the Talmud. Two rabbis who traveled around Babylon as teachers and judges would come into town and declare, "Who will be my wife for a night?"[40] The Gemara is divided as to whether this was literally the case or just a device for avoiding temptation. It was recognized that the sexual urge was a very powerful one: "Theft and sexuality are the things that man most strongly desires and wants."[41] This was one of the reasons that marriage was encouraged at as early an age as possible. The general rule was that eighteen was ideal, twenty at the latest, and according to Rav Chisda fourteen would be desirable.[42]

The *Shulchan Aruch* tries to incorporate both positions: "As a man's wife is permitted to him, he may do whatever he wants, to have intercourse at any time and to kiss anywhere he wants and to have intercourse in any position and in any way . . . but when he has intercourse it should be like someone paying a debt because of his duty to reproduce. . . . He should not have intercourse against his wife's wishes and if she is not in the mood he should try to win her over until she agrees."

5

Altogether sexuality is considered more favorably in Judaism than in other Western religions.[43] It is part of the very positive talmudic approach to life: The concept of joy is enshrined in the biblical instruction to rejoice on festivals,[44] and the idea of blessing God is an act of rejoicing in the good and giving expression to one's feelings.[45] The model of King David, combining a full material life with a deep spirituality, is the preferred Jewish role model, rather than the ascetic. A person should constantly thank God for the bad as well as the good. One should not derive any pleasure without thanking God,[46] though of course the corollary of this is that one should seek out pleasures so as to be able thank God as much as possible.

Not only should one enjoy pleasurable things but, "A person will have to give evidence and account in the future for anything his eye saw and he did not eat."[47] The Nazirite who deprives himself of wine for more than thirty days must bring a sin offering as atonement for having deprived himself of a legitimate pleasure: "Rabbi Elazar HaKappar said, 'In what way did he sin? Because he deprived himself of wine.

And there is a deduction to be made from this. If a man who deprives himself of wine is called a sinner, how much more so is a person who deprives himself of any thing (that is permitted)?"[48] Sex, in addition to being a means of procreation, is also, of course, a source of pleasure. So much so that the *Zohar* and the later kabbalists saw a sexual union as a metaphor of the union between God and man.

The relationship between a man and a woman is the ultimate human relationship. A man without a woman is without joy and not a complete person.[49] This is why talmudic rabbis who did not get married were unable to receive their due title. It is also why a judge may only be someone who has experienced marriage. Marriage is governed by the principle of love and the well-known phrase "And you should love your neighbor as yourself." One may not marry without first seeing his bride so that he may not come to despise her.[50] The reason offered against some sexual practices is that they may turn one against one's partner.[51] The justification for divorce is to avoid hatred and increase love. Of course, there are problems that may emerge from a whole range of decisions both within marriage and without, but the halachic approach is to enjoy life, to respect and care for one's partner, and to increase the amount of love in the world.

6

The restrictions that Jewish law imposes have been subjected to critical analysis by such giants as Marx and Freud. Freud saw them as means whereby authority could exercise psychological control over the masses using frustration as a tool, but this ignores the active encouragement of sex that underlies biblical and rabbinic law. On another level these laws have been used by some as an excuse for laxity. One often hears it said that since Judaism is so strict and sets such unattainable standards, then one can hardly be expected not to want to find an outlet. It certainly seems that sexuality is one of the major areas of backsliding, but sexuality is also the major area of hypocrisy given the tendency of some societies to suppress sexuality. The result is that even in Jewish life, which in principle is very positive about sexuality under controlled conditions, there are signs of distorted attitudes.

There is a myth in some circles that intercourse with non-Jews is not forbidden. The evidence of the Talmud does not support this: "Whoever has intercourse with an Aramean (non-Jewish) woman, the zealous ones are allowed to kill him."[52] This frightening example of young priests taking the law into their own hands shows how serious a threat to the social fabric (of both the priesthood and the laity) uncontrolled sexuality was considered. The debate about intercourse with a non-Jew has several aspects to it. There is the special law of Ezra against intermarriage: The Torah previously had forbidden intermarriage with the Canaanite tribes and Ezra extended it. But the law forbidding a male or female prostitute[53] was taken to apply beyond the "profession" to anyone having casual sex. Later rabbis specifically forbade intercourse with non-Jews.[54] The *Zohar* says, "There are three people who drive God's presence away from this world . . . he who sleeps with the daughter of a non-Jew."[55] The only issue was whether the ban was seen as a Torah law or as a rabbinic one. Still, this seemingly exclusivist legislation was utilitarian rather religious, designed to retain Jews within the community rather than allow them to disappear through intermarriage.

One of the issues on which Maimonides[56] puts great emphasis is that any intercourse that may lead to a forbidden marriage is forbidden. In effect he outlines five separate rabbinic laws against intercourse with a non-Jew. Thus suggestions that one may indulge oneself outside the confines of one's tradition find no support in halachic sources.

The ideal, of course, was to confine sex to a committed

relationship in marriage to create a stable environment in which to bring up children and be loyal to the Jewish religious tradition. The objection to intermarriage was not because of anything intrinsically objectionable in a non-Jew. It was simply based on concern for the weakening of the Jewish family atmosphere and involvement with Jewish life. But none of this is to be seen as being against sex as such. It was part of campaign to defend Judaism and to fight for Jewish survival in an atmosphere of assimilation and attrition. Within its prescribed boundaries, sex was overwhelmingly regarded as both an obligation and a pleasure. Its use by the kabbalists as a metaphor for union with God shows the positive attitude toward the sexual act that characterizes Jewish religious thinking. In effect, sex and the Jewish religion do indeed go together—but in a controlled alliance rather than in a loose pagan descent into self-indulgence.

Notes

1. Genesis 2.
2. Talmud Bavli *Sanhedrin* 80a–b.
3. Genesis 2:25.
4. Genesis 3:10–11.
5. Genesis 2:19.
6. Genesis 2:18.
7. Genesis 4:1.
8. Genesis 6:2.
9. Genesis 12:14.
10. Deuteronomy 9:5.
11. Leviticus 18:3.
12. Exodus 21:10.
13. Genesis 6:5.
14. Genesis 8:21.
15. Genesis 1:27.
16. Talmud Bavli *Brachot* 61a.

17. Midrash Rabba *Breishit* 9:9.
18. Midrash Rabba *Breishit* 22:11.
19. Talmud Bavli *Brachot* 5a.
20. Talmud Bavli *Chagigah* 11b.
21. Talmud Bavli *Moed Katan* 17a.
22. See note 27.
23. Numbers 31:21.
24. Leviticus 20:17.
25. Genesis 38.
26. Genesis 39:8.
27. Deuteronomy 21:10.
28. Talmud Bavli *Megillah* 13b. Vide *Tosefot Vetovelet*.
29. Exodus 21:10.
30. Exodus 24:1.
31. Exodus 24:4.
32. Talmud Bavli *Kiddushin* 81b.
33. Leviticus 20:18.
34. Mishna *Yevamot* 6.
35. Mishna *Ketubot* 5:6.
36. Talmud Bavli *Nedarim* 20b.
37. Talmud Bavli *Brachot* 62a.
38. Talmud Bavli *Nida* 16b.
39. Talmud Bavli *Eiruvin* 100b.
40. Talmud Bavli *Yoma* 18b.
41. Talmud Bavli *Chagigah* 11b.
42. Talmud Bavli *Kiddushin* 29b.
43. *Shulchan Aruch Even HaEzer* 25.
44. Deuteronomy 16:14–15.
45. Deuteronomy 8:10.
46. Talmud Bavli *Brachot* 35a.
47. Talmud Yerushalmi *Kiddushin* 4:12.
48. Talmud Bavli *Nedarim* 10a.
49. Talmud Bavli *Yevamot* 62a.
50. Talmud Bavli *Kiddushin* 41a.
51. Talmud Bavli *Nida* 13a.
52. Talmud Bavli *Sanhedrin* 91b.

53. Deuteronomy 23:18, Onkelos loc. cit.
54. Talmud Bavli *Avoda Zara* 36b, *Sanhedrin* 82a.
55. *Zohar Shemot* 3.
56. Maimonides' *Yad HaChazaka Issurei Biya* 12.

Chapter 16

Myth: You Can Identify a Good Jew

1

Is it better to be a good person or a good Jew? This question is one of the most frequently asked whenever Jews get together. One reason is because most Jews do not stick too closely to Jewish laws and customs and thus inevitably feel somewhat uncertain as to where they stand. The second reason is that there is a tendency in the Jewish community to continually up the ante. As society in general polarizes, standards within any religious community seeking to set itself apart, are rising and getting stricter, and conventions are becoming more demanding. We are witnessing throughout the world a reaction against the spiritual aridity of the advanced material and technological world we live in. Standards that were acceptable once no longer seem acceptable now. So where does a person stand? The problem is made even more confusing by the fact that those who profess outward strictness are sometimes seen behaving in an unethical way. What are the basic standards of Judaism? Does one have to be strict to be religious? Does one have to be

religious to be a good Jew? And what is better, to be a good
Jew or to be a good person?

There are plenty of examples in the Torah of good people
who are not Jewish: Malchizedek was a priest to El Elyon,[1]
the king Avimelech had strong standards of ethical behavior,[2] and Jethro was considered "good enough" to become
Moses' father-in-law. The word "good" is used to mean no
more than something approved of, usually by God but also
by others: "Good" in the eyes of God[3] and in the eyes of
Laban.[4] It is used to describe creation, the Tree of Knowledge, and gold.[5] "A good person" can mean different things,
depending on who is speaking. A good citizen may not be a
good employee. A good Catholic may not be a good Muslim.
A good Jew may not be a good rabbi—and a good person
may not be a good Jew. What is certain is that a bad person
cannot be a good Jew.

The word used in Jewish literature to describe the highest standard of human behavior is *tsadik*. The word is sometimes translated as "saint," but this is not really appropriate because the word "saint" has very definite Christian
connotations. Rather, it means an upright person who follows a set of spiritual and civil principles. Noah was an
upright and straight man in his generation who "walked with
God."[6] The word used to describe Noah is *tsadik*, "an upright man." The word is also used more generally in the
phrase *tsedek tsedek tirdof*, "You should pursue that which
is right (justice),"[7] and in the commandment that one should
only have "fair or just weights and measures."[8] There is
nothing in the use of the words "good," "straight," or"just"
that would indicate that it applies to someone simply because he or she carries out certain specific ritual tasks. These
words have much wider connotations and apply to the general standard of a person's behavior in regard to other human beings.

There is discussion in the Talmud as to whether or not
some basic moral laws are inherent to humanity, and there

are different standards that apply to different people. There are standards acceptable for a good non-Jew, the seven commands of Noah (One must not curse God, worship idols, murder, commit adultery, steal, take a limb from a living animal, and one must set up courts of law).[9] Adherence to these relatively basic principles enables a non-Jew to be treated as an equal citizen in this world and to be part of the World to Come,[10] which is the highest level of spiritual reward a person can achieve, as evidenced by the Mishna in *Sanhedrin*.[11] There are standards required of a "stranger dwelling amongst you." Even within Judaism there are different sets of standards. There are rules for a Cohen, rules for a Levite, and rules for a Nazirite. Interestingly, there are no specific rules applying to a rabbi that do not also apply to everyone else, though there is generally the feeling that someone in a high and public position ought to set a good example. The structure of Jewish law is such that in civil matters, matters *bein adam lachavero*, "between a person and his or her friend or neighbor," everyone is on the same level and has similar obligations. On the other hand, in ritual matters there are indeed different standards.

The Talmud records that at the time of the Temple there were some who could afford bigger and better sacrifices or a bigger and better *lulav* or *etrog*. In discussing the number of candles one lights for Chanukah, the Gemara says: "The commandment for Chanukah lights is one light for a man and his household, and that is for those who are particular; a light for each person is for those who want to be more particular than particular."[12] It is clear from this that there have always been those who wanted to be stricter than was really necessary. What was unacceptable to the great prophets of Judaism was that anyone should think himself or herself any better because of it.

There is indeed a principle found in the Midrash that "One should sanctify oneself through those things that are allowed"[13] and the notion of *kedusha*, holiness, is one that is

valued, but this does not mean that there is something inadequate in those who choose not to (sanctify). There is room
for everyone to rise as far or as little as they choose. This is
why some of the rabbis argued that "Good deeds need concentration."[14] There is still some value in the action itself
even if it is done out of habit, but no one would disagree
that *Kavanah*, focusing attention and thinking about what
one does, is the ideal. In effect, there are two levels of performing *mitzvot*: the behavioral and the cerebral.

2

We are tempted to classify laws into major and minor ones,
however, it is possible to argue that every law is special and
every law is Divine: "Be as careful about a minor command
as you would about a major one because you do not know
the reward for commands."[15] The issue of reward is secondary here; what is important is the idea that all actions have
relevance. After all, if one takes the source for Torah as
Divine then it is surely important to observe everything. If,
on the other hand, one believes that the commandments are
part of a national heritage then as well the more of the heritage one keeps, the more one can sustain and pass on.

Nevertheless it appears that certain laws were given a
great deal more emphasis than others as being crucial for
preserving the quality of good social life. The rabbis said,
"Groundless hatred between people is as bad as the three
most serious commands against idolatry, immorality, and
murder."[16] It is said of gossip that it is like denying God.[17]
Quite often the rabbis use hyperbole to make a point, but it
is interesting that although some of the commandments they
use to make these points are ritual in nature, like *Shabbat*
or *tsitsit*, the overwhelming majority are what we would call
ethical.

The rabbis were particularly sensitive about humiliating others: "Whoever humiliates a person in public has no share of the World to Come."[18] The famous chapter 19 of Leviticus (with its command to "Love your neighbor as yourself") lays down the fundamentals of ethical behavior with rules about gossip, taking advantage of a person's weakness (whether physical or because of a disadvantage, lack of information, or simple ignorance), and being insensitive to a stranger or an orphan. The rabbis of the Talmud made a point of emphasizing and underlining these particular issues and seeing them at the very root of Jewish existence and survival. Consider the reason the rabbis gave for the destruction of the Temple: "Jerusalem was destroyed only because there were no more honest people."[19]

The well-known episode of Kamtza and Bar Kamtza[20] is read on the Ninth of Av, commemorating the destruction of the two Temples. It is a lesson in how destructive needless antagonism can be: A man whom the host hated is invited by mistake to a banquet and then ejected, his humiliation was made worse because the rabbis present refuse to intervene. In his bitterness the victim sets in motion a chain of events that leads to the destruction of Jerusalem. The story emphasizes how the rabbis felt about internal divisions being responsible more than anything else for the destruction of Jerusalem. They did number ritual items among the things that contributed to the cataclysm, but overwhelmingly they were not what we would call a ritual law; they were social ones. This is also why the Day of Atonement is only for those sins between man and God. Anything a person has done to another person must be put right directly with that person himself or herself.

The rabbis were particularly concerned about how one's behavior is perceived. It was not just the concept of *marit ayin*, "appearances," and the idea that one should not behave in a manner in which actions might be misconstrued. They stressed the positive perspective of behaving in a manner that would bring positive reactions from others. The

Torah talks about the importance of how others see us: "This (the Torah) is what makes you wise and understanding in the eyes of the nations around you."[21] A repeated theme in the Mishna is what other people think of a person: "Rebbi said, 'What is the right path a person should choose for life? That which is glorious according to the doer and which brings him glory from others.'"[22]

You might think that Rebbi (Rabbi Yehuda HaNasi) could have simply said that one should follow the Torah, but clearly he is choosing a different level. One can keep the Torah and still be "an ugly person within the confines of the Law." Similarly, Rabbi Chanina ben Dosa said, "When the human spirit approves of a person this is a sign that God approves, and when people do not approve of a person this is a sign that God does not approve."[23] Once again, the way a person relates to and is perceived by other human beings, always assuming that they too have moral and spiritual standards, is put ahead of ritual correctness.

This is not to say that in any way the rabbis minimized the importance of ritual, just that it was important to have the intangible inter-human sensitivities as well. Ritual was still a means to an end, not an end in itself. The end was a better and closer relationship with God and humanity.

Related to this is the important concept of *kiddush haShem*, "sanctifying God's name," and its opposite *chillul haShem*, "desecrating God's name." This is a tremendously important notion in traditional thinking. The basis of acting in a way that brings respect to God is in Leviticus 19, where we are commanded, "You should be holy because I YHVH your God am holy." The word "holy," *kadosh*, is and unusual word, as has been noted in a previous chapter. The same word is used to describe objects and people set aside for special religious use, but it is also used to describe prostitutes, male[24] and female.[25] Literally, the word means "to set aside." The person or the object is neutral; what counts is how a person behaves or uses himself. Use that is dedicated to a higher order is holy and use that degrades is prostitution. The concept of *kedusha* is one that calls on us to raise our standards and try to be better human beings for our own sakes and to increase spirituality, goodness, and the presence of God in the world.

The Talmud gives some fascinating examples of both sides of the coin. A religious or a learned person has to be doubly concerned about the impression he or she may be giving. The Talmud says that desecrating God's name is so serious that even the Day of Atonement cannot remove the damage done. What is an example of this? "Rav said, 'In my case if I were not to pay the butcher on time.'"[26] This sounds rather petty, but Rav is saying that someone like he, a religious person and a leader, has a greater obligation, because of the way he is regarded, to make sure that his actions do not give rise to misunderstanding. The Talmud is scathing about a *Talmid Chacham* with stained or dirty clothing because of the bad impression this creates.[27] One could argue that nowadays anyone wearing manifestly Jewish religious clothing or claiming to be religious falls under this category.

The principle of sanctifying the name of God became a very important issue under conditions of oppression and forced conversions. How far was one supposed to go in refusing to make concessions? Was martyrdom required? Particularly in the wake of the Spanish Inquisition and expulsion, issues such as whether a Jew who became a Christian under duress had to convert back to Judaism became pressing. Maimonides is very strict about the necessity for standing on matters of principle, even to the point of death.[28] At the same time he was equally tolerant of those who were unable to withstand the pressure, as his "Letter to the Jews of Yemen" and "Document on Apostasy" attest.

This is not the matter under discussion; rather, we are concerned with how a person should behave toward others under normal conditions. The rabbis introduced the principle of "ways of peace," *darkei shalom*, which was used to require behavior above and beyond the letter of the law with regard to both Jews and non-Jews. The best known example of its use is in requiring landowners and charity committees to provide for non-Jewish poor even though, as non-citizens, they technically were not entitled to community support.[29]

3

Yet there remains the question of who is a Jew and how one defines an active and positive member of the Jewish community. A Jew has always been defined in Jewish Law as someone born of a Jewish mother or who converted to Judaism out of conviction. There is no doubt that historically there have been periods of varying severity or lenience; nevertheless this has been the defining characteristic for the past two thousand years. If "a good Jew" means someone born a citizen, then this is clear enough and no one would argue with it.

A Jew who sins remains a Jew.[30] A Jew who converts to another religion does not need to be converted back to Judaism. But what is the status of a nonpracticing Jew? His or her actions count. So, for example, ritual slaughter or marriage are effective even if carried out by someone not necessarily observant. However, according to Jewish Law someone who ignores or rejects Jewish Law cannot be relied upon to give evidence in a Jewish Court of Law.[31] Similarly, Jews whose occupations or reputations are unsavory can also be excluded. However, there is a difference in opinion about a Jew who disobeys out of self-indulgence and a Jew who disobeys out of conviction that Jewish Law is wrong. The rabbis were more indulgent of the former and more antagonistic against the latter.[32]

It is true that the rabbis extended their negative attitude to a whole range of people whose occupation or behavior they did not like and it is true that the Court of Law had great leeway to exercise discretion. It is very clear that at the time of the Talmud, Jewish society was very much divided between the *am ha'aretz*, the peasant or ignoramus who did not have an education, and the student of wisdom and his family who had studied Torah and kept it more punctiliously. This led to refusing to eat in an *am ha'aretz's* home because he might not have taken tithes or observed the laws strictly enough and to not wanting to intermarry with the children of an *am ha'aretz*.[33] There is even an opinion that one could kill an ignoramus.[34] This is not meant to be taken literally, of course, because it conflicts totally with Jewish Law, but the division went as far as restricting the wives of talmudic students, *eshet chaver* from preparing food with the wife of an *am ha'aretz*—although some rabbis allowed it on the grounds, mentioned earlier, of *darkei shalom*, to try to maintain good social relations even in the face of religious deficiency.[35]

The antagonism went both ways. Rabbi Akiva comments that when he was an *am ha'aretz* he said, "If only I could get hold of a *Talmid Chacham*, I would savage him like an ass." This quote illustrates the extent of the enmity that existed between the two "camps" in those days, but it was a battle for survival. The rabbis were very firm in their belief then (as now) that only with study and knowledge could Judaism survive the onslaught of the great cultures of those days. The rabbis at the time encouraged individuals to accept a higher level of practice. They created the title of *chaver*, "friend," and initiated a formal ceremony in front of witnesses to receive people onto this higher level.[36] Despite this, nowhere is it suggested that someone who keeps Jewish Law but does not attain a higher level is in any way inferior. A person is judged by his actions.

4

Within Halacha there are indeed different standards. Within the Jewish community around the world there are a confusing number of different levels of observance and strictness. Is there not just one law? How did we get to such different and confusing levels of what is kosher and what is not?

The Talmud defines the Jewish constitution, it expands and explains those laws that derive from the Torah and those that the rabbis instituted themselves, and it sets down a framework for dealing with situations that may arise. All this is done against a background of discussion and debate. What sets the Jewish system of law apart from so many others is the fact that the same principles and debates that apply to strictly ritual or spiritual matters also apply to the total spectrum of human activity, so a debate in a legal fashion developed by the rabbis may be about how much in damages one has to pay to an injured person or about how to define "work" on *Shabbat*. Certain principles for reaching decisions apply. In the general discussion of how to decide legal or ritual issues there is a principle that "The power to allow is preferable to the power to forbid."[37] As Rashi puts it in his commentary: "It is better to hear the opinion of one who allows because he relies on his arguments (his learning) and he is not frightened to allow. But the power of those who forbid is no proof because anyone can say something is forbidden even when it is allowed." Indeed, according to the Tosefta, "Whoever wants to be stricter, he has to bring the proof.[38]

This does not prevent a person from choosing to be stricter for himself. Often rabbis were lenient for others but strict for themselves. A well-known example of this leniency is that a bridegroom is not obliged to say the *Shema* on his wedding night because he will be unlikely to be able to concentrate. Rabbi Gamliel did so and replied to his students who questioned him, "I will not listen to you to give up the

acceptance of Divine Kingship even for a moment."[39] Yet the
rabbis were not keen on doing more: "Is it not enough with
what God has forbidden (that you want to add things on)?"[40]
On the contrary, they emphasized the preference to "Sanctify yourself with what is allowed."[41]

There has, nevertheless, particularly in recent centuries,
been a tendency to increase strictness incrementally. *Kashrut*
is a perfect example: In the Talmud something is either
kosher or not, but over the years people have chosen to
demand stricter standards. The term *glatt* is a Yiddish word
meaning "smooth or clear." It does not appear in halachic
sources until recent centuries. Its origin lies in the tendency
of animals in a wet European climate to develop tuberculo-
sis. Any defect or illness in an animal that may be life-threat-
ening makes the animal nonkosher. The tradition of examining the lungs to see if there were any signs of illness developed. If the animal passed this check it was declard kosher. Some people chose, as they became wealthier and more
discriminating, to eat only from those animals for which no
cxamination at all was necessary. This is no differrent than
people deciding to avoid certain foods for health reasons, but
sadly what has happened is that in a social game of one-
upmanship many suggest that ordinary kosher is not really
kosher—which of course is absurd. It is only symptomatic of
the widespread tendency toward hyper sensitivity. In the
notes on the *Shulchan Aruch*, written by Rabbi Moses
Isserles, the expression "He who is strict on this issue is only
to be amazed at," is often used. One example relates to laws
of mourning,[42] but in general this indicates that being stricter
is not always sensible or to be praised.

In his book *Sephardi and Ashkenazi*, Rabbi H. Zimmels
comments on the fact that the medieval Sephardi world was
very particular about issues of business ethics but less so on
matters of *kashrut*, while in the Ashkenazi world of Europe
it was the reverse. He suggests that the reason was because
in Spain Jews and non-Jews intermingled and many more

professions and means of earning a livelihood were open to
Jews. In Europe the reverse was the case. The struggle to
earn a living led to greater leeway and flexibility, even laxity, on matters of commerce, while on the other hand, Jews
and non-Jews hardly mixed and therefore the laws and customs regulating eating together were enforced much more
strictly. Whether or not this is true, his point is that there
has been a tendency to place much greater emphasis on
relatively minor issues of diet than on major issues of business ethics. Of course, dietary laws come from the Torah and
are therefore strict—but so are a great number of business
laws. If one is selecting which laws to keep strictly and which
not to base on convenience, then one is hardly in a position
to cast aspersions on those who likewise make choices,
though other ones. After all, the forbidding of gossip is as
much a part of the Torah as is the list of kosher animals.

There is the phrase in the Talmud that "He who is strict
will have long days and years,"[43] however, this did not become a feature of halachic literature until much later. The
phrase "The custom is to be stricter" may be found in the
Shulchan Aruch in the seventeenth century, but it is not
until the Mishna *Berura* in the twentieth century that it
became common to say "Whoever is stricter, may he be
blessed."

To illustrate the progression, consider the period of
mourning around Tisha B'Av, the Ninth Day of Av, that com-
memorates the destruction of both the First and the Second
Temples. In the Talmud, the only laws restricting eating and
imposing mourning apply to the week in which Tisha B'Av
falls.[44] Similarly, the *Shulchan Aruch* mentions only this
same time frame.[45] However it adds: "There are those who
have the custom not to bathe from the New Month of Av and
some who fast from the seventeenth of Tammuz." Another
custom is added later: "We have the custom not to get married between the Seventeenth of Tammuz and the Ninth of
Av."[46] It has now become universal to keep the "Three Weeks"

as a period of mourning. There is no reason why we should not choose to accept this extra degree of mourning, particularly in the light of what has happened to us in Europe this past century, but this is different from implying that those who do not keep the strict rules are poor Jews. That implication would sit ill on those who before the *Shulchan Aruch* did not have this custom at all.

5

Ultimately that is the crux of the matter: No person can judge another. Only God knows what goes on in the inner being of each one of us. The tendency of Jewish communities to judge and to judge hastily and often incorrectly is at the root of the problem. It is common to invoke the Law to prevent a less religious person from being called up to read from the Torah, but someone who appears outwardly religious may in fact be inwardly breaking far more laws. It is very dangerous to try to decide which selection is the less acceptable. It is true that we can judge only by appearances and that behavior is one of religious commitment, but the criteria for judgment are often faulty. This is why so many people think that being observant excuses a great deal and why observance becomes almost the only criterion of commitment.

In fact it may be that a Jew who keeps a great many commandments but disobeys just one may be in a qualitatively inferior position to a Jew who keeps very few but elects to do one or two very important ones. Judgment is dangerous. Similarly, a man may be a good Jew in the sense that he keeps a great deal of the Jewish tradition, but still not be as good a person as someone else who keeps less.

There is a difference between a good person and a good Jew. It has nothing to do with being better, just different. A Catholic differs from a Mormon. They are both Christians, but I suspect each would say the other is "wrong." Can a good Catholic be a good Mormon? Similarly, within Judaism there are many different sects and denominations. A good Satmarer Chassid cannot also be a good Lubavitch Chassid —but does it matter? To whom? Can a good Orthodox Jew be a good Reform Jew? It is arguable! If Reform requires total autonomy and Orthodoxy requires a degree of submission then the two are incompatible. It is irrelevant to debate which sect is more or less likely to guarantee continuity; we are simply discussing passing a value judgment— and value judgments depend entirely on who is making the judgment in the first place!

A Jew, to qualify as a Jew, has to show a degree of commitment to his Judaism, but I do not see how you can be a good Jew if you are not also a good person. Inherent in Jewish law is the obligation to be a caring, considerate human being toward others. On the other hand, a good person cannot automatically be a good Jew because of the specific requirements of living a Jewish life. In the end we make choices as to how we live and in accordance with what standards. Some of us will choose to be stricter and some more lenient, but passing judgment on others under any circumstance is fraught and dangerous given the nature of human error. "Do not judge your neighbor until you are in his position," said Hillel.[47] But passing judgment based on a pretense of religious superiority is simply not being religious. It is showing all the characteristics that genuine spirituality seeks to avoid. People love perpetuating the myth that a religious Jew is a good Jew, but not everyone who appears to be religious really is.

Notes

1. Genesis 14:19.
2. Genesis 20:9.
3. Genesis 1:4.

4. Genesis 29:19.
5. Genesis 2:12.
6. Genesis 6:10.
7. Deuteronomy 16:20.
8. Leviticus 19:36.
9. Talmud Bavli *Sanhedrin* 59.
10. *Tosefta Sanhedrin* 13.
11. Talmud Bavli *Sanhedrin* 90a.
12. Talmud Bavli *Shabbat* 21b.
13. *Sifri Parshat Reah* 104.
14. Talmud Bavli *Brachot* 13a.
15. Mishna *Avot* 2:1.
16. Talmud Bavli *Yoma* 9b.
17. Talmud Bavli *Erchin* 15b.
18. Talmud Bavli *Bava Metzia* 59a.
19. Talmud Bavli *Shabbat* 119b.
20. Talmud Bavli *Gittin* 55b–56a.
21. Deuteronomy 4:6.
22. Mishna *Avot* 2:1.
23. Mishna *Avot* 3:13.
24. Deuteronomy 23:18.
25. Ibid. and Genesis 38:21.
26. Talmud Bavli *Yoma* 86a.
27. Talmud Bavli *Shabbat* 114a.
28. Maimonides' *Yad HaChazaka Yesodei HaTorah* 5.
29. Mishna *Sheviit* 4:5, *Gittin* 5:5.
30. *Shulchan Aruch Yoreh Deah* 119:9, *Tur Choshen Mishpat* 283.
31. Talmud Bavli *Shavuot* 47a, *Kiddushin* 40b.
32. Talmud Bavli *Avoda Zara* 27b, *Chullin* 4a–b.
33. Talmud Bavli *Pesachim* 49b.
34. Ibid.
35. Talmud Bavli *Gittin* 61b.
36. Talmud Bavli *Bechorot* 30b.
37. Talmud Bavli *Beitza* 2b, et pass.
38. *Tosefta Sanhedrin* 7:3.

39. Mishna *Brachot* 2:5.

40. Talmud Bavli *Nedarim* 9:1.

41. *Sifri Reah* 104.

42. *Shulchan Aruch Yoreh Deah* 364:6.

43. Talmud Bavli *Brachot* 22a.

44. Talmud Bavli *Taanit* 26a, *Yevamot* 43a.

45. *Shulchan Aruch Orach Chayim* 551.

46. Ibid.

47. Mishna *Avot* 2:5.

Chapter 17

Myth:
Jewish Education
Guarantees Jewish
Survival

1

"Education" has become the key word of Jewish communal life because it is, belatedly in Western society, perceived as being the only way to guarantee survival. But what kind of education do we need? What kind of education works? Can we talk about a Jewish pedagogic tradition?

The Torah establishes a principle that has become embedded in Jewish Law. In the first paragraph of the *Shema* is the familiar phrase "And you will teach these laws to your children."[1] This is one of the obligations of the Torah, but what and to whom should we teach? Torah is the priority from a Jewish point of view, both because of its link with God and because of its intensification of Jewishness. Hence, "Rabbi Yochanan said in the name of Rabbi Meir, 'One does not sell a *Sefer Torah* except for learning Torah or to get a wife,'"[2] (an interesting balance between the wider issue of human continuity—marriage and having children—and the more specifically Jewish continuity issue of keeping Torah alive). To ensure Jewish education, according to later Jewish law, "The community can compel a father to hire a teacher for his son and can even confiscate his property to see that it is done."[3] The community is responsible for setting up schools too,[4] but here we are talking exclusively about schools for Torah.

What other educational obligations are there? A father is obliged (by law) to circumcise his son, to redeem him (all first born males are dedicated to God and have to be redeemed), to teach him Torah, to marry him off, and to teach him a profession. Some say also to teach him how to swim. Rabbi Yehuda says, "Whoever does not teach his son a profession teaches him to become a robber," (he will end up stealing because he will have no other way of earning a living, according to Rashi).[5] It seems pretty clear that a child must have both a Jewish education (Torah) and a means of support as well as other survival skills!

The issue of whether one must teach other skills and expertise is one of the major issues in the Talmud. If studying Torah is the will of God and if doing what God wants is the most important thing, then Torah—which is the means of getting closer to God—should be the only activity a person need be committed to. Yet, the Mishna is very definite about the need to combine Torah with other activity. Rabbi Gamliel the son of Rabbi Yehudah the Prince said, "It is good to combine Torah with work because being busy with both will keep a person out of trouble. And any study that has no work ends up being wasted and causing sin."[6] Or, as Rebbi Elazar Ben Azaria says, "If there is no Torah there is no work and if there is no work there is no Torah."[7]

Against this position stands Rebbi Nechunia ben HaKna, who says that the more one takes on Torah the fewer wordly matters he will have to be concerned about, and vice versa. However, his solution to the problem of who will do the necessary work to produce food and clothes is to suggest that "others" will do this for you. He does not specify if the others are Jewish or not.[8] The argument between Rabbi Shimon nar Yochai and Rabbi Yishmael is: "'And you will gather in your corn.' (Deuteronomy 18) But we have learnt, 'The Torah shall never depart from your lips.' (Joshua 1) Do we take this literally? The rabbis have said that 'Gather in your corn' means you should have to work, so says Rabbi Yishmael. Rabbi Shimon bar Yochai said, 'Is it possible that a man has to plow at the time for plowing and sow at the time for sowing and reap at the time for reaping and thresh the corn at the time for threshing and winnow when there is wind? When would he have time for Torah?' . . . Abaye said, 'Many tried Rabbi Yishmael's way and they succeeded. Many tried Rabbi Shimon bar Yochai's way and did not succeed.' Rava said to the rabbis, 'Please do not call upon me during the days of Nissan and Tishrei so that you do not disturb my making a living (during peak harvest times),'"[9] (which shows that he, himself, worked as well as studied).

A similar point is made after Rabbi Shimon bar Yochai and his son had been hiding in a cave to escape Roman persecution, spending all their time studying Torah. When Shimon and his son leave the cave they see people plowing. Shimon declares, "They are abandoning eternal life for transient life,"(instead of studying, they are working). Wherever they turned they looked at people and burnt them (with the mystical powers they developed through intense concentration on Torah). A voice came from Heaven and said, "Have you come out to destroy My world? Go back into the cave."[10] The issue here is a pragmatic one. Can one survive without a practical means of financial support?

2

The issue of studying something other than Torah became more complex with the connection between Greek wisdom and anti-Jewish ideology. The Greek philosophers were also the scientists of their day. Aristotle wrote about ethics and abstractions but he also wrote about scientific experiments and discoveries. We know that Jews took advantage of scientific progress then as now. The question of giving up time from Torah to study other things was a source of debate because it was not just learning to have work but an involvement in a different culture. "Ben Dama asked Rabbi Yishmael, 'Someone like me who has learnt all the Torah, am I allowed to study Greek wisdom?' He replied, 'It says "And you should study by day and by night," so find a time that is neither day nor night and study Greek wisdom then." But this disagrees with Shmuel bar Nachmani who says this quote is intended not as an obligation or a command but only as a blessing."[11]

The awful experiences suffered at the hands of Greek-speaking oppressors created a backlash. For example, at a time when two Hasmonean descendants, rivals for the monarchy, Hyrcanus and Aristobolus, were fighting among themselves, Greek sympathizers gave the besiegers advice on how to undermine Jewish law. As a result, the defenders issued "A curse on anyone who teaches his son the Wisdom of Greece."[12]

Against this, "Rabbi Shimon ben Gamliel said, 'In my father's house there were a thousand young men. Five hundred learned Torah and five hundred learned Greek wisdom. They were allowed because they were close to (non-Jewish) government.'"[13] Yet the Sanhedrin in general was made up of men who were expected to learn other languages and master other forms of knowledge. Indeed one opinion even has them learning about spirits and magic: "They said of Rabbi Yochanan ben Zakkai that he did not neglect Torah, Mishna, Gemara, Halacha, Haggada, deductions of Torah, deductions of the scribes, logical deductions, comparing texts, calendars, signs of the Zodiac, the language of angels and the language of spirits, the language of date palms, laundry parables and foxes parables, important matters and minor matters."[14] In other words, every area of knowledge was worth studying. Clearly the issue was a highly charged one because it recurs throughout the Talmud. However, it is not possible to say that there is only one position on it. Indeed, it is patently clear that some rabbis and students were studying subjects other than pure Torah.

3

There was also the question of whether education should be open to everyone or just the select few. When the aristocratic Rabbi Gamliel was the head of the academy he had a policy of restricted entry. He insisted that any student whose exterior was not matched by his interior should not be allowed in to study (one assumes he wanted spiritual excellence as well as intellectual). When he was deposed the rabbis from peasant stock, Rabbi Akiva and Rabbi Yehoshua, opened the study halls to everyone: "On that day (when Rabbi Gamliel was deposed as head of the academy) they removed the doorkeeper and allowed all students (who wanted to) to enter. Because Rabbi Gamliel had said that any student whose inner (self) did not match his outer could not come in to the house of study. On that day they added several rows of benches. Rabbi Yochanan said that Abba Yosef ben Dostai and the rabbis disagreed. One said they added four hundred benches and the other that seven hundred were added. Rabbi Gamliel grew depressed and said, "Maybe, God forbid, I have prevented Israel from learning Torah."[15] One cannot help but wonder why he had not thought of that before.

Similarly the question of women being taught was debated. Naturally this debate took place against a certain cultural background, but it does illustrate the possibility of divergence. The context for the most popular source is the law of the *sotah*.[16] The *sotah* is a woman who has been suspected of infidelity and has been warned not to consort with a particular man. In Jewish Law circumstantial evidence is not accepted, so even if the actual circumstances point to infidelity, the actual evidence required of two independent witnesses to convict is missing. If after a man has warned his wife she defies him by going into seclusion with the other man, there is once again only circumstantial evidence, but then the man has the right to take his wife to the priest who would make her drink some bitter water with God's name dissolved into it (from which the rabbis learn how important it is to try to preserve a marriage, since this is the only situation in which one may dissolve or "degrade" the Divine Name). This procedure was actually banned by Rabbi Yochanan ben Zakkai in the first century C.E. because he felt that men were not on a high enough level to deserve this special right: "The adulterers increased."[17]

If the woman was guilty, her body would begin to deteriorate and this would prove her guilt, according to the Torah. The Mishna says that a woman's good deeds might protect her from the effect of the waters: "From this Ben Azai said, 'A man has an obligation to teach his daughter Torah so that she will know, if she is forced to drink, what may protect her.' Rabbi Eliezer said, 'Whoever teaches his daughter Torah will be teaching her immorality.'"[18] I will not try to explain or justify Rabbi Eliezer's position here; it just emphasizes the fact that there was a debate and a difference of opinion (and let us not forget that women were not allowed to graduate from Oxbridge or Ivy League universities until this century).

Thus the two issues of education, secular as well as religious and open access to both sexes, is an ancient one and one in which Judaism was well ahead of its surrounding cultures.

4

In practice, how did Judaism deal with mass education? There is a tradition that the great High Priest and leader Shimon HaTsaddik introduced education to Israel. The Talmud records his visiting Alexander the Great on his way down the coast from Turkey to Egypt. He had been told by the Samaritans that the Jews were against him. The Samaritans had their own motives for wanting to see the Temple destroyed or at least desecrated. Alexander was not in general interested in challenging local religions, just in getting them to accept his authority. Shimon dressed up in his Day of Atonement clothes and with great ceremony approached Alexander. Alexander was so impressed—he had had a vision the night before that seemed to predict this encounter—that he granted Shimon's request to leave the Temple alone.[19] The Midrash adds that Shimon returned convinced that only through education could the Jews survive the cultural onslaught of Greece.

The Gemara also attributes national education to King Hezekiah, who had initiated a dramatic religious revival during the First Temple period: "(King) Hezekiah would go round every synagogue and study hall. What did he do? He placed a sword at the entrance to each one and said, 'Whoever does not study Torah will be pierced by this sword.' They checked from Dan to Be'er Sheva and they could not find one ignoramus from Givat to Antipars and they could not find one boy or girl, man or woman that was not expert (in the laws of) purity and impurity."[20] I have always been struck by two things about this narrative: First that Hezekiah's education program was aimed at everyone, including women, and second that it was both compulsory and aggressive. Perhaps the times required these methods.

The best known tradition credits the "national" education system to someone else: "Truly this man, called Yehoshua

ben Gamla, should be remembered for good! Originally whoever had a father, he taught him Torah. Whoever did not
have a father did not learn Torah. How did they justify this?
(On the basis of the quote) 'And you shall teach them,'
(Deuteronomy 11). And you shall teach, you, yourselves. They
instituted (a law) that they should establish teachers for
children in Jerusalem. How did they justify this? (On the
basis of the quote) 'And Torah shall go out from Jerusalem,'
(Isaiah 2). But still, whoever had a father, (the father) would
take him up to Jerusalem and teach him and whoever had
no father would not go up and learn. They instituted (a law)
that they should establish teachers for children in each area
for children of sixteen or seventeen. But whenever a teacher
got angry he (the pupil) would reject him and leave, until
Yehoshua ben Gamla arrived and instituted (a law) that they
should establish teachers for children in every area and every
city and bring in children of six or seven."[21]

5

There is also the issue of methodology. How did the rabbis
think one should teach? There are few hints in the Talmud,
ones that would astound both traditionalists and pro-
gressives in our educational academies nowadays. For example, "Rav visited this place and proclaimed a fast but no
rain came. The reader passed before (the ark) and when he
said, 'Let the winds blow,' the winds blew, and when he said,
'Let the rain fall,' the rain fell. He (Rav) said to him, 'What
is your business?' He replied, 'I teach children, and I teach
the children of the poor just the same way as I teach the
children of the rich. If someone cannot pay I do not take
anything. I have fish ponds and if (a child) is reluctant
(rebels) I bribe him with (fish from) them. I explain (everything simply) and I win him over until he comes and reads.'"[22]
Thus bribery was considered acceptable, but so too was en-

couragement. There is no tendency to blame the pupil, but rather the teacher, if things went wrong. Rabba said, "If you see a student who finds his studying as hard as iron, it is because his teacher did not explain things well to him. For it says (Ecclesiastes 10:10):"If it is as solid as iron (it is because there was) no explanation (no faces) that he went wrong."[23]

The *Shulchan Aruch* shows all the influences of a medieval academy: "One should not beat a pupil with cruel and harsh discipline, not with canes or sticks but with a small leather strap,"[24] and "There should be no breaks from study at all, apart from Friday evenings and the eves of festivals late in the day." On the other hand consider the ramifications of this statement: "If there is a teacher of children but a better one comes one may remove the first one and replace him with a better one. If there are two teachers, one who teaches a lot of text (covers ground) but does not check to see if the pupils have learned to understand properly and another who teaches less but makes sure they understand, we employ the one who checks more,"[25] which seriously emphasizes the importance of good teaching.

Nevertheless, none of this really addresses the major issues of Jewish education. On the traditional level the emphasis on covering ground, rote learning, and memorizing large amounts may be effective with some children, but too many are left with a sense of failure or a very limited sense of achievement. Certainly the talmudic tradition places great emphasis on intellectual skills, within a rather limited framework. For those able to adjust or accept, the traditional methods are great for training memory and powers of analysis with a defined structure. They are also excellent for getting students to study together because the *chavruta*, the partnership of two students to work out a text or to review one that has already been taught, encourages very different skills from those traditionally taught in Western schools. On the other hand, they are poor in encouraging open inquiry and, of course, secular skills. Nevertheless the Talmud recognizes different types and styles of study. The Talmud, at the end of *Horyot*, weighs the relative merits of the "Uprooter of Mountains" (the brilliant creative mind) and the "Sinai" (the systematic accumulator of texts and system).[26]

Jewish methodology is often contrasted with non-Jewish education, yet modern Western schools also have grave shortcomings. They suit those pupils able to accept structures and a certain type of curriculum but in general they are not good at stimulating open inquiry and free exploration either. The demands of a national curriculum or of university entrance may suit some pupils, but not all. Those pupils who are disadvantaged because of the home environment or internal limitations do not get the support and encouragement they need, while the particularly gifted tend to suffer in corporate structures.

There is also a fine distinction between "studying" and "learning." To study is a fine intellectual pursuit, but too often it is a means to an end. "Study" may be no more than the boring grind of amassing information to pass an exam. Rarely does one or is one permitted to pursue a line of inquiry as far or for as long as one wants. There is a syllabus and exams. The curriculum in most countries imposes restricted units of limited information required to pass exams, study often becomes a game in which the student seeks to outwit the examiner.

"Learning," the Yiddish word applied to Torah study, is study for its own sake. One spends as long as one wants on a page, an issue, a *sugya*. "Learning" is study for its own sake with no necessary end in mind. This is the ideal of the yeshiva world even though there are set folios (*masechtot*) that are scheduled each semester.

Sadly, many Jewish schools have lost the art of "learning" and have turned Jewish studies into "studying." This is the result of pressure from colleges and from parents who demand academic results, but it means that thousands of

Jewish children are turned off from Torah study because when Jewish study is no different from secular study, then the curriculum with the highest payoff in terms of career or money will always come out on top.

The old Jewish ideal of the parent being responsible for the child's education is not at all easy in our pressurized society. Yet more and more parents are opting for variations on the home schooling theme as a way of doing better for their children. Can a community take on responsibility for Jewish education if it raises conflicts with parental values?

6

Traditionally, education is a Divine command. Study has defined our people and sustained our tradition, so inevitably education is a condition of survival. The issue has arisen as a debatable one only with assimilation and the trend of vast numbers of Jews to abandon Jewish literacy for secular education. The committed Jewish world has never doubted the efficacy of study. Now, in order to win back to Judaism the major part of the Jewish population, education, is at the forefront of the Jewish agenda in every denomination.

Jewish education is supposed to answer the problem of Jewish survival, yet we see that many children who have a full Jewish education still show very little interest in Jewish life and in many cases abandon their tradition altogether. The record of Jewish schools in the English-speaking world over the past fifty years has not been that impressive. Why?

First of all, it should be obvious that simply having a school is no answer in itself. Without an appropriate structure and culture and without motivated teachers a school is likely to be no more successful in retaining Jewish identity than a beautiful, empty synagogue. However, agreeing on a shared vision is all but impossible in most Jewish communities around the world. What happens is that either a community bands together to produce a community school that tries to please all of the people all of the time or small sections of the community go it alone, stretching financial resources and failing educationally because of inadequate staffing or a too narrow vision.

The problem that the community school Jewish education meets is that most communities are comprised of a very wide range of Jews, all with varying standards and requirements, both religiously and in general. Where a school tries to be too many things to too many people it inevitably fails. The most successful schools I have come across around the world are those where the parents, pupils, and teachers all agree on every aspect of the curriculum. This applies to schools of different communities and different cultures. It is, for example, one of the strengths of the very Orthodox *chedarim*. In a typical Jewish community school, however, there are too many conflicting standards and goals. As a result, the declared position of the school may be undermined by teachers, pupils, and parents.

In addition we have expectations that Jewish schools will succeed in changing the commitment of their pupils to a more positive or intensive involvement in Judaism. This rarely works. The school is just one element in a range of elements that influence a child. Home, friends, and society are as influential as school. In general, a child will be loyal to his or her parents. If the school presents conflicting standards the norm is that the standards of the school will be ignored. It will only be in dysfunctional families that a child may look elsewhere for values.

A potent criticism of most Jewish community schools is that because they are so financially dependent on their host community they tend toward the safe and the conventional so as not to upset clients or donors. To burnish their image they tend to be too focused on results and nominal academic achievement and not enough on real learning and intellectual stimulation. Additionally, there is a real shortage of good, dedicated teachers at all levels. Teachers are often substandard and of such varied religious backgrounds that they themselves often contribute to a conflict of ideas and goals and indirectly undermine the vision of a school. The division into religious and secular departments creates an artificial divide that inevitably leads children to think of the Jewish religion as inferior or of less importance.

Schools are often religiously judgmental instead of being open. The aim should be to win students over by positive reinforcement rather than compulsion, but it takes a great deal in the way of manpower and resources to be able to provide variety and flexibility. Schools are too preoccupied with appearance and because they are so dependent on donations they reflect the very worst aspects of materialism that plague our communities and do so much to create the impression that money is worshipped more than God.

On the positive side, Jewish schools perform important social functions. They provide a Jewish child with a sense of belonging to a community as opposed to a feeling of alienation and difference. The confidence that comes from being part of a majority rather than a minority is very important in helping a child cope with the challenges of growing up and finding a place in society at large. Whether a child can then mix freely in an open society depends as much on the circumstances as it does on the attitudes and values absorbed. We have all met adults who lived in a closed environment when they were young and rebelled against it and now live in an open society. Conversely we often find those who lived in an open and possibly challenging society choosing to retreat into a closed and protective one.

The talmudic approach to education posits these important lessons: For education to work it must be seen as a religious commitment, connected to the reinforcement of Jewish values. Even where secular studies are taught they should not be seen as being in opposition to Judaism but as part of the total picture of a Jewish world that incorporates other disciplines and skills. The home and the school should be in complete agreement. The parent in handing over the obligation to teach his child must feel confident that the values of the home are the values of the school and its teachers, otherwise there will be conflict. If this is not possible the parent cannot leave to the school the religious or Torah education of the child. The school then has a social function, not just a religious one or an educational one, in the widest sense of word. Education is the responsibility of the parent. Delegation is a risk. It is up to the parent to try to minimize that risk.

The myth is that education by itself can ensure Jewish survival. It might in some cases—there are plenty of examples nowadays of rejuvenated Jewish life—but sadly there are too many examples of failure. Education has to be part of a wider agenda.

Notes

1. Deuteronomy 6:7.
2. Talmud Bavli *Megillah* 27a.
3. *Shulchan Aruch Hilchot Melamdim Yoreh Deah* 245:4.
4. *Shulchan Aruch Hilchot Melamdim Yoreh Deah* 7.
5. Talmud Bavli *Kiddushin* 29a.
6. Mishna *Avot* 2:2.
7. Mishna *Avot* 3:21.
8. Mishna *Avot* 3:6.
9. Talmud Bavli *Brachot* 35b.
10. Talmud Bavli *Shabbat* 33b.
11. Talmud Bavli *Menachot* 99b.
12. Talmud Bavli *Bava Kama* 82b.
13. Talmud Bavli *Bava Kama* 83a.
14. Talmud Bavli *Succah* 28a.
15. Talmud Bavli *Brachot* 28a.
16. Numbers 5.

17. Mishna *Sotah* 9:9.
18. Mishna *Sotah* 3:4.
19. Talmud Bavli *Yoma* 69a.
20. Talmud Bavli *Sanhedrin* 94b.
21. Talmud Bavli *Bava Batra* 21a.
22. Talmud Bavli *Taanit* 24a.
23. Talmud Bavli *Megillah* 8a.
24. *Shulchan Aruch Hilchot Melamdim* 245:10.
25. *Shulchan Aruch Hilchot Melamdim* 18:19.
26. Talmud Bavli *Horyot* 14a.

Chapter 18

Myth:
Ritual Sacrifices
Are Necessary

1

Sacrifices play a central part in the Torah. They are the main vehicle for worshipping God, for marking daily service, and for dealing with human activities and events. Jewish history is dominated by the two Temples, where sacrifice was the core of activity. Our prayers constantly repeat a desire to reinstate the sacrifices, yet for many the idea of animal sacrifice is difficult to be enthused about. How many people really want to see sacrifices return? How do we deal with this?

It was Cain who initiated the first sacrifice to God, a peace offering that was not an animal sacrifice. Is this why it was not accepted? No commentator suggests that this is the reason, but Abel's animal offering was accepted.[1] And was Abel's sacrifice to eat from as well or just to give to God?

Noah offered a sacrifice to God after coming out of the ark, but there had already been a distinction made between kinds of animals even before the flood as evidenced by the fact that Noah took in two of each animal described as "unfit." Unfit for what? One must assume that unfit means unfit both for human consumption and for sacrificing. The fact that Noah took seven each of the "fit" animals implies that by his time there was an established tradition about eating and sacrificing animals. According to a view in the Talmud, man was originally not permitted to eat meat. It was not until Noah that animal meat was allowed.[2] Was his sacrifice one that enabled him to eat meat as well as to thank God?

Later in the Torah the structure of sacrifices differentiated between those sacrifices in which a layman could participate and that were only for "higher" purposes. The *mincha*, or peace sacrifice, was one that was shared between man and God, whereas the *olah*, or burnt sacrifice, was usually offered completely to God and the priesthood. Cain offered a *mincha*; Noah, after the flood, offered an *olah*. Nevertheless the link between eating meat and sacrificing, according to Rashi, begins with Noah. If one wants to eat meat, one must kill within a controlled and spiritual framework and "share" the sacrifice with God and the priests. Thus one can begin to sense some of the lessons that the sacrificial system was designed to inculcate.

The idea that God "smells the offering"[3] is of course not meant literally any more than is "the finger of God" or "the anger of God." It is not that God "needs" sacrifices or any other ritual, but God is in a reciprocal relationship with humanity. Attempts by humans to connect with God have the effect of "pleasing" God and evoking a response if only because a human expressing deep inner feelings often understands better how to cope with life and to proceed.

God sealed His covenant with Abraham at the sacrifice that is divided into parts, one for Abraham and one for God.[4] Of course, the most important lesson about sacrifices was that learned by Abraham when he nearly offered up his son Isaac. Given the prevalence of human sacrifice throughout the world at that time there are two important points: One is that human sacrifice is unacceptable, and the second is that one can easily misunderstand Divine messages. Ultimately this is why instructions about what God requires are recorded in the Torah in detail rather than being left up to an "understanding."[5]

2

Once the system of sacrifices was clarified in the Torah certain issues emerged. On a personal level the sacrificial system emphasizes that it is not a system of automatic penance. One must put things right before one can come to the Temple. Whether it is correcting something one has done wrong to another person or to God, the first stage in the process is to confess—not to a priest but to oneself. One must then express and verbalize it to God. This is an amazing psychological innovation, this need to recognize, accept, and articulate what one has done. It is only since Freud that we have come to understand fully the human tendency to sublimate, to refuse to come to terms with reality or deal with what has happened. The confession, the *viduy*,[6] is designed precisely for this purpose. Then if restitution needs to be made, it must also be done as a precondition for bringing sacrifices. Finally, there must be a determination not to repeat what has been done. Only then, after restitution and after repentance, can the act seal the process.

This why the prophets so often criticized the misuse of the sacrificial system[7]—because people were taking shortcuts and assuming that an offering was enough. It is unlikely that the prophets opposed sacrifices altogether any more than they opposed the idea of kingship despite the legacy of bad kings. But they hated hypocrisy. Perhaps the people thought one could bribe the priesthood with a fat calf so that the priest would intervene with God. This idea still influences some people who are far from ethical yet make major donations to religious leaders in this "modern" era.

In addition to the process of sacrificing as a personal or communal atonement, the Torah describes communal sacrifices, personal sacrifices, and obligatory and voluntary sacrifices. Perhaps the most far-reaching is the biblical command that if one wants to eat meat one must bring it to the priests as a sacrifice and not just kill and eat it wherever one is. This would have created difficulties in a situation where an enlarged border would have made it impractical to travel to Jerusalem each time one wanted to eat meat, so accommodations were made.[8] Laymen were allowed to kill meat, but a distinction was made between *kodshim*, the holy, or sacred, and *chullin*, the workaday norm for the man in the street. Hunting is allowed, yet it is clear that the ideal is still to eat meat within the Temple framework. Why?

Anyone who has seen animals being slaughtered for meat will fully understand the horror of animal slaughter. It makes no difference what method is used or how hygienic and sanitized the abattoir may be. It is a horrible experience to which I can attest in the light of my experience, studying to qualify as a rabbi and having to learn the system of animal slaughter. I made it my business to observe different systems on different continents, both Jewish and non-Jewish. I have no doubt that if the ordinary person could see any method of animal killing he or she would have great difficulty in eating meat. The animals sense what is ahead of them and they are terrified. They are prodded with electrically charged sticks or worse to proceed to their deaths. The air is rank with the smell of blood and innards as they are poured out of the carcasses and run down the gutters. We in the twenty-first century simply hide these unpleasant scenes away and the average consumer has no inkling of what goes into bringing his steak to the table. It is far worse if one lives in the countryside and witnesses, as I used to in Oxfordshire, the way farmers hack animals to death either on their farms or at the back yard of the local butcher. Respect for animals or indeed for life seems totally absent.

The system of sacrifice was a vast improvement on these methods. Animals were led through courtyards by priests in clean ceremonial clothes. The mood was one of reverence and the air was filled with incense. The whole approach to killing was as an act of devotion restricted to a very few practitioners and within a religiously charged atmosphere of worship.

The Temple was the focal point of Jewish communal life. It was accessible to everyone. The king exercised political power, but the Temple was the place to which every person was entitled: man, woman, child, stranger, or alien. Certainly the priesthood performed the functions, but they performed them on behalf of and for the people of Israel and anyone from the world outside who wanted to participate. The Temple symbolized spirituality. It was the House of God even though God's name was mentioned in full only once a year, on the Day of Atonement. The Temple was not a house of prayer. It had singing, performed by the Levites, but this was a background to performance. In some ways every individual had more immediate access to God through prayer at home. The Temple was the place of the nation as opposed to the individual.

After the Babylonian exile the synagogues, which coexisted with the rebuilt Temple in Israel, continued to be the focal point of Diaspora life. The significance of the Temple for the nation was difficult to replace because its ceremonies were held on behalf of everyone regardless of language, level of commitment, place of residence, or affiliation. It was also the home of the legislative council, the Sanhedrin. When the Second Temple was destroyed the only way the rabbis could create some sort of replacement was through formal community prayer. This is the main reason why the prayers that they initiated refer so much to the sacrificial system. To them it represented the ideal cohesive system for the nation as a whole. Like the kingship, it was a symbol of self-determination, of cultural and religious independence, of a golden era. The darker the Diaspora became, the brighter shone the image of a freer and nobler past even if the reality of the time was not quite so perfect. One can understand the significance of the sacrifices in the rabbinic psyche of the generation that lost the Temple.

3

The question is whether it is necessarily the case that sacrifices will be reinstituted at a time in the future when the Temple may be rebuilt. There were many biblical laws that were either temporary or fell into disuse. The order to destroy the Canaanite tribes fell into abeyance both because with time they disappeared and because the Assyrians mixed all the tribes to the point where identification became impossible.[9] The laws of slavery applied to a slave society but when Jews were no longer in a position to have Canaanite slaves or when the societies they lived in did not allow Hebrew slaves the laws simply fell into disuse. The biblical law about prophets fell into disuse with the disappearance of prophecy. The laws of leprosy for people, clothes, and buildings were abandoned. The cities of refuge became inoperative and later unrealizable. Laws that allowed certain actions, such as the *sotah* for the suspicious husband, were simply stopped, as was capital punishment for certain crimes.[10] The list goes on. Of course, these laws were still studied. They represented ideas and ideals that merited poring over in the attempt to understand the underlying spiritual messages. They were studied to be retained with the possibility that they may yet function at a later date, but as effective aspects of Jewish life they had no function at all. Would the same thing apply to sacrifices with the destruction of the Temple?

The overwhelming body of rabbinic opinion was that sacrifices would indeed be restored. To this day that is the opinion to which the majority of the rabbis of the Orthodox world adhere. Nevertheless, many people still have difficulty reconciling themselves to animal sacrifices. This must also have been the case a thousand years ago because Maimonides tackles it in his philosophical masterpiece "The Guide to the Perplexed." I will quote Maimonides at length because his testimony on this subject is crucial.

> It is impossible to go suddenly from one extreme to another; it is therefore according to the nature of man impossible for him suddenly to discontinue everything to which he has been accustomed. . . . the custom which was in those days general amongst me and the general mode of worship in which the Israelites were brought up consisted in sacrificing animals in those temples which contained certain images, to bow down to those images, and to burn incense before them. Religious and ascetic persons were in those days the persons who were devoted to the service in the temples erected to the stars as has been explained by us. It was in accordance with the wisdom and plan of God as displayed in the whole creation that He did not command us to give up and discontinue all these manners of service; for to obey such a commandment would have been contrary to the nature of man who generally cleaves to that which he is used. It would in those days have made the same impression as a prophet would make at present if he called us to the service of God and told us in his name that we should not pray to him, not fast, not seek His help in time of trouble that we should serve Him in thought and not by any action. For this reason God allowed these kinds of service to continue. . . . I know you will at first reject this idea and find it strange; you will put the following question to me I your heart. . . . What prevented Him from making His primary object a direct commandment to us and give

us the capacity of obeying it? . . . It is contrary to man's nature that he should suddenly abandon all the different kinds of Divine service and the different customs in which he has been brought up. . . .

. . . The sacrificial service is not the primary object (of the commandments about sacrifice) whilst supplications, prayers, and similar kinds of worship are nearer the primary object and indispensable for obtaining it, a great difference was made in the Law between these two kinds of service. The one kind which consists in offering sacrifices although the sacrifices are offered to the name of God has not been made obligatory for us to the same extent as it had been before. We are not commanded to sacrifice in every place and in every time or to build a Temple in every place or to permit anyone who desires to become a priest and to sacrifice. On the contrary all of this is prohibited to us . . . except that prayers and supplication can be offered everywhere and by every person.[11]

According to this highly controversial position the sacrifices were a temporary stage in the process of weaning Israel away from pagan sacrifice and toward the ideal of communication with God through prayer. If this is the case then there is no reason to suppose that the sacrifices would be reinstated. It is often argued that Maimonides wrote his "Guide" for philosophers, assimilated Jews, or the non-Jewish world. A truer representation of his Jewish beliefs is his book of Jewish Law, the *Yad HaChazaka*. There, he discusses laws that form the essence of Judaism and includes those that while currently in abeyance, like the Sanhedrin or the kingship, might be reinstated. He details the sacrificial system, though the argument that Maimonides included only those laws that would still apply is disingenuous because he also covers laws about Canaanite slaves. Maimonides included the corpus of Jewish law not necessarily because everything would be reinstated but because it merited study and should not be forgotten because of its important role in the development of the people and its legal system. Nevertheless we can only hazard a guess, given that he is not here to reconcile these two apparently contradictory texts.

Of course it is possible that human attitudes may change. Fashionable ideas have fallen out of favor and vice versa. It will, anyway, take a superhuman intervention to turn anything to do with rebuilding the Temple into reality. The politics of the international community govern the Temple Mount. There is no realistic chance of demolishing the Mosque of Omar, and even if that were to happen the majority of the Orthodox world believes that one may not go onto the Temple Mount because we are in a state of ritual impurity. Within the Orthodox world itself the fissures are so profound that it is impossible to envision agreement on an architect, let alone on who would serve as a priest and how matters of ritual purity would be determined. It is not without reason that the rabbis believed that only a resurrected Elijah could possibly sort these things out. Thus it is possible that if the future is in the hands of God, so too is the solution, and we may change in our way of thinking too.

The rabbis sometimes came up with quite radical views about the nature of future worship: "In the Future to Come God will allow everything He has forbidden"[12] or "In the future all sacrifices will be annulled except for thanking God," (a similar statement is made about prayers as well).[13] Rabbi Yitschak said, "What is meant by the words 'This is the law (Torah) of the guilt offering,' 'This is the law of the sin offering?' Whoever studies Torah does not need a burnt offering nor a peace offering nor a guilt offering."[14] Rabbi Yitschak enumerates the different categories of sacrifices, personal and communal. For him Torah is the crucial issue because it is Torah rather than sacrifices that keeps the Jewish people alive. I am not suggesting that any of these rabbis did not wish to see the return of the sacrificial system. One simply does not know. One can see in their opinions some of the variety and openness that indicates that there are different ways of looking at this subject.

The fact is that no one knows how a messianic era would play itself out or how Divine intervention would work. For the present, the sacrificial system tells us a great deal about the past—but it also tells us a great deal about the nature of the sacrifices and national cohesion. There is a great deal to be learned from these ideas, structures, and procedures that, when applied to our daily concerns, can help us live our lives in the present. Perhaps two thousand or three thousand years ago Jews might have thought that sacrifices were necessary for the survival of Judaism. For the past two thousand years we have managed to survive without them. The future? God only knows.

Notes

1. Genesis 4:3–4.
2. Talmud Bavli *Sanhedrin* 59b.
3. Genesis 8:21.
4. Genesis 15.
5. Genesis 22.
6. Leviticus 5:5.
7. 1 Samuel 15:2, Isaiah 1:2, Jeremiah 7:22–23.
8. Deuteronomy 12:20.
9. Mishna *Yadaim* 4:4.
10. Mishna *Sotah* 9:9.
11. Maimonides' "The Guide to the Perplexed," iii, 32 (page 323 in Friedlander's translation).
12. Midrash *Tehillim* 146:4.
13. Midrash Rabba *Vayikra* 9:7.
14. Talmud *Menachot* 110a.

Chapter 19

Myth: Jews Believe in Luck

1

Are Jews forbidden to indulge in magic? Can Jews go to palmists or tarot card readers? What part does luck play in our religion? Is magic or spiritualism compatible with Judaism?

The first use of a word in the Torah that might hint at the world of magic is uttered by Laban, Jacob's father-in-law, when he says "I saw in my magic that God has blessed me because of you."[1] In modern Hebrew, the word *lenachesh* usually means "to guess." It is possible that Laban was saying something like "I took a risk in employing you but things have worked out well," but the Chaldeans were well known for their interest in the supernatural and that was probably Laban's world. There is even a Midrash that says that the rabbis agreed with Chaldean methods.[2] The same word is used of Joseph being able to guess, or divine the truth about his brothers.[3]

Within Egypt, Pharaoh calls upon his *chartumim*,[4] commonly translated "magicians," to interpret his disturbing dreams. Most scholars take the origin of the word to come from *cheret*, a stylus or engraver, and so the *chartumim* could be those who interpreted texts, perhaps the scientists of those days.

When Moses meets God at the burning bush,[5] God uses a variety of methods to persuade Moses to take on the assignment of going down to Egypt to rescue the Children of Israel. There was a burning bush that did not burn up, a staff that turned into a snake, and an arm that turned leprous. We might put all these down to miracles performed by God were it not for the fact that the Egyptian *chartumim* could—initially, at any rate,—imitate many of Moses's miracles, including the snake trick.[6] This situation reflects on the nature of miracles: Were they events that were part of the world order but used in specific ways and at crucial moments? Or were they then, and would be now, special and uniquely Divine interventions against the natural flow of the world. Why did God give Moses something that could be imitated unless He was delivering a message that there was something valid in Egyptian knowledge as well? Was the issue simply one of the application of this knowledge? However, the word *chartumim* is not used in the rest of the Torah in the context of magic again; it appears that it was intended as a specifically Egyptian phenomenon.

2

There are five different words that are used in the Torah for magic, wizardry, or the supernatural. *Nachash*—whose root suggests *lachash*, "to whisper" or "talk," or *nachash*, meaning "snake," with its hissing and slyness or its indirect way of moving forward—is the word used of Laban and Joseph and the one favored by Balaam when he is invited to curse the Children of Israel. Balaam declares that "There is no magic (*nachash*) in Jacob and no witchcraft (*kessem*) in Israel"—in other words that magic has no power over Israel, presumably because Israel is protected by God.[7] He discovers that God does not want him to curse and no longer returns to consult his *nachashim*,[8] so the most appropriate translation might be "fortune teller."

A word that is used in connection with *Nachash* is *onen*, which might refer to telling the future by reading the clouds (since the word for "cloud" is identical) or it could come from "answering," replying with words to requests for information. The word commonly used now for magic is *kishuf*, which indicates the ability to reveal secrets. It is used in Egypt together with wise men and so must have been one of their "sciences." "And Pharaoh called to his wise men and his magicians (*mechashefim*)."[9]

Connected and yet different is the word *kessem*, which is more a description of objects used in magic than a system. When the elders of Moab come toward Balaam they bring *kessamim*, "charms," in their hands,[10] and someone who uses charms is called a *kossem*. The word *kessem* also means "sticks," so possibly the art was in casting down sticks or wooden dice and reading them.

Another category involves making something, either an effigy or an image of someone. The relevant words are *ov* and *yidoni* and the Torah talks about not turning toward them (for answers) "Do not turn to the *ovs* and the *yidonis*,"[11] and "Do not ask of them"[12]—and here the context adds "asking of the dead," so it would appear that these elements were part of a procedure of calling up the spirits of the dead. The prophet Isaiah also forbids "asking "of them.[13] An *ov* might be an image, figurine, or effigy and a *yidoni* might be a spirit or a less material form having some special knowledge (given that *yidoni* has the same root as the word for knowledge). The Deuteronomy text adds another category, that of the *chover chaver*, literally meaning "friend." One can only assume this is a confidant or a private consultant on the affairs of the occult. It could also mean someone who has a special relationship with spirits or is on a higher level, like the honorific term *chaver* later given to scholars. Thus there is seemingly a series of very different categories.

When it comes to the laws of the Torah there is also a series of very specific ones that deal with magic and its allied areas. In Exodus there is a specific command to get rid of witches: "A witch (*mechashefa*) should not be allowed to live."[14] There are specific commands against individuals trying various things: "Do not try to make charms or tell the future," [15] and "Do not turn (for answers) to an image or a spirit and do not contaminate yourselves with them for I am God."[16]

Here we go a step further in specifying that this approach is a form of contamination that goes against God directly. The implication is that one must accept God's instructions and no one else's, but the same text goes on to say, "Do not eat over blood, do not make charms or tell the future." Eating blood was strictly forbidden in the Torah. It was a very important part of idolatrous rites in Canaan and has continued to play a role in magic rites, supposedly passing on the qualities of the previous "owner" of the blood. We have a clear indication that these practices were rooted in idolatry and the Torah's opposition is to the context as well as to the act itself.

The clearest evidence of the idolatrous context of these practices comes toward the end of the Torah: "When you come into the land that YHVH your God gives you, do not learn from them to do the abominations of those nations. There should not be amongst you anyone who passes his son or daughter through fire, a charmer of charms, a reader of clouds, a fortune teller, or a magician, nor a friendly fortune teller or someone who asks of an image or a spirit or asks of the dead, because God despises anyone who does these things and it is because of these abominations that YHVH your God is driving them out before you. You should be straight with YHVH your God. For these nations that you will displace, they listen to fortune tellers and charmers but you should not do so."[17]

The Torah goes on to talk about the prophet as the prototype of spiritual leadership and spiritual direction. He is the one to turn to for advice and for help in dealing with the unknown, the frightening, and the uncertainty of the future.

3

The most famous case in the Bible of asking after the dead concerns King Saul. Desperate for guidance after Samuel dies he asks his servants to find him a *baalat ov*, a woman who can produce images of the dead.[18] This, of course, gives us a clue to the meaning of *ov*, but it also raises a different question. The spirit of Samuel does indeed appear to rise, which seems to indicate that magic in one form or another can achieve results. Interestingly, the Torah does not say that magic is baseless, empty, or primitive. Its instructions are simply not to get involved in it in any way that might have some influence or power over a person. Clearly these practices were so ingrained and popular that they were all but impossible to wipe out. Shimon ben Shetach is reputed to have executed eighty women in a campaign he waged against witches.[19]

The name of the Festival "Purim" is based on the word for the magic lots that Haman cast to determine the appropriate time to destroy the Jews. Haman is portrayed as trying to use his "magic" to destroy the Jews, however Divine influence, even though hidden, is more powerful. Esther's name means "hidden" (and that is also why God's name is not mentioned directly in the story of Esther). As Haman's wife and wise men (paralleling the wise men and magicians of Pharaoh) tell him, "If you have begun to fall before him (Mordecai) you will not be able to overcome him."[20] This is a very obvious contrast to the Jewish historical experience, which often has included a decline before rising. It is an assertion of the superiority of the Jewish way of responding to challenges over the pagan way of feeling determined how to act and therefore more passive in the face of adversity.

By the time of the Talmud the debate centered more on astrology and *mazal*. There is a difference of opinion as to whether these "skills" count as idolatrous practices and therefore are banned under the general prohibition against anything to do with idolatrous practices, or whether they count as "wisdom"; "The men of the East know about *mazalot* and astrology."[21] Non-Jewish wisdom that has no heretical connotations is not prohibited—on the contrary, it is something to be appreciated and there is even a blessing to be said over wise men.[22]

There is also a major difference over to the extent to which the constellations or various forms of *mazalot* do or do not influence human behavior. It was at the time a universally accepted idea that the twelve signs of the Zodiac were an integral part of the way God's universe was made up. The role of the *mazalot* in determining the future seems bound up with magic and other esoteric practices: "What did they do wrong? They consulted the stars (signs of the Zodiac), magicians who look at birds and those expert in reading signs (*tayar*)."[23] Some commentators say these are the "auspices" of Roman tradition, the innards of birds; others suggest symbols, the origin of tarot.

In the creation process described in Genesis, there is no mention of *mazalot*. The Torah talks about the Sun, the moon, and the stars, but not until the Second Book of Kings is there a quote in which *mazalot* replaces the stars.[24] The fact that the *mazalot* are not mentioned in the Torah leads one opinion to argue that there are no such things as *mazalot* and *mazal* has no influence over Israel: "Abraham said to God, 'I can see the future in my *mazal* and I will only have one son.' God took him outside and showed him the Heavens and said to him, 'Ignore your astrology; *mazal* has no power over Israel."[25] The main discussion on this issue has Rebbi Yochanan, Rav, Rebbi Yehuda, Rebbi Nachman bar Yitzchak, Rebbi Akiva, and Shmuel all agreeing with different sources that *mazal* has no power over Jews.

On the other hand, Rebbi Channina says that both wisdom and wealth are influenced by *mazal* and that every hour of the day has its *mazal* exercising control over it.[26] The most famous quote supporting the influence of *mazal* is that "Life (how long a person lives), children (how many or how they turn out), and income do not depend on a person's desserts but on *mazal*."[27] Similarly, "There is not a blade of grass that does not have a *mazal* in the heavens,[28] and "*Mazal* affects people,"[29] seem to assert that something extra-terrestial has an influence, whether it is the constellations or the power of God working through various processes before it reaches mankind. If a person suddenly feels frightened it may be that even though he has not seen anything dangerous, his *mazal* has.[30] The Gemara responds that the answer is to say the *Shema*. In other words, having a direct connection to God is a protection against any sub-Divine powers or influences. The compromise position is that *mazalot* exist and have influence but that God controls everything: "There are twelve *mazalot* God created in the heavens,"[31] or "God controls the *mazal*."[32]

4

At the time of Maimonides the function of the signs of the Zodiac was still seen as a scientific truth. After describing the "heavens" and the spheres and the place of the Sun, moon, and stars in them Maimonides goes on to describe the names and the functions of the signs of the Zodiac.[33] The whole chapter reads very strangely to those of us brought up on a scientific model of how the universe is structured. For Maimonides the signs of the Zodiac are part of the world of astronomy. When it comes to what we call astrology, however, Maimonides is very definite in saying it has no place in Jewish life. The only question is whether or not the prohibition comes under the general category of idolatry.

In his list of the commandments in the Torah, Maimonides lists three separate laws in the idolatry category:

8. We have been forbidden to make an *ov*. This refers to offering well-known incense and performing special rituals to an effigy and then imagining that one hears replies to questions he asks it.
9. We have been forbidden to make a *yidoni*, which is a form of idol worship. This refers to taking a bird bone and putting it in the mouth and making smoke and going into a trance and behaving like someone who is sick and falling into a trance-like state and giving instructions.
10. We have been forbidden to get involved with spells, looking into the spirits of stars having an influence upon us, and making images and offering incense to them and acting in a particular way.

He then gives a further list of things that are forbidden because they divert a person from following Torah. They come after the prohibitions against listening to false prophets and against following non-Jewish customs and social values:

31. We have been warned against magic (*kossem*). This means allowing the powers of illusion that tell a person what events will happen before they do. The events actually do seem to happen because of the powers of their illusions and this leads people to become dependent on them and so slowly they take control of peoples' souls. . . . some of them strike the dust with a staff in particular ways and cry unusual cries and look at the ground for a long time until they see signs in the sand and foretell what will be and I have seen this sev-

eral times in the West. And others throw down small stones onto a leather curtain and they look at them for a long time and then tell things and this is common in places that I have been to. Others throw a leather girdle onto the ground and look at it and reveal secrets. The aim of this to make use of the powers of imagination. It is not that the action itself does anything or indicates anything but the masses are deluded by these things. . . .

32. We have been warned against making decisions like saying that this day will be good for doing this action or that on this day one should not do something. This is what is meant when He says, "You should have no *onen*" . . . but it is also forbidden to ask someone to tell the future and it is forbidden to act on what they say in the hope of succeeding or benefiting and included in this is all acts of magic. The rabbis have said that a future teller is an illusionist who can fool people into believing things that have no truth like putting a piece of rope into their cloaks and taking out a snake or throwing a ring into the air and taking it out of a person's mouth. . . .

33. We are forbidden to use omens (*lenachesh*) like empty minded people who say, "Since I turned back on my route I will not succeed," or "Today is the first day of the week and this was the day I saw something and that is why today I cannot succeed," . . .

34. We are forbidden from practicing magic. . . .

35. We are forbidden to be soothsayers, which means uttering combinations of words saying things that we think will help us. . . . this includes saying things over a scorpion or a snake bite in the hope that the words will cure. . . .

36. We are forbidden to ask things of an *ov* (the previous law was against making one). . . .

37. We are forbidden to ask anything of a *yidoni* (similarly, the previous law was against making one). . . .

38. We are forbidden to ask anything of the dead. . . .

Maimonides concludes his chapter on these practices by saying, "These are all lies and falsehood that are the nature of idolatry."[34]

In effect there are two issues that go toward explaining rabbinic opposition to these practices. The first is that anything associated with idolatry is forbidden. Insofar as one needs a reason, the reason is that idolatry requires of a person obedience to corrupt practices and symbols that traditionally destroyed the fabric of a moral, caring society that protected its citizens, and delivered them into the random and unpredictable power of priests and magicians who had control over life and death. Children were sacrificed, women were expected to perform as Temple prostitutes, and the instructions of "holy men" based on spells and "reading signs" had to be obeyed regardless of any law or any appeal. This conflicts with the Jewish concept of a clear commitment to a known constitution that preserves rights and protects the weak. In accepting Judaism one knows precisely in advance what is expected and what the rules are.

The second issue is the responsibility of a person to decide how to act. The opposition to idolatrous practices is because a person hands over the decision-making process either to another or to random or unknown criteria. This is not the same as asking for advice or seeking out expertise because one still has responsibility for the final decision. In Judaism, the expert advice of, say, a great rabbi is still based on clear set of assumptions and criteria. It is handing oneself over to unknown powers that conflicts with the Jewish principle of obedience to God and Torah.

5

Despite this very definite prohibition, the fact is that Jews around the world do pay a great deal of attention to "good luck" charms, things that supposedly protect from harm, and people who have special "gifts" for seeing into the future. Particularly in the Sephardi world, which ostensibly follows Maimonides as its major authority, the *chamsa* wards off the "evil eye" and there is a whole range of special formulae to be said. In the West many people pay attention to astrological charts and consult miracle workers to discover the appropriate times for deals and betrothals. It seems that almost everything Maimonides specifies as being wrong is popular in various Jewish circles. What of those who regard the *mezuzah* as a charm to protect homes? What is more, many people have had experiences with mind readers, palm readers, or psychics that are remarkably correct about both the past and the future. The Torah does not say these things are all nonsense, just that we should avoid them—and if the Bible can record Samuel's body returning does this not prove that there is something in it?

Just because people who present themselves as religious do things, this does not make them right. The *mezuzah* is not a charm. It simply reminds us of the principles and the commandments to which each home should be dedicated. The word on the exterior is the name of God. It is God who protects us, not the *mezuzah*. Yes, we have all heard of "wonders" that happen when we check a *mezuzah* and find a letter missing, but like all "miracles" there are other ways of interpreting what actually happened. Furthermore, we hear about the coincidences and the wonders but not about the cases where nothing happens at all. People are very gullible. That is precisely why so much of the Torah is devoted to attacking these sorts of practices.

The fact is that individuals should try to run their lives according to accurate information and well-thought-out decision-making. Sadly, there are people who need placebos in the medicine of the mind as much as in the medicine of the body. Even if there is something supernatural or a nether world that is different from ours, that does not mean we should pursue it. Indeed, as with idolatry, the Torah does not say there are no other gods, just that we should not allow them to influence us or be dominated by them.

Does this mean that it is all garbage? Not necessarily. Does this mean that one cannot study these practices out of interest? Not at all: "A person who learns anything from a sorcerer (associated with idolatry) deserves to die, but someone who learns from a magician (illusionist) it is written: 'You should not learn to do what these nations do.' To learn to do is forbidden but not to learn to understand and to teach, indeed anyone who knows about calendars or the signs of the Zodiac and does not use this knowledge, of him it is said: 'They pay no attention to the work of My (God's) hands.'"[35] There is room to study these phenomena in the effort to better understand the universe we inhabit. However, the guiding principle is: "Be straight with the Lord Your God."

We have the possibility of a direct and personal relationship with God: this is the route to take. It is, to give an analogy, like having direct access to the President but instead making appointments with his or her secretary. We have no need of intermediaries, only of wise and spiritual people who will help us make up our own minds.

The myth of *mazal*, as superstition, is a very widespread one. It is a good example of how an idea can take hold despite the overwhelming condemnation of most authorities.

Notes

1. Genesis 30:27.
2. Midrash Tanchuma Chukat 11; Zohar 1, 223.
3. Genesis 44:5.
4. Genesis 41:22.
5. Exodus 3, 4.
6. Exodus 8:3, 14.

7. Numbers 23:23.

8. Numbers 24:1.

9. Exodus 7:11.

10. Numbers 22:7.

11. Leviticus 19:31 and 20:6.

12. Deuteronomy 18:11.

13. Isaiah 8:19 and 19:3.

14. Exodus 22:17.

15. Leviticus 19:26.

16. Leviticus 20:27.

17. Deuteronomy 18:9–12.

18. 1 Samuel 28.

19. Mishna *Sanhedrin* 6.

20. Esther 6:14.

21. *Pesikta Rabtai* 14.

22. Talmud Bavli *Brachot* 58a.

23. Midrash Rabba *Kohelet* 7.

24. 2 Kings 23:5.

25. Talmud Bavli *Nedarim* 32a.

26. Talmud Bavli *Shabbat* 156a.

27. Talmud Bavli *Moed Katan* 28a.

28. Midrash *Bereshit Rabba* 10.

29. Midrash Rabba *Bereshit* 10.

30. Talmud Bavli *Megillah* 3a.

31. Talmud Bavli *Brachot* 32b.

32. *Pesikta Rabtai* 20.

33. Maimonides' *Yad HaChazaka Yesodei HaTorah* 3.

34. Maimonides' *Yad HaChazaka Avodat Cochavim* 11:16.

35. Talmud Bavli *Shabbat* 85a.

Chapter 20

Myth:
You Cannot Make
Decisions for Yourself

1

How much are we allowed to decide for ourselves under Jewish Law? There are some people who will not invest or make a personal decision without consulting a rabbi. Do we really have to do what rabbis tell us? Can we not find out what Jewish law requires for ourselves? Are the rabbis extending their authority beyond the original intention?

Jewish Law, like any legal system, is based upon authority. There is the authority of the source text—or the initial revelation or the compilation, whichever way one wants to understand the Torah—and then there is the authority of the interpreters and promulgators. Traditionally the "Sinai" experience, as transmitted through the text of the Torah, is the source authority for revealing how Jews believe God wants us to behave.

Let us assume that the Torah is the main text. How do we know that anyone is allowed to interpret it? The primary source for the right of later experts to interpret the Torah is sandwiched between the laws of the prophet, the priest, and the king in the last book, Deuteronomy. It is the law of the "halachic authority" which appears vested in both the priest and the judge. They are the precursors of the rabbis in that they were the people one turned to for answers on religious issues. However, in emphasizing the specific place where the Temple will be, the Torah hints at the future role of the Sanhedrin sitting in the *Lishkat HaGazit*, the Hewn Stone Court, which adjoined the Temple: "If an issue is beyond you in justice between two people, two claimants, two victims, issues of conflict in your gates then you should get up and go up to the place that YHVH your God will select for you. And you will come before the priests, the Levites or to the judge whoever he will be at the time and you will inquire and they will tell you what the judgment is. And you will do whatever they tell you from that place that YHVH will choose and you must be careful to do whatever they teach. According to the Torah as they teach you and according to the judgment that they tell you must do, you must not deviate from what they tell you right or left."[1]

Of course, there are problems with the meaning of this text. It implies that this only applies in cases of uncertainty that are brought before it and that judgment applies only when given "from the place." In practice this became the basic text for rabbinic authority. This authority, vested in whichever office it might be—priest, levi, or judge (read: "rabbis")—was such that it is cited as the reason the rabbis could institute the blessings for Chanukah and Purim using the phrase "Blessed are You YHVH our God and King of the Universe, Who has sanctified us through His commandments and has commanded us to light the lights of Chanukah," (or "to read the Megillah"). "'From where do we know that God commanded us?' (since these festivals originated long after the Torah was written) the rabbis ask. From 'And you will do as they teach you,' (Deuteronomy 17:8)."[2]

2

Authority originally was tripartite: the priests controlled the Temple ceremonies and were the guardians of the Law, the judge combined temporal and religious authority but was then replaced by the king, who held political power. And the king had to cope with the prophet, who was the moral authority and conscience of the people. During the Second Temple period, after Ezra restructured Jewish life in Israel, the rabbis, the Sanhedrin, in effect replaced prophecy—and with the destruction of the Temple and political autonomy, we were left with rabbinic authority as the arbiter of our religious constitution, the Halacha, even though there is no clear or obvious connection between the authority about which the Torah talks and an individual rabbi. Nevertheless, by the time of the medieval halachists it was accepted that "The judge in each generation" could be applied to the rabbi.

There is little dispute about the nature of halachic authority in Judaism among those who accept its constitution, in theory. The question is what precisely is the nature of current rabbinic authority and from where does it come?

The talmudic idea of *Semicha*, the laying on of hands, was the official rabbinic ordination. It originated with Ezra and was handed down by each rabbi to a select group of students who would then be relied upon to carry on the tradition. The attempt of the Romans to stop the handing on of this authority almost succeeded had not Bava ben Buta sacrificed himself to ensure its continuity.[3] Nevertheless this official process ended with the destruction of rabbinic hegemony in Israel somewhere around the third century C.E. (some argue a little later).

In fact, rabbinic authority has proceeded since then as a convention, with no biblically approved legal standing! Leadership has simply been accepted by the community of the committed. The chain continued via the *Tanaim*, who compiled the Mishna, and the *Amoraim*, who were the authorities of the postmishnaic period and eventually compiled the Gemara. On it went through the *Geonim*, who exercised authority in Babylonia during the latter part of the first century, and then to the *Rishonim*, the "earlier authorities," both Sepharadi and Ashkenazi, whose often differing opinions were codified in the *Tur Shulchan Aruch*, which in turn was condensed into the *Shulchan Aruch* of Rabbi Joseph Karo. The experts who followed were called the *Acharonim*, the "later authorities," on whose views current decision-making relies very heavily but not exclusively. And so we come to the present state of affairs.

Nowadays the traditional rabbinic experts, judged on their scholarship and mastery of the sources, vie with each other via the very public medium of the *she'ela utshuva*, the written responsum. We as laymen or rabbis ally ourselves to our own chosen rabbi or expert, and it may depend on the issue as to which expert we turn. Some rabbis specialize in medical issues, others in civil law. There are no appointments. Expertise is achieved in a very public and open way based entirely on a person's mastery of the sources. Those rabbis who have public appointments, as chiefs or heads for instance, have no automatic authority in matters of Jewish Law. On the contrary, they are rarely experts because their involvement in public affairs has given them little time to specialize. Theirs are often political or diplomatic positions. The greatest of experts rarely have public appointments.

Halachic authority in itself is not an issue for those of us who live our lives according to Halacha in all its facets. The issue is how far this authority extends. Within the Chassidic world and its Lithuanian equivalent there is a new orthodoxy that insists that rabbinic opinion is absolute. One has to submit ones decisions to superior authority. This authority extends to areas previously considered metahalachic, such as whether to buy a home, to invest, or have an operation; how to deal with personal problems; and how to vote in secular elections. This orthodoxy has come, during the past hundred years, to be known as Torah Opinion (*Daat Torah*) and appears to be vested in individual rabbis either by affiliation if one is a Chassid, or by studying under a rabbi in a particular yeshiva, or by general reputation. The actual term *Daat Torah* first appears in rabbinic literature in the eighteenth century and simply means "the halachic position." Only recently has it come to mean officially, rabbinically sanctioned policy.

This submission to authority is partly a result of the influence of Church authority on medieval Jewry. In general, no opinion could be held without Church approval. Take Gallileo for example: The church did not like his scientific conclusions so it tried to silence him. Jewish communities existed under the model of Church authority and in effect were subservient to it. Although medieval examples of Jewish self-government were not always autocratic, all the models around them were. In part, this new submission to authority is the result of the way the Chassidic movement developed, with its hereditary hierarchy and internal authority.

The fact is that this authority is a powerful tool in Israeli and American politics (and the ambiguity of Church and State separation in the United States still allows for powerful bloc votes and politicians scrambling to be seen with religious authorities for the votes they bring). It is also a crucial element of Ultra-Orthodox self-definition in its current fundamentalist mood (not confined to Jewish groups but typical of the worldwide trend in religious movements already noted in an earlier chapter).

The issue that underlies this presentation is that halachic expertise often appears to be subject to an "agreed" agenda in areas that range from politics to relations with minorities to attitudes to change. These agendas do not call on texts (traditionally the basis of halachic decision making) to justify themselves, but rather on internally received ideas.

3

Although Halacha should in theory cover every aspect of one's life, in the past the obvious assumption was that this was confined to its laws, which were clearly defined. One could study and discover the Law for oneself—and indeed this was the stated aim of the compilers of both of Maimonides' *Yad HaChazaka*, the first comprehensive code of Jewish Law, and Rabbi Joseph Karo's *Shulchan Aruch*, which was set out in sections to be studied by the layman. So how can halachic authority be said to extend beyond definitive law to matters of faith, politics, or commerce? To what extent does it allow or disallow autonomous ideas and opinions to find legitimate expression?

In classic halachic situations there have always been disagreements, some of them fundamental as in the case of Rabbi Yossi HaGlili, who held that one could eat fowl with milk.[4] After the decision was made to include fowl under the general category of "meat," he ordered his family to follow the new decision. Similarly Akavya ben Mehallalel,[5] who argued with the majority of the rabbis at the time on four important issues (there was even a move made to remove his authority). They begged him to change his opinion and offered him the position of *Av Beth Din*, but he refused to abandon his principles: "Better I should be called an idiot all my life than that I should be a wicked person for a moment before God because people would then say that I changed my mind in order to benefit." Yet he too accepted the majority vote. When he was dying he said to his children, "Change your opinion on these issues that you followed my opinion on." They said, "Why did you not change your opinion?" He replied, "I followed the opinion that I heard from a majority of rabbis and they followed an opinion they heard from a majority. I stood by my tradition and they stood by their tradition. But you now are hearing my opinion as that of a single person against a majority opinion and therefore you have to abandon the opinion of the minority and follow the majority."[6]

Elazar ben Chanoch argued with his peers about *netilat yadayim*—whether washing hands before meals was an obligation or a recommendation.[7] The issues that separated Hillel and Shammai covered almost the whole range of legal thought. Most well known of all was the conflict between Rabbi Eliezer and the *Chachamim* over Achinai's oven and its status as far as ritual purity was concerned. He was able to call on a range of miracles and finally a Divine voice to support his position but the rabbis stood firm by the principle derived from the Torah itself that a majority of rabbis decides the law, not miracles or a Divine voice.[8]

In all these issues the rabbis agreed to make a decision, to vote on what the law would be from that moment on. Then, even those who disagreed would follow the majority decision. In all these cases the use of the *cherem*, or ban, as a tool of enforcement is threatened. Two tractates in the Babylonian Talmud, *Eduyot* and *Horyot*, deal primarily with authority, its process and its limitations.

In matters of law, a decision is vital. The principle that "A *Beth Din* cannot overrule the decision of another *Beth Din* unless it is greater in wisdom and number"[9] held sway. This device has been the single strongest bulwark against change in Halacha. It has also been a major factor in inhibiting reassessments of laws even when the original reasons for the enactments may have fallen away. The classic formulation of this process of halachic debate has been the famous phrase "Both these views and the other views are the words of the Living God."[10] This is designed to accord respect for minority views, but it does not mean that all views are equal. In the end a decision, arbitration, is required. Once this has happened the ordinary person no longer needs to consult anything or anyone other than the legal text to know what to do.

4

No such decision-making process seemed to apply to the theological or political arenas in talmudic literature. There, an individual must find his or her own way of understanding, of believing, and of enhancing the relationship with God. I have found no source in rabbinic literature for the use of the *cherem*, a sort of excommunication, over a theological issue. It is true that a *min*, a heretic, is excluded from a range of functions and roles, but in essence this is confined to saying that people who have no commitment to a system should not be allowed to participate in its legal processes. The rabbis seem concerned only with the negative, with the heretic or the rejectionist, with he who has no part of the World to Come on the one hand and he who defies authority publicly and aggressively on the other. "He who desecrates *Shabbat* in public acts is as though he is rejecting Judaism"[11] is typical of a behavioral exclusion, but there does not appear to be any attempt to define in positive terms what exactly should be believed and how. There is simply a statement of what the unacceptable position is.

A fascinating situation that shows how major differences were accommodated is that of the Sadducee High Priests. They were known to disagree with the rabbis on issues such as the afterlife and the Oral Law as well as details of Temple procedure. Still, their officiation in the Temple was accepted provided they adhered to the Pharisee understanding of how the tradition required the ceremonies to proceed. The Mishna in the first Chapter of *Yoma*[12] movingly talks about how the *Beth Din* would prepare the High Priest (who was often a political appointment and totally ignorant of Judaism). They tactfully warn the High Priest not to try any tricks when performing the Day of Atonement ritual in the Temple: "My Lord the High Priest we are the representatives of the Court of Law and you are the representative of the Court of Law. We want you to swear by He Whose Name dwells in this house that you will not change anything from what we tell you to do!" Then they would both cry, the *Beth Din* for suspecting and the High Priest for being suspected. The rabbis accepted the correct behavior even if the thought was not correct.

In the political battle over the fate of Jerusalem, Yochanan ben Zakai defected from the zealots and negotiated a compromise with the Romans, saving the tradition, but not everyone agreed with his stance. Similarly, Zecharia ben Avkilas's fateful decision was to risk losing the Temple rather than compromise Halacha.[13] Rabbi Akiva's support of Bar Cochba in the second century was criticized by his contemporaries and he was held up to ridicule.[14] There is plenty of dissension but no indication of any need to take a vote. In the whole of midrashic literature there is no evidence of needing to decide. Indeed, although the phrase "One does not need to find a reply to matters of interpretation or matters of traditional story" is found not in the Talmud itself but later,[15] it certainly reflects the atmosphere of talmudic discourse, which agrees that one does not have to take too precisely or literally comparisons of texts.[16]

This does not mean that anyone can say or think whatever he or she likes and still stay within a Jewish format of thought. Midrash does in its own way describe Jewish thinking though the range is vast and incidentally includes within it a great deal of what is now characterized as Christian thought ("Turning the other cheek" finds plenty of resonance in midrashic thought).[17] It is clear that both the Torah and the rabbis held certain ideas as fundamental to a specifically Jewish outlook. The Unity of God, benevolence, and revelation are specified in the Torah and the afterlife, resurrection, and messianism in rabbinic sources (though attributed to earlier tradition). But the framework for defining or articulating these issues was Midrash, not Halacha—and as we know Midrash is a totally different process from Halacha.

It is indeed heard in *yeshivot* nowadays that Midrash too has its authority, but no one has carried out the systematic scheme of priority and precedent that we find in Halacha with a clear cut hierarchy of authority. Whereas halachically there is an elaborate structure of authority, a clear demarcation of hierarchy, a clear statement of what constitutes rebellion against authority, no such clearly defined position exists on what we might call theological issues.

Whereas the Rambam is accepted as an absolutely crucial voice, a *rishon*, in the halachic process, any disagreement falling within defined parameters, no such respect is accorded his Aristotelian philosophic system. While his Thirteen Principles have come to be accepted as a handy guide or menu of "Jewish Thinking" (despite the theoretical opposition of giants like Crescas and Albo), there is no obligation to accept an Aristotelian description of what constitutes a Perfect Unity as opposed to a Platonic or, indeed, (anachronistically) a Wittgensteinian one. In my yeshiva we were explicitly warned not to read Maimonides' philosophical work "The Guide to the Perplexed." On the other hand, we were expected to study and master the halachic authorities and to get to know for ourselves what Jewish Law requires of us. We did not think of going to the Rosh Yeshiva to ask something that could be found in black and white in a well-known text book.

5

The question is how much of an individual choice may one exercise within the framework of commitment to halachic

Judaism. This varies, the issue being one of degree and personal comfort. Manifestly there is some room for autonomy, even within the strictest interpretation of the confines of Halacha, simply because of the terminology that says: "He who wishes to be strict, may he be blessed."[18] Of course, there is the counter phrase "He who is strict is questionable!"[19] There are various options for praying and degrees of strictness over and above the basically approved. Kosher food is a prime example.

A clue to the answer of how much choice one has lies in the concept of "free will," or freedom to choose. Free will has, since ancient Greek times, been a major problem for philosophers both in general and in Jewish philosophy specifically. If God knows everything, if "Everything is in the hands of God, except for (catching) colds and (falling into) traps,"[20] then what choice do we have, apart from taking care of our health or making sure we do not fall into traps? Yet, as *Pirkei Avot* has it, "Everything is foreseen and permission is given."[21] Maimonides says, "Every person has permission (freedom to act)."[22]

It has always been an article of Jewish thought, both philosophic and antiphilosophic (let us say both midrashic and mystical) that we are free. We may argue about the degree of freedom. We may argue that we are conditioned and influenced by a myriad of different causes and circumstances. But the fact is that we have a system of punishment. Such a system implies a degree of responsibility. We may say that a child has no responsibility. We may even say that someone brought up in a place where there are no standards is "A child captured and brought up by pagans." But we still expect a person to exercise various degrees of self-control. "Freedom" does not mean an absence of any influence; rather it means an absence of restraint.

If, therefore, we have a punitive system, we must also to some degree be held accountable. If we are held accountable we have a responsibility to try to understand something about our actions, about ourselves and why we act the way we do. The authoritarian exhortation to "Get oneself a rabbi (mentor)"[23] requires the individual to make a choice, to take the initiative. It is not a statement of passive acceptance. Some argue that the punitive system was never meant to be carried out exactly as stated. Indeed, it was so hedged about that in many cases it could not. The *ben sorer umoreh*, or "rebellious son," described in the Torah,[24] for example, is so circumscribed and qualified that according to the Talmud it could never have happened in reality.[25] Still, even if this system exists in theory more than in practice, even if it exists to give a scale of values and priority rather than to have causal punitive impact, it exists and it implies choice. You cannot punish someone who has no choice.

God's prior knowledge, or omniscience, Rambam argued, does not necessarily imply predetermination. This freedom of choice applies equally to thought as to action—I would argue more so. We are all limited behaviorally one way or another, by our families or by society. It is our freedom to think what we want that is crucial to our independence. The real test of autonomy comes with regard to the major theological principles of Jewish spirituality. If an individual is asked to assent to certain ideas, then by the very nature of "idea" as opposed to "action," in the absence of defining details describing the idea, one must concede that it is up to the individual to reach his or her own conclusions in a manner suited to his or her own intellect and intellectual tendencies, so long as those conclusions fall within the loose, general parameters of the tradition.

After all, while it may be true that around the world every man and every woman, eats, sleeps, and performs similar bodily functions and therefore it is possible to come up with a system of behavioral commands that apply equally to a range of humans of varying intellect and education, the same cannot be said of the intellect. In terms of both mental ca-

pacity and cultural training, there are vast differences between peoples, cultures, and individuals on earth. There is
no way that one system of thought could possibly be understood or accepted by everyone in the way that legal imperatives can.

One need think only of the very deep and important differences between the mystical and the rational in Judaism.
Indeed, the divide between the rational and the mystical led
to several bitter schisms, most notably between the Vilna
Gaon and the Besht and between Rabbi Yonatan Eybeshutz
and Rabbi Yaacov Emden. Yet the very fact that divergent
traditions have continued within the framework of a commitment to Halacha is proof in itself of the permissibility in
practice of some differences.

6

What, then, is the nature of the contrasting concepts of respect for rabbinic or saintly opinion, *Daat Torah* and the earlier expression, *Emunat Chachamim*, "Belief in the Wise?"
It is clear that asking the wise for advice, accepting that
some are on a higher spiritual and intellectual level and
should be deferred to or consulted, is an important part of
our tradition. We have always revered the "elder." Indeed,
this a Torah law. Is this not what differentiates Orthodoxy
from Heterodoxy—a recognized system of authority as
opposed to individualized arbitrariness? The issue is not
one of respect or willing deferral to greater authority. It is
one of obligation. Are we obliged to accept authority, and if
so to what extent? It is my position that Judaism allows
for a modified, limited, low level of autonomy in matters
of Halacha, but it allows for a high level of autonomy in
the realms of ideas and thought. It is up to the individual
how much autonomy, in both areas, he or she chooses to
exercise.

So if we accept halachic authority, if we accept the superiority of those endowed with a higher level of understanding and learning, what does this entail? Whereas I cannot try to change Halacha on a personal whim, I do actually make everyday decisions such as when to pray and sometimes even if to pray, with or without a *minyan*, or sitting or standing over the Atlantic? In practice do we not see decisions to move into Chassidism, with its myriad variations of custom and even Halacha—and Chassidism itself? Jews born into Sephardi homes or Mitnaged homes experience very different manifestations of Jewish religious life. Certainly the range is limited, and some choose to make it more limited. On the other hand, out of respect for rabbinic stature (I will not be negative by calling it a fear of taking responsibility) many choose to make a whole range of decisions solely on the basis of rabbinic approval, from buying a house to doing a deal to getting married. This may be no different from asking the expert advice of a doctor, psychiatrist, or broker. It may not be my style of behavior, but it is a legitimate expression of Jewishness.

I have no argument with someone choosing submission. My argument is only with those who insist on this submission as a criterion of halachic commitment to Judaism. Technically anyone can decide halachically, if he has the information and the skill. Anyone can engage in halachic discourse and debate. The approach of Halacha is to look at a text, see the precedent, and reach a conclusion. If one cannot, then one consults. If one is innovating, then he should check his judgment against the experts'.

Submitting a view for approval does not mean that one can never make a personal decision. The *Shulchan Aruch* was divided into handy sections so that individuals could know the Law and by reviewing it regularly not need to consult an expert on every issue. One turns to a rabbi after one has covered the material but still does not have the expertise to reach a conclusion. Indeed, expert rabbis themselves consult other experts on difficult issues, and nowadays experts may be so only in limited areas. A rabbi familiar with technological issues may not be so familiar with financial ones.

Everyone has the capacity to study and decide but decisions should be based on textual information and analysis, not on whims and preferences. Nevertheless, the constitution, by its nature, restricts and limits the extent of individual freedom precisely because it lays down an overall framework.

7

In matters of faith and thought we have a "high level" of autonomy. Do I not every day engage in a struggle of faith and reach out to God sometimes more successfully and sometimes less? Do I never wonder how the God I experience and encounter every day was capable of not intervening when millions of Jewish children met their unspeakable deaths? Am I supposed to blindly accept without thought? That is not the Rambam's approach in either the *Yad HaChazaka*, his halachic magnum opus, or "The Guide to the Perplexed!" Am I an automaton who acts and thinks without consideration? If I have to blindly accept authority both in action and thought then where is the room for freedom of individual thought?

Indeed what then is the meaning of *Ani maamin*, "I believe," if I am not allowed to wonder if I really do and what exactly it is that I believe in? Or do we say that just as *mitzvot lav tsrichot kavana* (a required action does not require considered intent), so too thoughts do not require *kavana* (conscious intent)? This is not said anywhere in the Talmud, otherwise what would be the nature or the value of a thought that is not a thought but a mechanical recitation? The first paragraph of the *Shema* requires *kavana*, concentration and thought.[26] What is *kavana* if not an exercise in autonomous thinking?

When Moses is faced with Eldad and Medad prophesying in the camp his response is, "If only everyone was a prophet": "And two men were left in the camp, one called Eldad and the other called Medad and the spirit of God rested on them and they were among the appointed ones (as judges chosen to assist Moses) but they had not gone out to the Tabernacle and they prophesied in the camp. And the young man ran and told Moses and said, 'Eldad and Medad are prophesying in the camp.' And Joshua, the assistant of Moses, one of his young men, answered and said, 'My master Moses, destroy them.' And Moses said to him, 'Are you worried for me? If only all the people of God were prophets. If only God would give His spirit to everyone.'"[27] The whole nation has the capacity to be a "Nation of Priests," and it would seem from this that every individual has both the capacity and the right to explore his own spirituality and to converse with the Almighty. Yet when Miriam makes a similar statement in the very next chapter, she is punished and God restates the uniqueness of His relationship with Moses.[28] The reason is that there are limitations.

There is a typical tension between these two positions. In principle everyone can be special; in practice, only a few are. In the same way that there is in Halacha a tension between a command to kill and a command to protect life, a command to respect the fetus and a command to respect the mother's existent life, so too in Halacha we are often faced with a sort of relativism, a situation in which conflicting halachic principles clash. The situation decides in which direction we lean when giving a *psak*, a halachic decision. Sometimes it is just not possible to say, "This will always be the Halacha regardless of circumstances."

This is the genius of Halacha. This is the brilliance of Revelation. It is the Greek absolutism—only one Truth—that leads to a position of compulsion, of forced conversion.

Contrast that with Jewish acceptance of the varieties of humanity and religious experience, which leads us to find room for and to value the *ger toshav* (the stranger in our midst who is given equal civil rights in return for adherence to a basic set of laws), the "Son of Noah," and the *chassidei umot ha'olam*, (the pious of the nations of the world). Another paradigm is *dina di malchuta*, "The Law of the Land is accepted as law," by Jews in civil matters even if it conflicts with Halacha. Of course, a priori we prefer our system of civil law, but we are allowed to accept other systems depending on where we live. This relativism allows and indeed encourages respect both for authority on one hand and individuality on the other.

There is, by way of contrast, a lower level of decision-making when it comes to Jewish Law precisely because the boundaries have always been more clearly defined. "Authority" and "autonomy" are, similarly, two imperatives that coexist in Judaism in a state of tension. I argue that this is healthy and positive. The danger is always in moving too far in either direction. When people attack a religious position that seeks to reconcile two different points of view they forget that it was the great Rambam who said that this is precisely how you achieve the *Shvil HaZahav*, the "Golden Mean." You lean in the opposite direction further than you might otherwise want, in order to correct an imbalance. The Golden Mean is finding a balance between the necessary obedience to a system and preservation of one's individuality and the very personal responsibility of answering to God for one's thoughts and one's deeds.

Rabbis should be giving guidance. They can point out directions and give sources. They can study and discuss. But in the end the individual must make up his or her own mind, not the rabbi. "The words of the Master or the words of the pupil, whose words do we obey?"[29] It is obvious that in this context it is God and not the rabbi who is the Master.

There is a myth in some quarters that it is not right for individuals to make their own decisions on religious matters. If this is meant to counter the idea that an individual can invent or create new laws and change the structure, then of course it is no myth; it is the reality. But if it means that individuals cannot study and discover the law for themselves, and that every single sphere of their daily activity requires rabbinic sanction, then this is indeed a myth.

Notes

1. Deuteronomy 17:8.
2. Talmud Bavli *Shabbat* 23a.
3. Talmud Bavli *Sanhedrin* 14a.
4. Talmud Bavli *Shabbat* 130a.
5. Talmud Bavli *Sanhedrin* 78a
6. Talmud Bavli *Eduyot* 5:7.
7. Talmud Bavli *Brachot* 19a.
8. Talmud Bavli *Bava Metzia* 59a.
9. Mishna *Eduyot* 1:5.
10. Talmud Bavli *Eiruvin* 13b etc.
11. Talmud Bavli *Eiruvin* 69b.
12. Mishna *Yoma* 1:5.
13. Talmud Bavli *Gittin* 56a.
14. Talmud Yerushalmi *Taanit* 4:5.
15. *Siftei Chachamim Devarim* 1:4, *Beer HaGolah* 135.
16. Talmud Bavli *Menachot* 82b.
17. Talmud Bavli *Yoma* 23a.
18. Talmud Bavli *Brachot* 22a, *Shulchan Aruch Orach Chayim* 640.
19. *Shulchan Aruch Yoreh Deah* 374.
20. Talmud Bavli *Avoda Zara* 3b.
21. Mishna *Avot* 3:19.
22. Maimonides' *Yad HaChazaka Hilchot Teshuva* 5:1.
23. Mishna *Avot* 1:6.

24. Deuteronomy 22.
25. Talmud Bavli *Sanhedrin* 61a.
26. Talmud Bavli *Brachot* 13b.
27. Numbers 11:29.
28. Numbers 12.
29. Talmud Bavli *Kiddushin* 42b.

Index

About the Author

Jeremy Rosen is an orthodox rabbi who has occupied prominent pulpits in Scotland, Africa, and London. He was principal of Carmel College in England for thirteen years and is currently director of YAKAR Educational Center in London and professor of comparative religion at and chairman of the Faculty for Comparative Religion in Antwerp, Belgium. He is a philosophy graduate of Cambridge University, England, and has *semicha* from Mir Yeshiva in Jerusalem. Rabbi Rosen has always been committed to bridging gaps both between Jews of different backgrounds and between Jews and non-Jews. He is married and has four children.